ASIA BOND MONITOR
JUNE 2021

ASIAN DEVELOPMENT BANK

ADB

© 2021 Asian Development Bank
6 ADB Avenue, Mandaluyong City, 1550 Metro Manila, Philippines
Tel +63 2 8632 4444; Fax +63 2 8636 2444
www.adb.org

Some rights reserved. Published in 2021.

ISBN 978-92-9262-922-9 (print), 978-92-9262-923-6 (electronic), 978-92-9262-924-3 (ebook)
ISSN 2219-1518 (print), 2219-1526 (electronic)
Publication Stock No. SPR210232-2
DOI: http://dx.doi.org/10.22617/SPR210232-2

The views expressed in this publication are those of the authors and do not necessarily reflect the views and policies of the Asian Development Bank (ADB) or its Board of Governors or the governments they represent.

ADB does not guarantee the accuracy of the data included in this publication and accepts no responsibility for any consequence of their use. The mention of specific companies or products of manufacturers does not imply that they are endorsed or recommended by ADB in preference to others of a similar nature that are not mentioned.

By making any designation of or reference to a particular territory or geographic area, or by using the term "country" in this document, ADB does not intend to make any judgments as to the legal or other status of any territory or area.

Please contact pubsmarketing@adb.org if you have questions or comments with respect to content, or if you wish to obtain copyright permission for your intended use that does not fall within these terms, or for permission to use the ADB logo.

Corrigenda to ADB publications may be found at http://www.adb.org/publications/corrigenda.

Note:
ADB recognizes "Hong Kong" and "Hongkong" as Hong Kong, China; "China" as the People's Republic of China; "Korea" as the Republic of Korea; "Siam" as Thailand; "Vietnam" as Viet Nam; and "Saigon" as Ho Chi Minh City.

Cover design by Erickson Mercado.

Contents

Emerging East Asian Local Currency Bond Markets: A Regional Update

Highlights

Local currency (LCY) government bond yield movements diverged across emerging East Asia between 28 February and 21 May due to market-specific factors.[1] Uncertainty regarding the COVID-19 pandemic and government containment efforts influenced the economic outlook in the region, affecting investment sentiment and bond yields.

The economic performance of all emerging East Asian markets improved in the first quarter (Q1) of 2021 relative to the fourth quarter (Q4) of 2020. Most economies—the People's Republic of China (PRC); Hong Kong, China; the Republic of Korea; Singapore; and Viet Nam—reported positive GDP growth in Q1 2021. Other regional markets contracted in Q1 2021 but at a slower pace than in the fourth quarter (Q4) of 2020.

Investor sentiment remained subdued amid looming uncertainties brought about by the COVID-19 pandemic and inflation fears in the United States (US). This led to volatilities in financial markets, especially in March. Equity market performances were mixed across emerging East Asia. The resurgence of COVID-19 cases in some markets triggered new social distancing restrictions that affected consumer sentiment. Exchange rates and risk premiums remained roughly stable.

The COVID-19 pandemic remains the largest downside risk. In addition to rising cases in some markets and new variants, the slow pace of the vaccine rollout is also hampering economic recovery in some regional markets. Another potential risk is the possibility of tightening liquidity conditions globally, specifically that the Federal Reserve might tighten US monetary policy in response to growing inflationary pressure.

Local currency bonds outstanding in emerging East Asia rose to USD20.3 trillion at the end of March.

Emerging East Asia's LCY bond market expanded to reach a size of USD20.3 trillion at the end of March. However, the overall growth of the bond market moderated somewhat in Q1 2021 as governments sought to balance fiscal policy and corporates weighed uncertainty over the economic recovery. On a quarter-on-quarter (q-o-q) basis, overall growth in the region's bond market slipped to 2.2% in Q1 2021 from 3.1% in Q4 2020. Similarly, growth on a year-on-year (y-o-y) basis slowed to 15.9% from 18.2%. As a share of GDP, emerging East Asia's bond market was equivalent to 96.4% of the region's economic output in Q1 2021, slightly down from 97.7% in Q4 2020.

The outstanding amount of government bonds totaled USD12.6 trillion at the end of March, representing 61.8% of emerging East Asia's total bond stock. Government bonds grew 2.1% q-o-q and 18.0% y-o-y in Q1 2021, down from the 3.6% q-o-q and 19.5% y-o-y growth in Q4 2020. The corporate bond market reached a size of USD7.8 trillion, accounting for 38.2% of the regional LCY bond stock. Corporate bond market growth was 2.4% q-o-q and 12.6% y-o-y in Q1 2021, compared with 2.2% q-o-q and 16.2% y-o-y in Q4 2020.

The PRC had the largest LCY bond market in emerging East Asia at the end of March, accounting for 77.8% of the region's bonds outstanding. The Republic of Korea had the next largest market, with a regional share of 11.7%, followed by members of the Association of Southeast Asian Nations with an aggregate share of 9.0%.[2]

New bond issuance during Q1 2021 totaled USD1.9 trillion, slightly down from USD2.0 trillion in Q4 2020. Overall issuance volume declined 1.7% q-o-q in Q1 2021, following a 14.7% q-o-q contraction in Q4 2020. On a y-o-y basis, issuance growth moderated to 8.6% in Q1 2021 from 32.3% in Q4 2020.

---

[1] Emerging East Asia comprises the People's Republic of China; Hong Kong, China; Indonesia; the Republic of Korea; Malaysia; the Philippines; Singapore; Thailand; and Viet Nam.
[2] LCY bond statistics for the Association of Southeast Asian Nations include the markets of Indonesia, Malaysia, the Philippines, Singapore, Thailand, and Viet Nam.

Recent Developments in the ASEAN+3 Sustainable Bond Market

The aggregate amount of sustainable bonds outstanding in ASEAN+3 markets reached USD301.3 billion at the end of March, accounting for nearly 20.0% of the global sustainable bond total.[1] Overall growth quickened to 13.2% q-o-q in Q1 2021 from 6.3% q-o-q in Q4 2020. Green, social, and sustainability bonds accounted for 74.6%, 11.7%, and 13.6% of the regional sustainable bond market, respectively, at the end of Q1 2021.

ASEAN markets accounted for 5.1%, 0.05%, and 15.9% of the outstanding stock of regional green, social, and sustainability bonds at the end of March. The PRC continued to dominate the regional green bond market, accounting for 70.0% of green bonds outstanding in ASEAN+3 at the end of March. At the same time, the Republic of Korea and Japan accounted for 57.4% and 40.1% of regional social bonds outstanding, and 36.3%, and 39.3% of regional sustainability bonds outstanding, respectively.

At the end of Q1 2021, corporate issuers dominated regional green and sustainability bond markets, accounting for 88.1% of green bonds and 72.5% of sustainability bonds. Public sector issuers, including governments and corporates with government links, accounted for 59.2% of social bonds outstanding. The financial sector was the largest issuing sector of regional sustainable bonds at the end of Q1 2021. A majority of regional green and social bonds were issued in LCY, while more than half of regional sustainability bonds were denominated in foreign currencies.

The June issue of the *Asia Bond Monitor* includes a box discussing how some regional markets have been using green *sukuk* (Islamic bonds) to fund environment-friendly investments. Another box analyzes how technological advances such as digital finance can facilitate the financing of sustainable investments for a green and inclusive recovery. This issue also contains a theme chapter on the governance of sustainable finance.

Box 1: Green *Sukuk* Market

Green *sukuk* are used to fund environment-friendly projects. They are similar to green bonds but are Shari'ah-compliant. The global green *sukuk* market is not as well established as the global conventional *sukuk* and green bond markets. As of 21 May, over USD10 billion of green *sukuk* had been issued by 16 entities from around the world, with 65% of the total issuance coming from Malaysia and Indonesia. Global issuance of green *sukuk* grew from 2017 to 2019 before declining in 2020. Investors in green *sukuk* come from 19 economies, led by the US, the European Union, Canada, and the United Kingdom. Since most issuances of green *sukuk* rely on international demand, 88% of them were issued in either US dollars or euros. LCY-denominated green *sukuk* in Malaysia and Indonesia mainly attract domestic investors.

Box 2: Scaling Up Sustainable Investments through Fintech

This box provides an overview of how fintech, or digital finance, solutions can facilitate sustainable investments and improve project implementation by enhancing information flows and transparency. Fintech solutions are dedicated to making financial services more efficient through internet-related technologies. Blockchain technology, a fintech application, helps address major concerns in the three key phases of an infrastructure project's life cycle: (i) inception and fundraising, (ii) realization, and (iii) operation. This box discusses blockchain-based project bonds issued through a digital crowdfunding platform as an example to show how fintech applications provide novel solutions for financing sustainable infrastructure investments.

Theme Chapter: Governing Sustainable Finance

This theme chapter discusses developments in the private and public sectors to integrate sustainability factors into financial systems and investment frameworks to mitigate sustainability risks and align finance with the United Nations Sustainable Development Goals. The study outlines some challenges such as defining sustainable finance and related financial instruments, and developing a commonly accepted taxonomy, impact matrix, and disclosure standards. Public policies and cooperation between monetary and financial authorities are needed to address these challenges.

---

[3] For the discussion on sustainable bonds, ASEAN+3 includes ASEAN members Indonesia, Malaysia, the Philippines, Singapore, and Thailand, plus the People's Republic of China; Hong Kong, China; Japan; and the Republic of Korea.

Global and Regional Market Developments

Bond yields were mixed in emerging East Asia amid divergent recovery paths and looming uncertainties.

Between 28 February and 21 May, government bond yields posted divergent patterns across both advanced economies and emerging East Asian markets.[1] Most emerging East Asian markets witnessed a continued decline in yields on 2-year local currency government bonds as liquidity conditions remained accommodative, supported by easy monetary stances. Yields on 10-year government bonds presented a mixed picture, tracking uneven recovery paths and market-specific economic fundamentals. Overall investment sentiment in the region remained subdued during the review period amid looming uncertainties in the fight against COVID-19 and inflationary pressure in the United States (US), as well as the related implications for monetary stances and financial conditions (**Table A**).

From 28 February to 21 May, 10-year government bond yields inched up in all major advanced economies except for Japan (**Figure A**). Long-term bond yields rose significantly in the US over an improved economic outlook and additional fiscal stimulus. In addition, concerns over inflationary pressure introduced volatility into financial markets.

In the US, the Federal Reserve acknowledged that the domestic economy has strengthened but risks remain and the future direction of the economy will be shaped by the ongoing pandemic. The US posted an annualized GDP growth rate of 6.4% in the first quarter (Q1) of 2021, up from 4.3% in the fourth quarter (Q4) of 2020. In June, the Federal Reserve upgraded its economic forecasts to 7.0% and 2.4% for 2021 and 2023, respectively, from 6.5% and 2.2% in March. The forecast for 2022 remained unchanged at 3.3%. The US labor market has so far been stable. Nonfarm payroll additions improved to 559,000

Table A: Changes in Global Financial Conditions

	2-Year Government Bond (bps)	10-Year Government Bond (bps)	5-Year Credit Default Swap Spread (bps)	Equity Index (%)	FX Rate (%)
Major Advanced Economies					
United States	3	22	–	9.0	–
United Kingdom	(9)	1	(4)	8.2	1.6
Japan	(1)	(8)	2	1.6	(2.2)
Germany	0.9	13	0.4	12.0	0.9
Emerging East Asia					
China, People's Rep. of	(18)	(21)	7	(0.6)	0.6
Hong Kong, China	(4)	(12)	–	(1.8)	(0.1)
Indonesia	(22)	(15)	(0.5)	(7.5)	(0.8)
Korea, Rep. of	5	15	(5)	4.8	(0.3)
Malaysia	22	13	6	(1.0)	(2.2)
Philippines	5	23	6	(8.8)	1.3
Singapore	(2)	19	–	5.7	0.05
Thailand	(13)	6	2	3.7	(3.0)
Viet Nam	(8)	(2)	8	9.9	(0.1)

( ) = negative, – = not available, bps = basis points, FX = foreign exchange.
Notes:
1. Data reflect changes between 28 February 2021 and 21 May 2021.
2. A positive (negative) value for the FX rate indicates the appreciation (depreciation) of the local currency against the United States dollar.
Sources: Bloomberg LP and Institute of International Finance.

---

[1] Emerging East Asia comprises the People's Republic of China; Hong Kong, China; Indonesia; the Republic of Korea; Malaysia; the Philippines; Singapore; Thailand; and Viet Nam.

Figure A: 10-Year Government Bond Yields in Major Advanced Economies (% per annum)

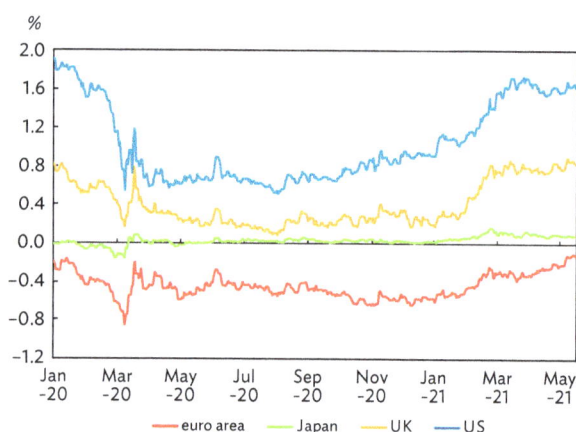

UK = United Kingdom, US = United States.
Note: Data coverage is from 1 January 2020 to 21 May 2021.
Source: Bloomberg LP.

in May from 278,000 in April but was lower than the 785,000 in March. The unemployment rate fell slightly to 5.8% in May from 6.1% in April and 6.0% in March.

The Federal Reserve left its monetary policy unchanged during its meeting on 27–28 April. The federal funds target range was kept at between 0% and 0.25%, and monthly asset purchases were maintained at a minimum of USD80 billion per month for US Treasuries and USD40 billion for agency mortgage-back securities. Consumer price inflation accelerated to 5.0% year-on-year (y-o-y) in May from 4.2% y-o-y in April and 2.6% y-o-y in March. On 4 May, US Treasury Secretary Janet Yellen said that interest rates may need to rise to prevent overheating due in part to government stimulus spending measures. She later walked back her comments, saying she does not see an inflation problem in the US. Adding to the concerns over inflation, additional economic stimulus measures have been passed or are being contemplated for later this year. On 11 March, President Biden signed a USD1.9 trillion stimulus package. On 15 April, President Biden unveiled plans for a USD2.0 trillion infrastructure bill. While the Federal Reserve noted that inflation has risen largely due to transient factors, markets are increasingly concerned by possible early changes to the easy monetary stance and new stimulus packages. More recently, while the Federal Reserve largely left monetary policy unchanged during its 15–16 June meeting, the updated forecasts showed that it expects two policy rate hikes in 2023, which is earlier than the dot plot indicated in the April FOMC meetings.

In addition, during the press conference, Chairman Powell indicated that the Federal Reserve would begin discussions on scaling back its asset purchases.

In the euro area, GDP recorded consecutive declines of –4.7% y-o-y in Q4 2020 and –1.3% y-o-y in Q1 2021, partly driven by rising COVID-19 cases and subsequent containment measures. The European Central Bank (ECB) noted that the euro area's short-term outlook was affected by rising COVID-19 cases, but it expects the economy to recover later in 2021. In June, the ECB updated its economic forecasts to 4.6% and 4.7%, respectively, for 2021 and 2022, from 4.0% and 4.1% in March. The 2023 forecast was left unchanged at 2.1%. On 22 April, the ECB maintained its current monetary policy—leaving key policy rates unchanged at 0% (main refinancing rate), –0.5% (deposit facility rate), and 0.25% (marginal lending facility rate)—and continued its asset purchase program at a total amount of EUR1,850 billion until at least the end of March 2022. The ECB indicated that it would accelerate the pace of bond purchases in the second quarter of this year to boost the economy given a weak performance in Q1 2021. It also noted a rise in inflation due to temporary factors. Subsequenly, the ECB again left monetary policy unchanged on 10 June.

In Japan, the economy is expected to recover as the pandemic abates. However, rising COVID-19 cases led the government to extend its state of emergency several times, with the latest extension lasting until 20 June. This weighed on Japan's recovery, with annualized GDP contracting 3.9% in Q1 2021 after a gain of 11.7% in Q4 2020. The Bank of Japan (BOJ) noted in its April meeting that the domestic economic outlook has improved, although it remains in a "severe" situation. The BOJ also updated its GDP forecasts for fiscal years 2021 and 2022 to 4.0% and 2.4%, respectively, from forecasts made in January of 3.9% and 1.8%. During its 27 April meeting, the BOJ left its monetary policy unchanged, with the policy rate balance held at –0.1% and the target yield on 10-year Japanese Government Bonds at zero. The BOJ's asset purchase program was also continued through the end of September, with annual purchases of JPY12.0 trillion of exchange-traded funds, JPY180.0 billion of real estate investment trusts, and JPY20.0 trillion of commercial paper and corporate bonds. The BOJ indicated that risks remain tilted to the downside and that it will continue to monitor the effects of the pandemic and undertake additional easing as needed. On 18 June, the BOJ left monetary its policy rates unchanged but extended the duration of its purchases of

Table B: Policy Rate Changes

Economy	Policy Rate 1-Jun-2020 (%)	Rate Change (%)												Policy Rate 21-May-2021 (%)	Change in Policy Rates (basis points)
		Jun-2020	Jul-2020	Aug-2020	Sep-2020	Oct-2020	Nov-2020	Dec-2020	Jan-2021	Feb-2021	Mar-2021	Apr-2021	May-2021		
United States	0.25													0.25	0
Euro Area	(0.50)													(0.50)	0
Japan	(0.10)													(0.10)	0
China, People's Rep. of	2.95													2.95	0
Indonesia	4.50	↓0.25	↓0.25				↓0.25			↓0.25				3.50	↓100
Korea, Rep. of	0.50													0.50	0
Malaysia	2.00		↓0.25											1.75	↓25
Philippines	2.75	↓0.50					↓0.25							2.00	↓75
Thailand	0.50													0.50	0
Viet Nam	4.50					↓0.50								4.00	↓50

( ) = negative.
Notes:
1. Data coverage is from 1 June 2020 to 21 May 2021.
2. For the People's Republic of China, data used in the chart are for the 1-year medium-term lending facility rate. While the 1-year benchmark lending rate is the official policy rate of the People's Bank of China, market players use the 1-year medium-term lending facility rate as a guide for the monetary policy direction of the People's Bank of China.
Sources: Various central bank websites.

securities other than Japanese Government Bonds from September 2021 to March 2022.

Emerging East Asia witnessed divergent bond yield movements that tracked market-specific factors, including uneven economic recoveries, varying vaccine rollout progress, and different monetary and fiscal policy measures.

The largest decline in 2-year bond yields was in Indonesia, which posted a decline of 22 basis points (bps). This was supported by a rate cut of 25 bps by Bank Indonesia on 18 February to further boost liquidity (**Table B**) . The yield for Indonesian 10-year bonds also declined by 15 bps during the review period amid ample liquidity and the return of foreign capital inflows into the bond market following outflows in February and March. The People's Republic of China (PRC) had the second-largest decline in short-term yields in the region, with its 2-year bond yield falling 18 bps and its 10-year yield falling 21 bps. The PRC's strong economic recovery continued in Q1 2021, with GDP growing 18.3% y-o-y after expanding 6.5% y-o-y in the previous quarter. Foreign investment in the PRC bond market increased on the strong economic performance and attractive yields. In addition, as part of measures to mitigate a possible build-up of credit risk in the financial system, the PRC has taken steps to slow the issuance of bonds by local governments, which weighed on bond yields through supply-side pressure. Hong Kong, China and Viet Nam both experienced a decline in their respective 2-year and 10-year bond yields during the review period.

In the Republic of Korea, Malaysia, and Singapore, increases in 10-year bond yields reflected positive economic outlooks. The Republic of Korea recorded GDP growth of 1.9% y-o-y in Q1 2021, reversing a contraction of 1.1% y-o-y in Q4 2020. Singapore posted a 1.3% GDP growth rate in Q1 2021, reversing a contraction of 2.4% in Q4 2020. In Malaysia, Bank Negara Malaysia expects the economy to recover to pre-COVID-19 levels by the middle of 2021 and is forecasting 2021 GDP growth in the range of 6.0%–7.5%. In Q1 2021, Malaysia recorded negative GDP growth of –0.5% y-o-y, which was an improvement from the –3.4% y-o-y growth recorded in Q4 2020. Malaysia's economic recovery may be impacted by the latest 2-week mobility restrictions starting in June due to a rise in COVID-19 cases.

The Philippines posted the region's largest increase in the 10-year bond yield, which gained 23 bps. In March, rising COVID-19 cases and containment measures weighed down the economic recovery. In Q1 2021, the Philippines' GDP contracted 4.2%, the largest quarterly decline in emerging East Asia. The rise in bond yields was also driven by inflation concerns as the average inflation rate of 4.4% y-o-y in January–May exceeded the Bangko Sentral ng Pilipinas' 2021 target of 2.0%-4.0%. The Philippines reported y-o-y inflation of 4.5% each in March, April, and May.

Consistent with bond market performances, other key indicators of regional financial conditions posted mixed patterns during the review period of 28 February to 21 May. Among equity markets, five out of nine markets recorded

Figure B.1: Equity Indexes in Emerging East Asia

1 Jan-20 = 100

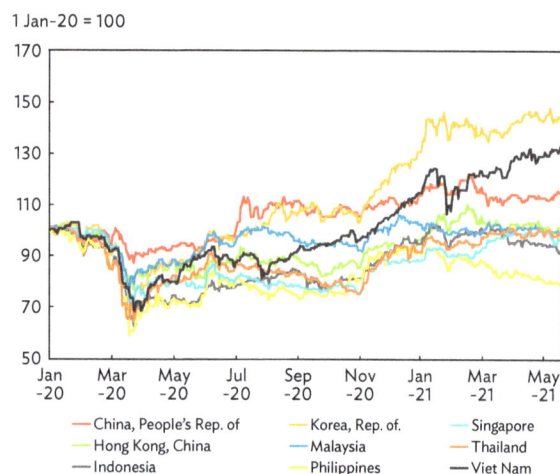

Note: Data coverage is from 1 January 2020 to 21 May 2021.
Source: *AsianBondsOnline* computations based on Bloomberg LP data.

Figure B.2: Changes in Equity Indexes in Emerging East Asia

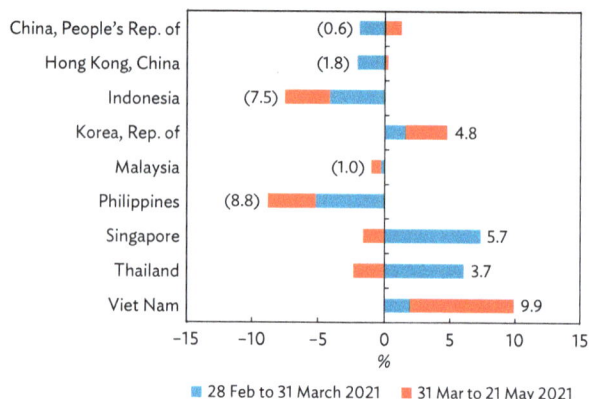

( ) = negative.
Notes:
1. Changes from 28 February to 31 March 2021 and from 31 March to 21 May 2021.
2. Figures on the chart refer to the net change between the two periods.
Source: *AsianBondsOnline* computations based on Bloomberg LP data.

declines, while the other four posted gains. Equity market movements diverged across emerging East Asia beginning in March, as some markets experienced a resurgence of COVID-19 cases (**Figure B.1**). The equity market of Viet Nam recorded the largest gain, rising 9.9% on the back of positive GDP growth in Q1 2021. This was followed by Singapore (5.7%) and the Republic of Korea (4.8%). Although Thailand's equity market was up 3.7% during the review period, this was largely due to gains through the end of March before the market retreated in April and May as COVID-19 cases surged and additional containment measures were declared (**Figure B.2**). Thailand posted negative GDP growth of –2.6% y-o-y in Q1 2021, up from –4.2% y-o-y in Q4 2020.

The equity market in the Philippines posted the region's largest decline during the review period, falling 8.8% on a weaker economic outlook, as rising COVID-19 cases led to the re-imposition of mobility restrictions starting in March, and on the GDP contraction of 4.2% y-o-y in Q1 2021. Rising inflation in the Philippines also limited additional easing measures by the Bangko Sentral ng Pilipinas. Indonesia's equity market fell 7.5% on the back of the weak economic performance in Q1 2021 when GDP contracted 0.7% y-o-y.

Regional currencies were largely stable between 28 February and 21 May, posting divergent patterns that followed market-specific factors (**Figure C.1**). Between 28 February and 31 March, regional currencies weakened against the dollar on the back of a strengthening

Figure C.1: Currency Indexes in Emerging East Asia and the United States

1-Jan-20 = 100

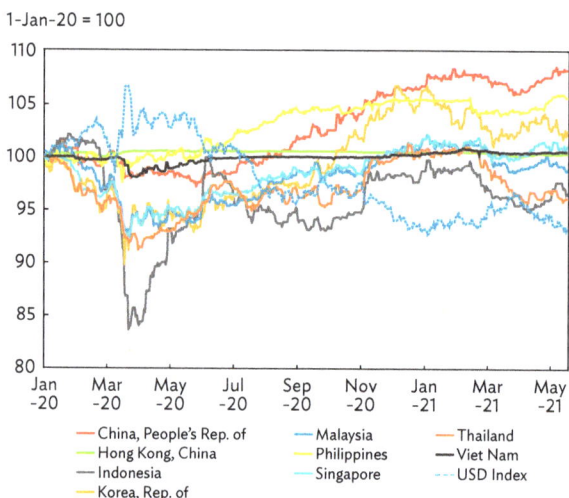

USD = United States dollar.
Note: Data coverage is from 1 January 2020 to 21 May 2021.
Source: *AsianBondsOnline* computations based on Bloomberg LP data.

US economy and the impact of inflation concerns on monetary stances. From 31 March to 21 May, most regional currencies recovered as the Federal Reserve indicated that US inflation was largely transitory, reducing the likelihood of either tapering or tightening (**Figure C.2**). The Philippine peso gained 1.3% versus the US dollar from 28 February to 21 May, as the weak domestic economic performance reduced demand for US dollars. The peso was also buoyed by strong

Figure C.2: Changes in Spot Exchange Rates vs. the United States Dollar

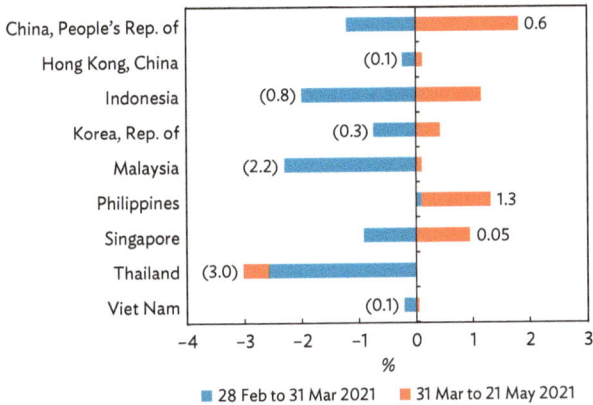

Notes:
1. Changes from 28 February to 31 March 2021 and from 31 March to 21 May 2021.
2. Figures on the chart refer to the net change between the two periods.
3. A positive (negative) value for the foreign exchange rate indicates the appreciation (depreciation) of the local currency against the United States dollar.

Source: Bloomberg LP.

Figure D: Credit Default Swap Spreads in Select Asian Markets (senior 5-year)

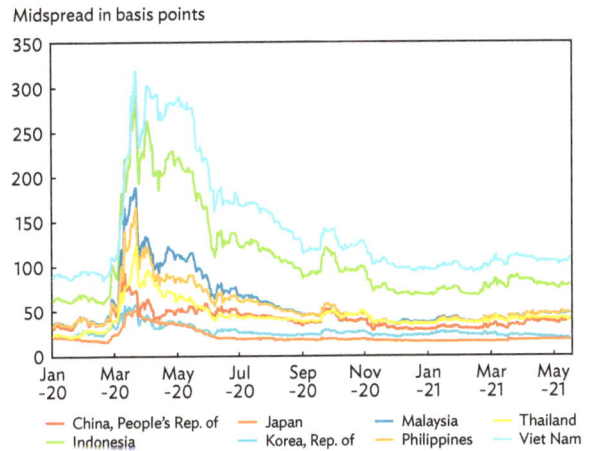

USD = United States dollar.
Notes:
1. Based on USD-denominated sovereign bonds.
2. Data coverage is from 1 January 2020 to 21 May 2021.
Source: Bloomberg LP.

overseas Filipino worker remittances, which grew 12.7% y-o-y in April and 4.9% y-o-y in March. The region's largest currency depreciation was in Thailand where the baht declined 3.0% over growth concerns as the economic recovery was derailed by the resurgence of COVID-19 cases.

Risk sentiment, as captured by credit default swap spreads and sovereign stripped spreads, rose across the region in March due to heightened risk aversion on global inflationary pressure and rising US yields, before declining in April. A few markets witnessed only slightly higher credit default swap spreads by the end of the review period and sovereign stripped spreads were largely calm after a spike in March (**Figures D, E**).

Foreign capital flows into the region's bond markets were volatile in March and April 2021 (**Figure F**). While the PRC market attracted a sizable share of the region's foreign capital inflows, it experienced outflows in March on heightened concerns of a possible "Taper Tantrum" effect over inflation concerns and rising interest rates in the US. As the region's current account performance remained fundamentally solid, foreign reserve buffers were maintained, currency valuations were relatively stable, and with the Federal Reserve indicating that US inflation was mostly transitory, risk sentiment partly recovered, and most regional bond markets recorded positive capital inflows in April.

Figure E: JP Morgan Emerging Markets Bond Index Sovereign Stripped Spreads

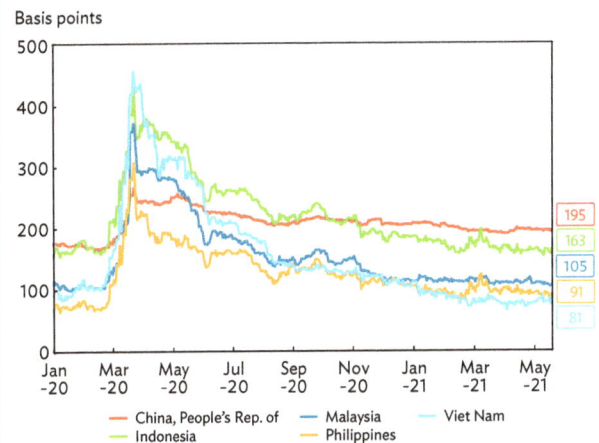

USD = United States dollar.
Notes:
1. Based on USD-denominated sovereign bonds.
2. Data coverage is from 1 January 2020 to 21 May 2021.
Source: Bloomberg LP.

Foreign holdings as a share of regional bond markets were lower at the end of March compared with the end of January in a few markets, resulting from heightened risk aversion amid inflation concerns (**Figure G**). After hitting a high of 10.6% in February, the foreign holdings share in the PRC's bond market slipped to 10.1% at the end of March, as rising US yields limited regional bonds' attractiveness to foreign investors. The delay in the

Figure F: Foreign Bond Flows in Select Emerging East Asian Economies

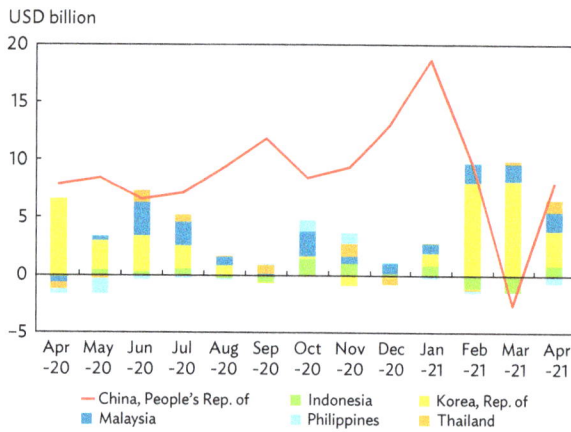

USD = United States dollar.
Notes:
1. The Republic of Korea and Thailand provided data on bond flows. For the PRC, Indonesia, Malaysia, and the Philippines, month-on-month changes in foreign holdings of LCY government bonds were used as a proxy for bond flows.
2. Data as of 30 April 2021.
3. Figures were computed based on 30 April 2021 exchange rates to avoid currency effects.
Sources: People's Republic of China (Bloomberg LP); Indonesia (Directorate General of Budget Financing and Risk Management, Ministry of Finance); Republic of Korea (Financial Supervisory Service); Malaysia (Bank Negara Malaysia); Philippines (Bureau of the Treasury); and Thailand (Thai Bond Market Association).

Figure G: Foreign Holdings Share in Select Emerging East Asian Markets

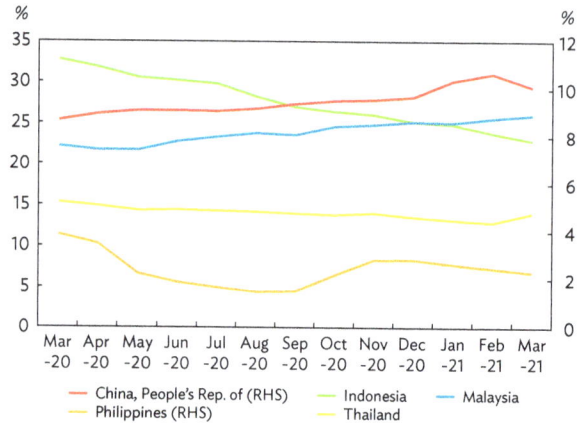

RHS = right-hand side.
Source: *AsianBondsOnline*.

inclusion of Chinese bonds in the World Government Index of FTSE Russell and JP Morgan also contributed to the decline in foreign holdings. The foreign holdings share has steadily declined in both the Philippines and

Indonesia since January on weak domestic economic performances. Malaysia's bond market recorded steady gains in its foreign holdings share, buoyed by its removal from the FTSE Russell watch list in March 2021.

A diversified investor base is very important to the resilience of regional bond markets. Many regional markets—including the Republic of Korea, Thailand, Malaysia, and Viet Nam—enjoy sizable participation by long-term domestic investors such as insurance companies and pension funds (**Figure H**). Banks are the

Figure H: Investor Profiles of Local Currency Government Bonds in Select Emerging East Asian Markets

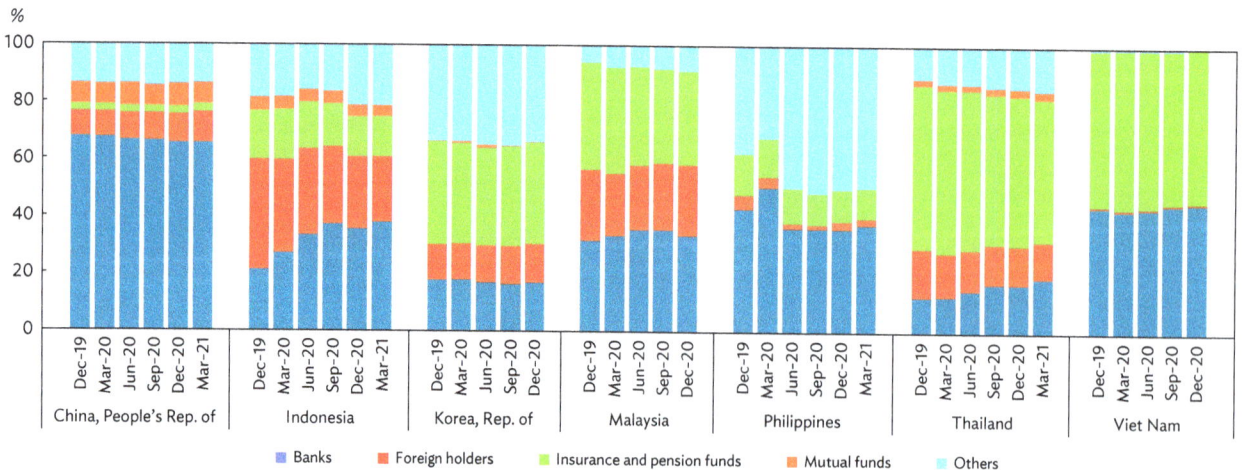

Notes:
1. Data coverage is from December 2019 to March 2021 except for the Republic of Korea, Malaysia, and Viet Nam (December 2020).
2. Others include central banks, governments, individuals, securities companies, custodians, private corporations, and all other investors not elsewhere classified.
Source: *AsianBondsOnline* computations based on local market sources.

major market player in the PRC's bond market. However, a number of bond markets in emerging East Asia are dominated by only a few investor groups. Greater diversification of the investor base is needed in the region's bond markets. This was also evident in the results of the annual *AsianBondsOnline* bond market liquidity survey conducted in late 2020, where survey participants cited the importance of greater diversity of the investor profile among the structural issues that need further development in the region's bond markets.

Economic Outlook

Let us now turn to the regional economic outlook, which affects the outlook for regional financial markets. A number of safe and effective COVID-19 vaccines arrived in late 2020, giving rise to hopes that the world would soon return to pre-pandemic normal. Those hopes proved too sanguine because the pace of vaccination has been substantially slower than expected in not only developing economies but also in some advanced economies. As of 17 June, over 2.5 billion vaccine doses had been administered, representing 16.1% of the global population.[2] Furthermore, vaccination rates varied widely across the world, with advanced economies generally performing better than developing economies.

Although global COVID-19 vaccination has been slow and uneven, the world is gradually moving toward global herd immunity. Notwithstanding the slower-than-expected progress of vaccination, both business and consumer confidence are gradually improving. Furthermore, even when there are renewed pandemic outbreaks, governments have generally not resorted to lockdowns or other draconian measures. The world has learned to live with COVID-19, which explains why economies remain open to varying degrees even in the face of fresh COVID-19 case surges.

The improvement of business and consumer confidence around the world due to the slow but steady progress on vaccination has lifted economic activity. Greater mobility due to less stringent restrictions is also having a positive effect. In light of these favorable developments, the International Monetary Fund (IMF) upgraded its projected 2021 growth for the world economy to 6.0% in its latest *April 2021 World Economic Outlook* from 5.5% in its January 2021 forecast and 5.2% in its October

2020 forecast. The IMF also upgraded its projected 2022 global growth forecast to 4.4% from 4.2% in both its January 2021 and October 2020 forecasts. In its April report, the IMF estimated that the world economy shrank by 3.3% in 2020, a tad smaller than its estimate of a 3.5% contraction in January. The growth forecast upgrade was more pronounced for advanced economies, which the IMF expects to expand by 5.1% in 2021 and 3.6% in 2022, following a contraction of 4.7% in 2020. Growth forecasts for emerging markets and developing economies are −2.2%, 6.7%, and 5.0% for 2020, 2021, and 2022, respectively. A powerful engine of global economic recovery is world trade, which is forecast to expand 8.4% in 2021 and 6.5% in 2022 after contracting 8.5% in 2020.

In its *April 2021 Asian Development Outlook*, the Asian Development Bank predicted that developing Asia will also stage a robust recovery from the COVID-19 crisis. Despite limited progress on vaccination and major COVID-19 outbreaks in India and elsewhere, the region is projected to grow by 7.3% in 2021 and 5.3% in 2022, following a marginal contraction of 0.2% in 2020. Developing Asia's turnaround is broad-based and well-balanced, with both domestic demand and exports contributing to the growth momentum. The projected 2021 growth figures for the PRC; the Association of Southeast Asian Nations (ASEAN); the Republic of Korea; and Hong Kong, China are 8.1%, 4.4%, 3.5%, and 4.6%, respectively. The corresponding figures for 2022 are 5.5%, 5.1%, 3.1%, and 4.5%.

To conclude, the economic outlook for both the world and for emerging East Asia is clearly positive. Although progress on global vaccination has been slow and uneven, vaccination campaigns have nevertheless given a fillip to business and consumer confidence, lifting economic activity. As vaccinations proceed and the world gradually moves toward global herd immunity, we can expect the global growth momentum to further strengthen.

There is increasing awareness within the region of the importance of a green and inclusive recovery. Many innovative financing solutions can contribute to a sustainable recovery. **Box 1** discusses how regional markets and policy makers have been using green *sukuk* (Islamic bonds) to finance environment-friendly investments.

[2] Bloomberg. 2021. More Than 2.51 Billion Shots Given: Covid-19 Tracker. https://www.bloomberg.com/graphics/covid-vaccine-tracker-global-distribution/.

Box 1: Green *Sukuk* Market

Green *Sukuk* Issuance

Similar to green bonds, proceeds of green *sukuk* (Islamic bonds) can be used to fund environment-friendly projects; but unlike green bond, green *sukuk* are Shari'ah-compliant securities backed by a specific pool of assets (Azhgaliyeva 2021).[a] Green *sukuk* have two labels: Islamic and green. Similar to conventional bonds, green *sukuk* are usually labeled green following the International Capital Market Association's Green Bond Principles and the Association of Southeast Asian Nations Capital Market Forum's Green Bonds Standards.

Most green *sukuk* in the world are issued in Southeast Asia, led by issuances in Malaysia and Indonesia. Global issuance of green *sukuk* grew from 2017 to 2019. However, there was a large decline beginning in 2020, probably due to the outbreak of COVID-19 (**Figure B1.1**). The issuance of green *sukuk* is not yet as well established as the issuance of conventional *sukuk* or green bonds. At the time of writing, there were only 16 green *sukuk* issuers around the world.

As of 21 May 2021, over USD10 billion of green *sukuk* had been issued by 16 entities from four countries—Indonesia, Saudi Arabia, the United Arab Emirates, and Malaysia (in descending order)—and the Islamic Development Bank (**Figure B1.2**).

Green *Sukuk* Policy Support in Malaysia

The Securities Commission Malaysia introduced national green *sukuk* standards in 2019 in the form of the Sustainable and Responsible Investment *Sukuk* Framework. The list of eligible green *sukuk* projects is provided in **Table B1.1**. Issuers of green *sukuk* that are compliant with the framework receive a subsidy of 90% of the cost of an external reviewer (up to MYR300,000), income tax exemption, and a tax deduction (Azhgaliyeva, Kapoor, and Liu 2020). Although comprising only 11% (USD1.2 billion) of global total green *sukuk* issuance, Malaysia has the largest number of private green *sukuk* issuers in the world, and they are supported by green bond grant and tax incentives.

Figure B1.1: Green *Sukuk* Issuance

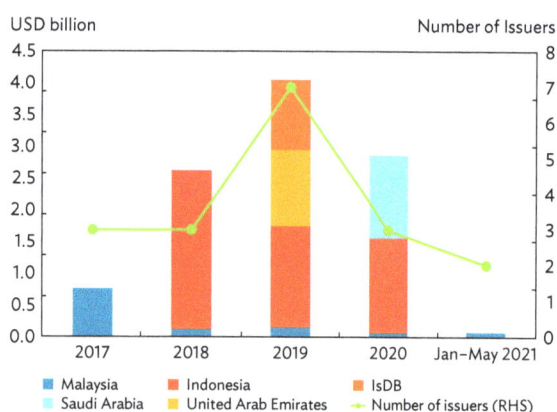

IsDB = Islamic Development Bank, RHS = right-hand side, USD = United States dollar.
Note: Data as of 21 May 2021.
Source: Author's compilation based on data from Bloomberg.

Figure B1.2: Green *Sukuk* Issuance by Country
(USD billion)

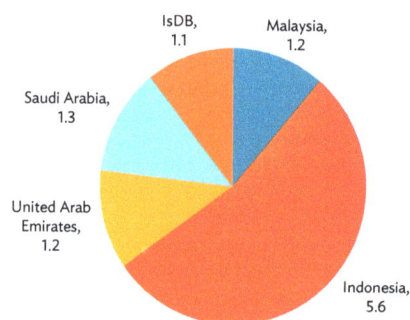

IsDB = Islamic Development Bank, USD = United States dollar.
Note: Data as of 21 May 2021.
Source: Author's compilation based on data from Bloomberg.

[a] This box was written by Dina Azhgaliyeva, research fellow of the Asian Development Bank Institute.

continued on next page

Box 1: Green *Sukuk* Market   *continued*

Table B1.1: Green *Sukuk* National Policies in Malaysia

Policy	Description
SRI *Sukuk* Framework, 2014	Eligible projects include natural resources, renewable energy and energy efficiency, and community and economic development or *waqf* (donated properties and assets)
SRI *Sukuk* and Bond Grant Scheme, 2018–2025	The cost of an external reviewer for issuing green bonds compliant with the SRI *Sukuk* Framework or ASEAN Green, Social, or Sustainability Bond Standards is subsidized at 90% (up to MYR300,000)
Tax Deduction, 2016–2023	Tax deductions for expenditures incurred on issuances that are compliant with the SRI *Sukuk* Framework and approved or authorized by, or lodged with, the Securities Commission Malaysia through 2023
Income Tax Exemption, 2018–2025	Income tax exemptions for recipients of the SRI *Sukuk* and Bond Grant Scheme

ASEAN = Association of Southeast Asian Nations, MYR = Malaysian ringgit, SRI = Sustainable and Responsible Investment *Sukuk* Framework.
Sources: Azhgaliyeva, Kapoor, and Liu (2020); Securities Commission Malaysia (2019); and https://www.sc.com.my/development/sri.

Green *Sukuk* Policy Support in Indonesia

Indonesia also has a national regulatory framework for green bond issuance and, specifically, a national Green Bond and Green *Sukuk* Framework. The list of eligible and excluded projects is provided in **Table B1.2**. Since 2018, more than half (USD5.5 billion) of all green *sukuk* issuance globally has come from a public issuance by the Government of Indonesia.

Table B1.2: National Green *Sukuk* Policies in Indonesia

Policy	Description
Green Bond and Green *Sukuk* Framework, 2017	Eligible projects include renewable energy, energy efficiency, resilience to climate change and disaster risk reduction, sustainable transport, waste-to-energy and waste management, sustainable management of natural resources, green tourism, green buildings, and sustainable agriculture. Excluded projects include new fossil-fuel-based electric power generation capacity, large-scale hydro plants, and nuclear and nuclear-related assets.
Sovereign Green *Sukuk*, 2018	From March 2018 to May 2021, Perusahaan Penerbit SBSN Indonesia III issued USD5.5 billion of sovereign green *sukuk*, or more than half of total global green *sukuk* issuance.

Note: Perusahaan Penerbit SBSN Indonesia III is a special purpose vehicle incorporated by the Government of Indonesia.
Source: Azhgaliyeva, Kapoor, and Liu (2020).

Demand for Green *Sukuk*

Green *sukuk* help investors meet their targets of investing in environment-friendly projects. Although the supply of green *sukuk* comes entirely from markets in Southeast Asia (Malaysia and Indonesia) and the Middle East (Saudi Arabia and the United Arab Emirates), investors in green *sukuk* come from 19 economies, led by the United States (US),

Figure B1.3: Demand for Green *Sukuk* across Issuing Economies and Currencies

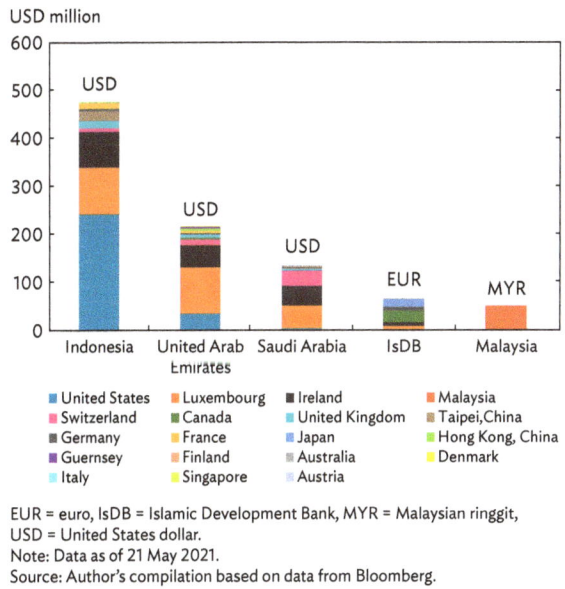

EUR = euro, IsDB = Islamic Development Bank, MYR = Malaysian ringgit, USD = United States dollar.
Note: Data as of 21 May 2021.
Source: Author's compilation based on data from Bloomberg.

the European Union, Canada, and the United Kingdom (**Figure B1.3**).

Most issuers of green *sukuk* rely on international demand, which is why 88% of green *sukuk* are issued in either US dollars or euros. US dollar-denominated issuance has comprised 77% of total green *sukuk* issuance since 2017, followed by the euro (11%), Malaysian ringgit (11%), and Indonesian rupiah (1%) (**Figure B1.4**).

Figure B1.4: Green *Sukuk* Issuance by Currency

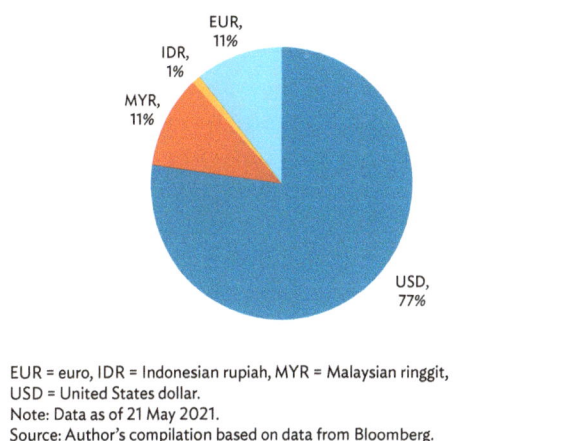

EUR = euro, IDR = Indonesian rupiah, MYR = Malaysian ringgit, USD = United States dollar.
Note: Data as of 21 May 2021.
Source: Author's compilation based on data from Bloomberg.

continued on next page

Box 1: Green *Sukuk* Market   *continued*

Malaysia and Indonesia dominate local-currency-denominated green *sukuk* issuance. Green *sukuk* denominated in US dollars and euros attract international investors, while green *sukuk* denominated in Malaysian ringgit so far have attracted local investors only. A green *sukuk* issuance in Indonesian rupiah in November 2019 has yet to attract investors.

From the first issued green *sukuk* in June 2017 until 2019, green *sukuk* issuance grew steadily. Last year was challenging for green *sukuk* issuers as annual issuance declined in 2020 and continued to fall in the first 5 months of 2021. Green *sukuk* issuance in Malaysia and Indonesia is driven by supply-side policy support. Policies supporting green *sukuk*—national standards, grants, sovereign bonds—are similar to green bond supporting policies.

References

Azhgaliyeva, D. 2021. Green Islamic Bonds. *Asian Development Outlook 2021 Background Paper*. https://www.adb.org/documents/asian-development-outlook-2021-background-papers.
Azhgaliyeva, D., A. Kapoor, and Y. Liu. 2020. Green Bonds for Financing Renewable Energy and Energy Efficiency in South-East Asia: A Review of Policies. *Journal of Sustainable Finance & Investment*. 10 (2). pp. 113–40.
Securities Commission Malaysia. 2019. *Sustainable and Responsible Investment Sukuk Framework: An Overview*. https://www.sc.com.my/api/documentms/download.ashx?id=84491531-2b7e-4362-bafb-83bb33b07416.
World Bank. 2020. *Pioneering the Green Sukuk: Three Years On*. https://openknowledge.worldbank.org/handle/10986/34569.

Risks to Economic Outlook and Financial Stability

Both downside and upside risks loom on the horizon. The risks to emerging East Asia's economic outlook and financial stability are broadly balanced. The COVID-19 pandemic is the source of both the biggest upside risk and the biggest downside risk. It is true that an elevated degree of uncertainty surrounds the future trajectory of the pandemic. But it is also true that economies around the world and the region have learned to live with the virus. Governments now largely avoid automatically imposing lockdowns or other stringent restrictions at the first sign of a renewed outbreak. Instead, they allow their economies to remain open to varying degrees even when there is a fresh resurgence of new cases. Somewhat paradoxically, although developing Asia has lagged the rest of the world in vaccination progress and is a long way from reaching herd immunity, it is projected to grow strongly by 7.3% this year. The paradox fades once we recognize that mobility restrictions have been eased out of sheer economic necessity. COVID-19 or not, governments in the region and elsewhere are realizing that they cannot shut down their economies forever. Put differently, in the tradeoff between lives versus livelihoods, governments are increasingly favoring livelihoods.

However, governments have little choice but to reimpose stringent restrictions in the face of virulent new waves of the pandemic, such as the one that has ravaged India since March. At a broader level, a resurgence of the pandemic remains the single biggest negative risk facing emerging East Asia's economy and financial markets. An especially worrisome trend is the emergence of new COVID-19 variants that may potentially be resistant to vaccines. This makes it all the more imperative for the global community to work closely together to produce and distribute as many vaccines as possible and vaccinate as many people as possible. As long as a large share of the global population remains unvaccinated, new vaccine-resistant COVID-19 strains might continue to emerge, frustrating efforts to bring the pandemic under control. Protracted delays in the production and distribution of vaccines thus pose a major downside risk, especially in developing countries with weaker medical infrastructures.

At the same time, COVID-19 poses the single biggest positive risk to economic growth and financial stability. As noted earlier, vaccine rollout has been slow and uneven, not only in developing countries but also in some advanced economies such as Japan. However, the weakness that has been hindering global recovery could unleash global recovery. Specifically, accelerated production and rollout of vaccines would move the world much closer to its pre-COVID-19 status of 2019 or something reasonably close to that. Even the limited progress on global vaccination so far has tangibly improved business and investor confidence, lifting both investment and consumption. This implies that the acceleration of global vaccination campaigns, and hence the acceleration of progress toward global herd immunity, would provide a huge boost to global consumption, investment, and growth. In this optimistic scenario, the light at the end of the COVID-19 tunnel would no longer remain a hope but a reality, and growth could surpass forecasts by a wide margin.

While the overarching upside and downside risk is both closely related to the evolution of COVID-19 and global vaccination campaigns, a number of other risks loom. In particular, geopolitical tension between the PRC and the US remains at elevated levels despite the advent of a new administration in Washington, DC. Given the structural and multifaceted nature of the tension between the world's two biggest economies, it is unclear if relations will improve substantially in the near future. This is not only harmful for the PRC's growth prospects but also those of its neighbors that have close trade, investment, and other economic links with both giants. On the other hand, if PRC–US relations were to suddenly improve, the regional and global economies stand to gain from the mitigation of a major source of uncertainty in the economic landscape.

A low-probability risk to emerging Asia's financial stability arises from a possible tightening of global financial conditions. The region currently enjoys relatively benign financial conditions relative to 2013, as evident in robust current account balances, foreign reserve levels, currency valuations, and relatively low inflation rates. However, given that the robust US economy is showing signs of incipient inflationary pressure, the Federal Reserve might react by suddenly and sharply raising interest rates. Such a monetary policy shock from the US could trigger capital outflows from the region and destabilize regional financial markets. However, given the strong fundamentals of emerging East Asian economies, evident in healthy current account positions, large foreign exchange reserves, and macroeconomic stability, a repeat of something like the 2013 Taper Tantrum is highly unlikely. To sum up, the primary upside and downside risks to the region's growth and financial stability both stem from COVID-19 and are broadly in balance.

While there have been discussions on the rapid buildup of debt in many emerging markets during the pandemic, it is important to mobilize more domestic resources to broaden funding sources. **Box 2** analyzes how technological advances such as digital finance can help mobilize more domestic resources to finance needed investments.

Box 2: Scaling Up Sustainable Investments through Fintech

Although the international discourse on financing for development has highlighted the need for unlocking domestic resources, much of the discussion has centered around incentivizing private capital from advanced countries to finance investment in developing and emerging economies.[a] While foreign aid and foreign private capital can play an important role in financing development, it is important to acknowledge the limits of foreign investment in financing infrastructure, as well as the financial vulnerability risks associated with foreign finance. It is also important to make better use of domestic savings in developing and emerging economies, many of which invest significant amounts of their savings in low-yielding assets in the financial centers of advanced economies due to underdeveloped capital markets at home and a scarcity of "safe" assets denominated in local currency (LCY). Strengthening domestic resource mobilization is therefore crucial, and concerted efforts to this effect are needed.

Financial technologies, or fintech, can complement conventional banking and capital markets, and facilitate domestic resource mobilization for sustainable investments (Chen and Volz 2021). Fintech, which is also known as digital finance, is a business approach dedicated to making financial services more efficient through internet-related technologies. Fintech comprises different applications, including lending, blockchain and cryptocurrency, regulatory technology (regtech), personal finance, payment service and billing, insurance, capital market solutions, wealth management, money transfer and remittances, and mortgage and real estate financing (**Table B2.1**).

The G20 Sustainable Finance Study Group (2018) highlighted the emerging practice and opportunities of applying digital technologies to sustainable finance. As pointed out by the Sustainable Digital Finance Alliance (2018), digital finance can help overcome challenges to connecting the financial

[a] This box was written by Yushi Chen, doctoral researcher of the Science Policy Research Unit at the University of Sussex, and Ulrich Volz, director of the Centre for Sustainable Finance at SOAS University of London and senior research fellow at the German Development Institute.

continued on next page

Box 2: Scaling Up Sustainable Investments through Fintech *continued*

Table B2.1: Overview of Fintech Solutions

Category	Example
Lending solutions	Online marketplace lending and alternative underwriting platforms such as peer-to-peer lending platforms and digital crowdfunding platforms
Blockchain and cryptocurrency	Companies leveraging blockchain technologies for financial services
Regulatory technology (regtech)	Audit, risk, and regulatory compliance software
Personal finance	Tools to manage bills and track personal and/or credit accounts
Payment service and billing	Payments processing, payments transferring, card developers, and subscription billing software tools (a major function of mobile banking)
Insurance solutions	Online insurance services or data analytics and software for (re)insurers
Capital market solutions	Sales and trading, analysis, and infrastructure tools for financial institutions
Wealth management	Investment and wealth management platforms and analytics tools
Money transfer and remittances	International money transfer and tracking software
Mortgage and real estate financing	Mortgage lending and financing platforms

Source: Chen and Volz (2021) based on CB Insights (2019).

sector with the real economy by improving information flows and the efficiency of financial services, and by overcoming information asymmetries through better systems and data. It can foster inclusion and innovation in the real economy by broadening sustainability choices and providing new sources of finance. Digital finance can also help to unlock the full potential of sustainable finance by facilitating better use of sustainability-related data for financial decision-making

and by supporting nascent business models by enabling better access to funding. The United Nations Secretary General's Task Force on Digital Financing of the Sustainable Development Goals recently emphasized the development of financial inclusion into citizen-centric finance as one of the transformational opportunities brought about by digitalization (Digital Financing Task Force 2020).

Chen and Volz (2021) show how fintech and blockchain-based solutions can facilitate domestic resource mobilization for sustainable infrastructure investments and at the same time improve the implementation of infrastructure projects throughout the entire life cycle by facilitating processes and enhancing transparency. Blockchain technology, which is based on distributed ledger technology, provides an encrypted, tamper-proof, and transparent system that can be used to implement innovative solutions for financing sustainable infrastructure.

Chen and Volz (2021) propose a comprehensive blockchain-based approach that integrates multiple fintech applications to mobilize domestic financing for sustainable infrastructure investment. In particular, blockchain-based project bonds could be issued through a digital crowdfunding platform that transparently records and certifies the use of proceeds, sustainability impact, and revenue streams of the project by combining timestamp, public and private key mechanisms, and smart contract technologies. Blockchain technology could be used to address key concerns in the three key phases of an infrastructure project's life cycle: (i) inception and fundraising, (ii) realization, and (iii) operation (**Figure B2**).

Figure B2: Key Phases of the Infrastructure Project Life Cycle and Advantages of a Blockchain-Based Finance Approach

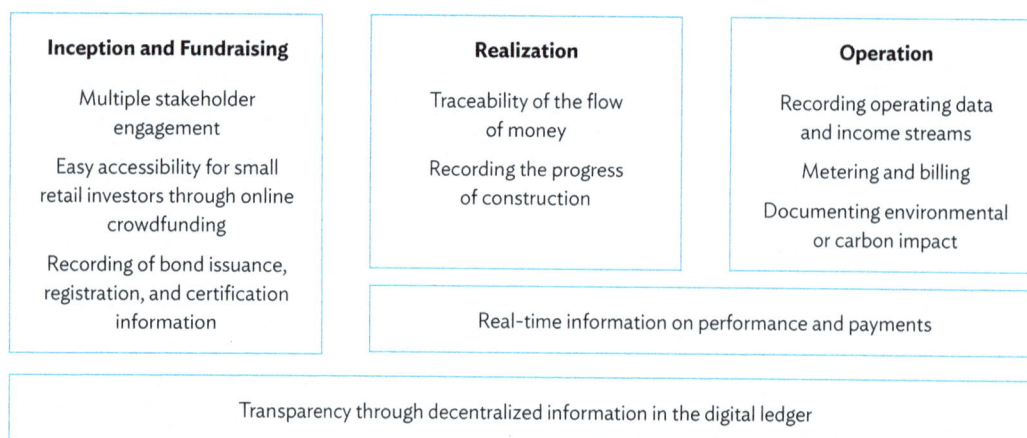

Inception and Fundraising
Multiple stakeholder engagement
Easy accessibility for small retail investors through online crowdfunding
Recording of bond issuance, registration, and certification information

Realization
Traceability of the flow of money
Recording the progress of construction

Operation
Recording operating data and income streams
Metering and billing
Documenting environmental or carbon impact

Real-time information on performance and payments

Transparency through decentralized information in the digital ledger

Source: Chen and Volz (2021).

continued on next page

Box 2: Scaling Up Sustainable Investments through Fintech   *continued*

In the inception and fundraising phase, blockchain can be coupled with a digital crowdfunding platform to mobilize domestic savings for investment in LCY project bonds. Mobile-based fintech solutions could enable small-scale retail investors to buy bonds on their phone, providing investment opportunities for people who would traditionally have neither the means nor the expertise and access to invest in securities. By applying blockchain technology, the bond issuing entity can record the bond issuance, registration, and certification information in the blockchain network, which enhances the credibility of the project.

In the realization phase, the blockchain can record information on the flow of money and the progress of construction in the digital ledger, enabling investors and other stakeholders to trace the use of proceeds and obtain information on the construction status in a transparent way in real time. The International Monetary Fund (2020) estimates that globally around one-third of funds dedicated to public infrastructure investment is lost to inefficiencies or corruption. Enhanced transparency can reduce the risk of misappropriation of proceeds and help identify problems early on.

Last but not least, blockchain can also facilitate project management once the project is operational, e.g., through metering and billing. By recording operating data on the blockchain, stakeholders can receive transparent information on project revenue streams and reduce the risk for investors. It also provides the option of documenting environmental or carbon impacts, which could be used for receiving carbon credits through carbon emission trading schemes. The issuing entity can leverage the blockchain to build an impact investing information platform, which documents the carbon certification or emission reductions, or any other positive impacts—be they ecological or social—that the project may have.

Overall, such a fintech approach would not only provide investors of different sizes the opportunity to purchase LCY assets and issuers such as municipalities to raise funds for sustainable infrastructure investment. It would also facilitate project management once the project is operational and create full transparency across the life cycle of the investment, reducing problems with misuse of funds. This approach could be configured in multiple ways to suit different situations. The main idea is to leverage the strength of a decentralized governance model backed by blockchain to achieve project-level financial inclusion. By replicating this approach, multiple projects could be aggregated to create a larger portfolio that would be attractive to institutional investors, including impact investors.

References

CB Insights. 2019. *FinTech Trends to Watch*. https://www.cbinsights.com/research/report/fintech-trends-2019/.

Chen, Y. and U. Volz. 2020. Scaling Up Sustainable Investment through Blockchain-Based Project Bonds. *ADBI Working Paper* No. 1247. Tokyo: Asian Development Bank Institute. https://www.adb.org/sites/default/files/publication/696276/adbi-wp1247.pdf

Digital Financing Task Force. 2020. *People's Money: Harnessing Digitalization to Finance a Sustainable Future. Final Report of the UN Secretary General's Task Force on Digital Financing of the Sustainable Development Goals*. New York: United Nations.

G20 Sustainable Finance Study Group. 2018. *Sustainable Finance Synthesis Report*. New York.

International Monetary Fund. 2020. *Fiscal Monitor: Policies to Support People during the Covid-19 Pandemic*. Washington, DC: International Monetary Fund.

Sustainable Digital Finance Alliance. 2018. *Digital Technologies for Mobilizing Sustainable Finance: Applications of Digital Technologies to Sustainable Finance*. Geneva.

Bond Market Developments in the First Quarter of 2021

Size and Composition

Emerging East Asia's local currency bond market expanded in the first quarter of 2021 to reach a size of USD20.3 trillion at the end of March.

The local currency (LCY) bond market in emerging East Asia continued to grow in the first quarter (Q1) of 2021, reaching an aggregate size of USD20.3 trillion at the end of March.[3] Overall growth eased to 2.2% quarter-on-quarter (q-o-q) from 3.1% q-o-q in the fourth quarter (Q4) of 2020 (**Figure 1a**). The region's government and corporate bond segments continued to expand in Q1 2021, albeit at a weaker pace than in the prior quarter as governments balanced fiscal policy with risk control and corporates weigh uncertainties surrounding the pace of economic recovery in the region.

The q-o-q growth rate of bonds outstanding moderated in five of the region's nine markets from Q4 2020 to Q1 2021. All markets except for Thailand and Viet Nam posted positive q-o-q growth in Q1 2021. Among those that recorded an expansion, the Philippine and Indonesian bond markets posted the fastest q-o-q growth in Q1 2021, while markets in Hong Kong, China and the People's Republic of China (PRC) had the weakest growth.

On a year-on-year (y-o-y) basis, the region's LCY bond market grew at a weaker pace of 15.9% in Q1 2020 versus 18.2% in Q4 2020 (**Figure 1b**). All emerging East Asian bond markets except Hong Kong, China; Indonesia; and Singapore experienced a slowdown in y-o-y growth in Q1 2021 compared to the previous quarter. Nonetheless, all nine emerging East Asian markets posted positive y-o-y growth in Q1 2021, led by Indonesia and the Philippines.

The PRC's bond market remained the largest in the region at the end of March with outstanding bonds of USD15.8 trillion. The PRC's share of the region's total

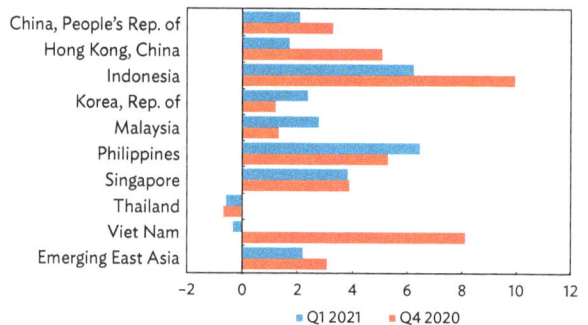

Figure 1a: Growth of Local Currency Bond Markets in the Fourth Quarter of 2020 and First Quarter of 2021 (q-o-q, %)

q-o-q = quarter-on-quarter, Q1 = first quarter, Q4 = fourth quarter.
Notes:
1. For Singapore, corporate bonds outstanding are based on *AsianBondsOnline* estimates.
2. Calculated using data from national sources.
3. Growth rates are calculated from local currency base and do not include currency effects.
4. Emerging East Asia growth figures are based on 31 March 2021 currency exchange rates and do not include currency effects.
Sources: People's Republic of China (CEIC); Hong Kong, China (Hong Kong Monetary Authority); Indonesia (Bank Indonesia; Directorate General of Budget Financing and Risk Management, Ministry of Finance; and Indonesia Stock Exchange); Republic of Korea (The Bank of Korea and KG Zeroin Corporation); Malaysia (Bank Negara Malaysia); Philippines (Bureau of the Treasury and Bloomberg LP); Singapore (Monetary Authority of Singapore, Singapore Government Securities, and Bloomberg LP); Thailand (Bank of Thailand); and Viet Nam (Bloomberg LP and Vietnam Bond Market Association).

market slipped slightly to 77.8% of bonds outstanding at the end of March from 77.9% at the end of December. Overall growth in the PRC's bond market moderated to 2.1% q-o-q in Q1 2021 from 3.3% q-o-q in Q4 2020.

Growth in the PRC's government bond segment dropped to 1.6% q-o-q in Q1 2021 from 3.8% q-o-q in Q4 2020, dragged down largely by weaker issuance of local government bonds and a contraction in the issuance of Treasury bonds. To manage risk in the financial system, the Government of the PRC scaled back its pandemic stimulus measures. The government also reduced the full-year quota for local government bonds in 2021 to CNY3.65 trillion from CNY3.75 trillion in 2020. While the local government bond stock increased during Q1 2021, the government sought to limit the utilization of this

---

[3] Emerging East Asia comprises the People's Republic of China; Hong Kong, China; Indonesia; the Republic of Korea; Malaysia; the Philippines; Singapore; Thailand; and Viet Nam.

**Figure 1b: Growth of Local Currency Bond Markets
in the Fourth Quarter of 2020 and First Quarter of 2021
(y-o-y, %)**

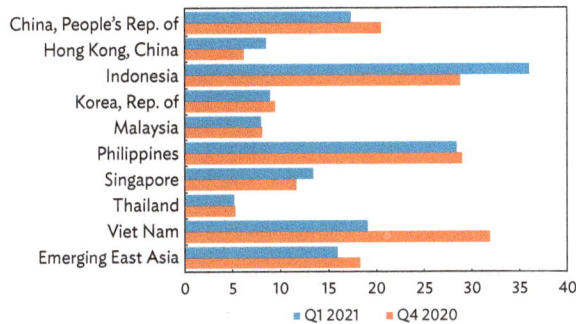

Q1 = first quarter, Q4 = fourth quarter, y-o-y = year-on-year.
Notes:
1. For Singapore, corporate bonds outstanding are based on *AsianBondsOnline* estimates.
2. Calculated using data from national sources.
3. Growth rates are calculated from local currency base and do not include currency effects.
4. Emerging East Asia growth figures are based on 31 March 2021 currency exchange rates and do not include currency effects.
Sources: People's Republic of China (CEIC); Hong Kong, China (Hong Kong Monetary Authority); Indonesia (Bank Indonesia; Directorate General of Budget Financing and Risk Management, Ministry of Finance; and Indonesia Stock Exchange); Republic of Korea (The Bank of Korea and KG Zeroin Corporation); Malaysia (Bank Negara Malaysia); Philippines (Bureau of the Treasury and Bloomberg LP); Singapore (Monetary Authority of Singapore, Singapore Government Securities, and Bloomberg LP); Thailand (Bank of Thailand); and Viet Nam (Bloomberg LP and Vietnam Bond Market Association).

type of bond for fundraising. Unlike the usual practice of speeding up issuance upon replenishment of the quota at the start of the year, local governments slowed their debt issuance during the quarter, thus contributing to the slowdown in the growth of the government bond stock.

Growth in the PRC's corporate bond stock quickened to 2.9% q-o-q in Q1 2021 from 2.4% q-o-q in Q4 2020 amid a brisk economic recovery. On a y-o-y basis, the PRC's bond market expanded 17.3% in Q1 2020, down from 20.5% in the previous quarter.

The Republic of Korea was home to the second-largest LCY bond market in emerging East Asia at the end of March with an outstanding bond stock of USD2.4 trillion. Its share of the regional total was steady from Q4 2020 to Q1 2021 at 11.7%. Overall growth in the bond market doubled to 2.4% q-o-q in Q1 2021 from 1.2% q-o-q in Q4 2020, supported by faster growth in the government bond segment. Growth in outstanding government bonds jumped to 4.0% q-o-q in Q1 2021 from 0.9% q-o-q in

the previous quarter, bolstered by an expansion in the stock of central government bonds. Issuance of Treasury and other government bonds supported this growth, as the government frontloaded expenditures for 2021 to strengthen the domestic economic recovery. Growth in the stock of corporate bonds dipped to 1.2% q-o-q in Q1 2021 from 1.4% q-o-q in Q4 2020 due to maturities and a contraction in issuance. On an annual basis, the Republic of Korea's bond market expanded 8.9% y-o-y in Q1 2021, down from 9.4% y-o-y growth in the prior quarter.

Hong Kong, China's LCY bond market reached a size of USD314.6 billion at the end of March. Overall, the bond market expanded 1.7% q-o-q in Q1 2021, driven largely by growth in the corporate bond segment. The tepid 0.2% q-o-q growth in outstanding government bonds was driven solely by an expansion in the stock of Hong Kong Special Administrative Region bonds, as the outstanding stock of Exchange Fund Bills and Exchange Fund Notes remained unchanged. The corporate bond segment posted a 3.1% q-o-q increase in Q1 2021, supported by strong issuance. On a y-o-y basis, the bond market of Hong Kong, China expanded 8.4% in Q1 2021, up from 6.1% in the previous quarter.

The aggregate amount of LCY bonds outstanding among member economies of the Association of Southeast Asian Nations (ASEAN) stood at USD1.8 trillion at the end of March.[4] Overall growth slipped to 3.0% q-o-q in Q1 2021 from 3.4% q-o-q in Q4 2020. The total government bond stock reached USD1.3 trillion, while corporate bonds outstanding stood at USD0.5 trillion at the end of March. The bond markets of Thailand, Malaysia, and Singapore remained the three largest among all ASEAN members.

Thailand's LCY bonds outstanding stood at USD443.1 billion at the end of March. The bond market continued to contract, declining 0.6% q-o-q in Q1 2021 after a 0.7% q-o-q drop in the previous quarter. Government bonds outstanding declined 0.8% q-o-q in Q1 2021 due to a contraction in Bank of Thailand (BOT) bonds that outpaced the growth in government bonds and state-owned enterprise and other bonds. The stock of outstanding corporate bonds saw a marginal decline of 0.1% q-o-q during the review period due to a high volume of maturities. The y-o-y growth in the Thai bond market fell slightly to 5.1% in Q1 2021 from 5.2% in Q4 2020.

---

[4] LCY bond statistics for ASEAN include the markets of Indonesia, Malaysia, the Philippines, Singapore, Thailand, and Viet Nam.

The outstanding amount of Malaysia's LCY bonds totaled USD397.8 billion at the end of March. Overall growth more than doubled to 2.8% q-o-q in Q1 2021 from 1.3% q-o-q in Q4 2020. Government bonds outstanding expanded 4.3% q-o-q during the review period, boosted primarily by strong growth in central government bonds that outpaced the contraction in central bank bills. Growth in corporate bonds outstanding slowed to 1.0% q-o-q in Q1 2021 from 2.2% q-o-q in Q4 2020. On a y-o-y basis, Malaysia's LCY bond market growth rate was hardly changed, expanding 7.9% in Q1 2021 versus 8.0% in Q4 2020.

The largest *sukuk* (Islamic bond) market in emerging East Asia is in Malaysia, with a total of USD251.3 billion of *sukuk* outstanding at the end of March. *Sukuk* accounted for 63.2% of Malaysia's LCY bond market. At the end of March, the outstanding stock of government *sukuk* totaled USD103.1 billion, or 48.0% of Malaysia's government bond market. Outstanding corporate *sukuk* stood at USD148.2 billion, or 80.9% of the corporate bond market.

Singapore's LCY bonds outstanding reached USD388.3 billion at the end of March, as growth eased to 3.8% q-o-q in Q1 2021 from 3.9% q-o-q in Q4 2020. Government bonds outstanding expanded 6.0% q-o-q in Q1 2021, driven by growth in outstanding Singapore Government Securities and Monetary Authority of Singapore (MAS) bills and notes. The growth in MAS bills was spurred by the issuance of 1-year floating-rate notes in March in addition to existing 6-month floating-rate notes. A contraction of 0.3% q-o-q in the corporate bond segment dragged down growth in government bonds, leading to slightly slower q-o-q growth in Q1 2021 compared with Q4 2020. On an annual basis, Singapore's bond market growth quickened to 13.4% y-o-y in Q1 2021 from 11.6% y-o-y in Q4 2020.

The outstanding amount of Indonesia's LCY bonds stood at USD330.4 billion at the end of March on growth of 6.2% q-o-q. The government bond segment posted growth of 6.7% q-o-q, which stemmed primarily from an expansion in central government bonds. Meanwhile, the stock of Bank Indonesia instruments contracted during the review period due largely to a decline in issuance. The corporate bond segment, which expanded 1.7% q-o-q, also contributed to overall growth in Q1 2021. On a y-o-y basis, Indonesia's LCY bond market growth accelerated to 36.0% in Q1 2021 from 28.7% in the previous quarter.

The Philippines' LCY bond market reached a size of USD187.9 billion at the end of March, as growth quickened to 6.5% q-o-q in Q1 2021 from 5.3% q-o-q in Q4 2020. The growth was driven by the government bond segment, which posted an 8.4% q-o-q expansion in Q1 2021 following a 7.0% q-o-q increase in the prior quarter. Treasury bills and bonds and Bangko Sentral ng Pilipinas securities contributed to the growth, with the latter posting a 35.2% q-o-q gain. The stock of corporate bonds continued to contract, declining 2.0% q-o-q in Q1 2021 after a 1.3% q-o-q drop in Q4 2020, as weak market sentiment persisted amid a resurgence of COVID-19 cases during the review period.

The LCY bond market in Viet Nam remained the smallest in emerging East Asia with an outstanding bond stock of USD71.0 billion at the end of March. Viet Nam's LCY bond market contracted 0.3% q-o-q in Q1 2021, driven largely by a decline in the stock of government bonds, which offset the growth in the stock of corporate bonds. Government bonds contracted 1.1% q-o-q in Q1 2021 due to declines in Treasury bonds and government-guaranteed and municipal bonds. Corporate bonds expanded 3.3% q-o-q during the review period. On a y-o-y basis, Viet Nam's bond market grew 19.0% in Q1 2021, down from 31.9% in the previous quarter.

At the end of March, government bonds continued to account for the majority of emerging East Asia's total LCY bond stock, representing a 61.8% share. In nominal terms, the outstanding amount of government bonds in the region climbed to USD12.6 trillion on growth of 2.1% q-o-q and 18.0% y-o-y (**Table 1**). Except for Thailand and Viet Nam, all government bond markets in the region posted positive q-o-q growth in Q1 2021. Nonetheless, the q-o-q growth of the region's government bond stock slowed in Q1 2021 versus Q4 2020, as growth moderated in most of the region's markets including that of the PRC.

The PRC and the Republic of Korea maintained their positions as the first- and second-largest government bond markets in the region, respectively, with a combined share of 88.3% of the region's total government bond stock at the end of March. ASEAN economies held 10.5% of the region's government bond total. Among ASEAN economies, the largest government bond markets were those of Thailand, Indonesia, and Singapore.

Table 1: Size and Composition of Local Currency Bond Markets

	Q1 2020		Q4 2020		Q1 2021		Growth Rate (LCY-base %)				Growth Rate (USD-base %)			
							Q1 2020		Q1 2021		Q1 2020		Q1 2021	
	Amount (USD billion)	% share	Amount (USD billion)	% share	Amount (USD billion)	% share	q-o-q	y-o-y	q-o-q	y-o-y	q-o-q	y-o-y	q-o-q	y-o-y
China, People's Rep. of														
Total	12,464	100.0	15,537	100.0	15,799	100.0	4.9	16.1	2.1	17.3	3.1	10.1	1.7	26.8
Government	7,886	63.3	9,978	64.2	10,102	63.9	3.5	13.8	1.6	18.5	1.7	7.9	1.2	28.1
Corporate	4,577	36.7	5,559	35.8	5,697	36.1	7.3	20.3	2.9	15.2	5.5	14.0	2.5	24.5
Hong Kong, China														
Total	291	100.0	310	100.0	315	100.0	(0.5)	0.3	1.7	8.4	0.1	1.6	1.4	8.1
Government	151	51.9	153	49.3	153	48.6	(1.1)	0.7	0.2	1.5	(0.6)	2.0	0.03	1.2
Corporate	140	48.1	157	50.7	162	51.4	0.2	(0.2)	3.1	15.9	0.7	1.1	2.8	15.5
Indonesia														
Total	216	100.0	322	100.0	330	100.0	0.6	6.4	6.2	36.0	(14.5)	(7.1)	2.8	52.7
Government	189	87.4	291	90.6	301	91.0	0.7	6.7	6.7	41.5	(14.4)	(6.8)	3.2	58.9
Corporate	27	12.6	30	9.4	30	9.0	(0.5)	4.4	1.7	(2.3)	(15.4)	(8.8)	(1.6)	9.8
Korea, Rep. of														
Total	2,032	100.0	2,424	100.0	2,382	100.0	2.8	8.7	2.4	8.9	(2.4)	1.3	(1.7)	17.2
Government	814	40.1	993	41.0	992	41.6	4.2	6.6	4.0	13.1	(1.1)	(0.7)	(0.1)	21.8
Corporate	1,218	59.9	1,430	59.0	1,390	58.4	1.9	10.2	1.2	6.0	(3.3)	2.7	(2.8)	14.1
Malaysia														
Total	354	100.0	399	100.0	398	100.0	2.9	6.0	2.8	7.9	(2.6)	0.2	(0.3)	12.5
Government	186	52.6	212	53.1	215	54.0	3.9	4.9	4.3	10.7	(1.6)	(0.9)	1.2	15.4
Corporate	168	47.4	187	46.9	183	46.0	1.7	7.3	1.0	4.8	(3.7)	1.3	(2.0)	9.3
Philippines														
Total	140	100.0	178	100.0	188	100.0	6.9	7.9	6.5	28.4	6.8	11.8	5.4	34.1
Government	109	77.8	145	81.2	155	82.7	7.5	6.2	8.4	36.5	7.4	10.1	7.3	42.6
Corporate	31	22.2	34	18.8	33	17.3	5.0	14.0	(2.0)	0.01	4.9	18.2	(3.0)	4.5
Singapore														
Total	324	100.0	380	100.0	388	100.0	2.2	11.8	3.8	13.4	(3.3)	6.5	2.1	19.9
Government	206	63.6	249	65.5	260	66.9	2.5	14.6	6.0	19.3	(3.0)	9.3	4.2	26.1
Corporate	118	36.4	131	34.5	129	33.1	1.7	7.1	(0.3)	3.1	(3.7)	2.1	(1.9)	9.0
Thailand														
Total	402	100.0	465	100.0	443	100.0	(0.5)	4.1	(0.6)	5.1	31.3	44.7	(4.7)	10.2
Government	286	71.0	342	73.5	325	73.3	(1.0)	2.7	(0.8)	8.5	26.4	37.3	(4.8)	13.8
Corporate	117	29.0	123	26.5	118	26.7	0.8	7.9	(0.1)	(3.3)	45.2	66.8	(4.2)	1.4
Viet Nam														
Total	58	100.0	71	100.0	71	100.0	10.4	14.4	(0.3)	19.0	8.3	12.2	(0.2)	22.0
Government	53	91.6	59	82.7	58	82.1	10.5	15.4	(1.1)	6.6	8.3	13.2	(0.9)	9.2
Corporate	5	8.4	12	17.3	13	17.9	9.9	4.1	3.3	154.9	7.8	2.1	3.4	161.3
Emerging East Asia														
Total	16,281	100.0	20,086	100.0	20,314	100.0	4.2	14.0	2.2	15.9	2.4	8.8	1.1	24.8
Government	9,881	60.7	12,422	61.8	12,560	61.8	3.3	12.3	2.1	18.0	1.6	7.3	1.1	27.1
Corporate	6,400	39.3	7,664	38.2	7,754	38.2	5.7	16.8	2.4	12.6	3.6	11.3	1.2	21.1
Japan														
Total	11,079	100.0	12,115	100.0	11,604	100.0	0.04	1.4	2.7	7.8	1.0	4.5	(4.2)	4.7
Government	10,282	92.8	11,250	92.9	10,793	93.0	0.01	0.9	2.9	8.1	1.0	4.1	(4.1)	5.0
Corporate	797	7.2	865	7.1	811	7.0	0.4	7.9	0.4	4.7	1.4	11.3	(6.3)	1.7

( ) = negative, LCY = local currency, q-o-q = quarter-on-quarter, Q1 = first quarter, Q4 = fourth quarter, USD = United States dollar, y-o-y = year-on-year.

Notes:
1. For Singapore, corporate bonds outstanding are based on *AsianBondsOnline* estimates.
2. Corporate bonds include issues by financial institutions.
3. Bloomberg LP end-of-period LCY–USD rates are used.
4. For LCY base, emerging East Asia growth figures based on 31 March 2021 currency exchange rates and do not include currency effects.
5. Emerging East Asia comprises the People's Republic of China; Hong Kong, China; Indonesia; the Republic of Korea; Malaysia; the Philippines; Singapore; Thailand; and Viet Nam.
6. For Indonesia, data for government bonds include nontradable bonds.

Sources: People's Republic of China (CEIC); Hong Kong, China (Hong Kong Monetary Authority); Indonesia (Bank Indonesia; Directorate General of Budget Financing and Risk Management, Ministry of Finance; and Indonesia Stock Exchange); Republic of Korea (The Bank of Korea and KG Zeroin Corporation); Malaysia (Bank Negara Malaysia); Philippines (Bureau of the Treasury and Bloomberg LP); Singapore (Monetary Authority of Singapore, Singapore Government Securities, and Bloomberg LP); Thailand (Bank of Thailand); Viet Nam (Bloomberg LP and Vietnam Bond Market Association); and Japan (Japan Securities Dealers Association).

LCY corporate bonds outstanding in emerging East Asia reached USD7.8 trillion at the end of March. On a q-o-q basis, growth in the region's corporate bond market quickened to 2.4% in Q1 2021 from 2.2% in the previous quarter. The faster growth rate was driven mostly by growth in the PRC's corporate bond market. Six out of the region's nine markets showed positive q-o-q growth in their corporate bond segments during the review period. The Philippines, Singapore, and Thailand posted contractions in the stock of their corporate bonds. On a y-o-y basis, growth in the region's LCY corporate bond stock moderated to 12.6% in Q1 2021 from 16.2% in Q4 2020.

The PRC and the Republic of Korea accounted for the majority of emerging East's Asia's corporate bond stock with a combined share of 91.4% at the end of March. ASEAN economies accounted for 6.5% of emerging East Asia's corporate bond stock. Within ASEAN, Malaysia had the largest corporate bond market at the end of March, followed by Singapore and Thailand.

The aggregate amount of LCY bonds outstanding in emerging East Asia was equivalent to 96.4% of the region's GDP at the end of March, down from 97.7% at the end of December 2020 but up from 88.1% in March 2020 (**Table 2**). The GDP shares of both government and corporate bonds decreased in Q1 2021 from Q4 2020: the government bond market's GDP share was down to 59.6% from 60.4%, and the corporate bond market's share fell to 36.8% from 37.3%. While total outstanding bonds in the region increased, the lower bonds-to-GDP shares were mainly due to the accelerated expansion of the PRC's exceptionally large economy pulling up the region's aggregate GDP. To a smaller extent, growth in the economies of Viet Nam and Hong Kong, China also lifted the region's overall GDP.

All of the region's economies saw increases in their bonds-to-GDP shares from Q4 2020 to Q1 2021 except for the PRC and Viet Nam, which saw declines, and Thailand, where the share was practically unchanged.

The Republic of Korea, Malaysia, and Singapore had the largest bonds-to-GDP shares in the region, with all exceeding 100%. The Republic of Korea's bond market remained the largest, as measured by this metric, at 146.1%, while Viet Nam's bond market remained the smallest at 23.3%.

Table 2: Size and Composition of Local Currency Bond Markets (% of GDP)

	Q1 2020	Q4 2020	Q1 2021
China, People's Rep. of			
Total	90.5	99.8	97.7
Government	57.3	64.1	62.5
Corporate	33.2	35.7	35.2
Hong Kong, China			
Total	80.6	89.4	89.5
Government	41.8	44.1	43.4
Corporate	38.8	45.4	46.0
Indonesia			
Total	22.1	29.3	31.0
Government	19.3	26.5	28.2
Corporate	2.8	2.8	2.8
Korea, Rep. of			
Total	133.2	143.4	146.1
Government	53.4	58.7	60.8
Corporate	79.8	84.6	85.2
Malaysia			
Total	107.1	119.4	122.8
Government	56.3	63.4	66.3
Corporate	50.8	55.9	56.6
Philippines			
Total	36.4	47.8	51.1
Government	28.3	38.8	42.3
Corporate	8.1	9.0	8.9
Singapore			
Total	90.6	107.2	111.0
Government	57.6	70.2	74.2
Corporate	33.0	37.0	36.8
Thailand			
Total	78.2	88.7	88.7
Government	55.6	65.2	65.0
Corporate	22.7	23.5	23.6
Viet Nam			
Total	22.5	26.1	23.3
Government	20.6	21.6	19.2
Corporate	1.9	4.5	4.2
Emerging East Asia			
Total	88.1	97.7	96.4
Government	53.5	60.4	59.6
Corporate	34.6	37.3	36.8
Japan			
Total	213.4	232.2	239.6
Government	198.1	215.7	222.8
Corporate	15.4	16.6	16.7

GDP = gross domestic product, Q1 = first quarter, Q4 = fourth quarter.
Notes:
1. Data for GDP are from CEIC.
2. For Singapore, corporate bonds outstanding are based on *AsianBondsOnline* estimates.
Sources: People's Republic of China (CEIC); Hong Kong, China (Hong Kong Monetary Authority); Indonesia (Bank Indonesia; Directorate General of Budget Financing and Risk Management, Ministry of Finance; and Indonesia Stock Exchange); Republic of Korea (The Bank of Korea and KG Zeroin Corporation); Malaysia (Bank Negara Malaysia); Philippines (Bureau of the Treasury and Bloomberg LP); Singapore (Monetary Authority of Singapore, Singapore Government Securities, and Bloomberg LP); Thailand (Bank of Thailand); Viet Nam (Bloomberg LP and Vietnam Bond Market Association); and Japan (Japan Securities Dealers Association).

By segment, Singapore's government bonds had the highest bonds-to-GDP share in the region at 74.2% in Q1 2021, while Viet Nam's government bonds had the lowest at 19.2%. The Republic of Korea had the highest corporate bonds-to-GDP share at 85.5%, while Indonesia had the smallest at 2.8%.

Foreign Investor Holdings

The trends of the foreign holdings share of local currency government bonds in emerging East Asian markets were mixed in Q1 2021.

The foreign investor holdings share increased in the PRC, Malaysia, and Thailand, while it declined in Indonesia and the Philippines, from Q4 2020 to Q1 2021 (**Figure 2**). The divergence in economic recoveries and COVID-19 resurgences and containment measures in some economies affected investor decisions about fund allocations in the region's government bond markets.

Foreign investors continued to increase their holdings of PRC government bonds, with the share rising to 10.1% at the end of March from 9.7% at the end of December 2020. Investors continued to expand their positions in the PRC's government bond market because of its high yields. Moreover, the PRC's economic growth potential, the size and rapid growth of its LCY bond market, and the ease of access for foreign investors make it an attractive investment destination.

In Malaysia, the foreign investor share of government bond holdings continued its uptrend, climbing to 26.0% at the end of March from 25.2% at the end of December 2020. Foreign holdings remained supported by strong fund inflows as high yields kept Malaysian government bonds appealing to investors. Additionally, FTSE Russell's decision to retain Malaysia's membership in its World Government Bond Index boosted demand. At the end of March, Malaysia surpassed Indonesia for the region's largest share of foreign holdings in its LCY government bond market.

The ongoing downtrend in the share of foreign ownership in Thailand's government bond market reversed in Q1 2020, as the foreign holdings share rose to 14.0% at the end of March from 13.6% in December 2020. The Q4 2020 foreign holdings share was at its lowest level since Q1 2016.

Foreign holdings of government bonds in Indonesia declined to 22.9% at the end of March, posting an 11-year low. While the Government of Indonesia is borrowing heavily in the LCY bond market, most of this new debt is being absorbed domestically. Bank Indonesia's holdings of sovereign debt climbed to 10.7% at the end of March from 9.0% a year earlier, because of its bond-buying program to finance the government's pandemic relief measures. In addition, foreign investor interest in Indonesian government bonds remained weak, with fund outflows seen in Q1 2021.

The share of foreign ownership of government bonds in the Philippines slid to 2.3% at the end of March from 2.9% at the end of December 2020. The decrease was underpinned by foreign fund outflows as investors reduced their risk exposure on worries that the resurgence of COVID-19 cases could derail the economic recovery.

At the end of December 2020, the Republic of Korea's foreign holdings' share of government bonds outstanding increased to 13.6%, sustaining the upward trend in place since June 2019. Foreign investors continued to build their positions in the Republic of Korea's government bond market as they viewed the bonds as a safe asset on the back of attractive yields, low fiscal deficits, and a strong external account. Viet Nam's foreign holdings' share increased in Q4 2020, though marginally, to 0.56% at the

Figure 2: Foreign Holdings of Local Currency Government Bonds in Select Asian Markets (% of total)

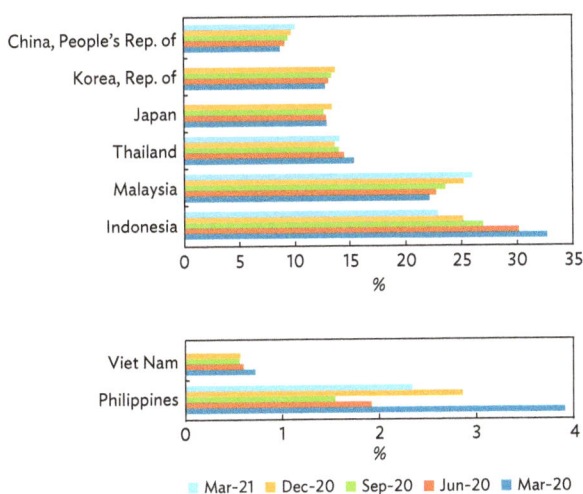

Note: Data for Japan, the Republic of Korea, and Viet Nam are as of 31 December 2020.
Source: *AsianBondsOnline*.

end of December from 0.55% at the end of September. Viet Nam's bond market is the smallest in the region, thus limiting opportunities for foreign investors.

Foreign Bond Flows

Foreign funds continued to flow into the government bond markets of most emerging East Asian economies in Q1 2021.

Emerging East Asia received total net inflows of USD45.2 billion in Q1 2021, continuing the sustained increase in place since the third quarter of 2020 (**Figure 3**). All of the region's markets recorded net foreign buying of government bonds in Q1 2021 except for Indonesia and the Philippines. During the quarter, the largest monthly inflows occurred in January (USD21.3 billion), and the smallest were in March (USD6.0 billion). In April, net inflows picked up to USD14.0 billion. High global liquidity, yield premiums, and better recovery prospects in the region were the main drivers of the positive flows. Even with the surge in yields in the US, emerging East Asian government bonds maintained their overall attractiveness.

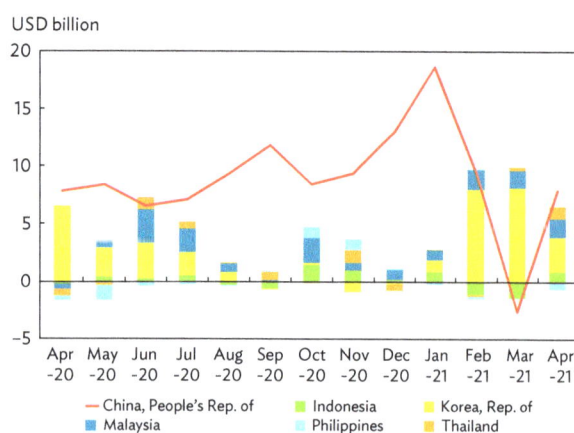

Figure 3: Foreign Bond Flows in Select Emerging East Asian Economies

USD = United States dollar.
Notes:
1. The Republic of Korea and Thailand provided data on bond flows. For the PRC, Indonesia, Malaysia, and the Philippines, month-on-month changes in foreign holdings of LCY government bonds were used as a proxy for bond flows.
2. Data as of 30 April 2021.
3. Figures were computed based on 30 April 2021 exchange rates to avoid currency effects.
Sources: People's Republic of China (Bloomberg LP); Indonesia (Directorate General of Budget Financing and Risk Management, Ministry of Finance); Republic of Korea (Financial Supervisory Service); Malaysia (Bank Negara Malaysia); Philippines (Bureau of the Treasury); and Thailand (Thai Bond Market Association).

The PRC drew in a total of USD25.7 billion of foreign funds in Q1 2021. This was, however, lower than the inflows in Q4 2020 of USD31.0 billion due to outflows in March amounting to USD2.6 billion. The monthly drop in March can be traced to rising yields and good economic recovery prospects in the US, which narrowed the yield spread and weakened the Chinese yuan against the US dollar, dimming some of the appeal of PRC government bonds. The sell-off in March ended the 2-year foreign buying spree in the government bond market. Nonetheless, the market quickly recovered with inflows amounting to USD8.0 billion in April. Foreign interest in government bonds is expected to be resilient following the final approval of FTSE Russell's inclusion of PRC bonds in its World Government Bond Index starting in October. The inclusion period, however, will take 36 months rather than 12 months as previously announced.

In the Republic of Korea, net inflows amounted to USD17.3 billion in Q1 2021, reversing the USD0.8 billion of net outflows in the preceding quarter. The Republic of Korea's quarterly inflows were the region's largest next to the PRC and the largest quarterly foreign buying in the Republic of Korea's bond market since data are available. Throughout Q1 2021, the Republic of Korea recorded monthly foreign fund inflows. In April, foreign investors added a net USD3.0 billion of funds into the government bond market. The inflows were traced to the reinvestment of funds following a large volume of maturities toward the end of 2020. Moreover, returns on the Republic of Korea's government bonds were still higher than those of US Treasuries even if the latter's yields have been rising. The local bond market's appeal also remained supported by the Republic of Korea's manageable fiscal deficits and a strong external account position.

Foreign investments in the Malaysian and Thai government debt markets continued to climb in Q1 2021. Malaysia received total inflows of USD4.1 billion during the quarter, continuing the steady increase in inflows since a rebound in the second quarter of 2020. In April, Malaysia posted its 12th consecutive month of net inflows, amounting to USD1.6 billion. The resilience of foreign demand was sustained by optimism over Malaysia retaining its inclusion in the FTSE Russell World Government Bond Index and on the improving economic recovery. In Thailand, total inflows in Q1 2021 were modest at USD0.1 billion, the smallest quarterly amount since the return of foreign fund inflows in Q2 2020. It was also the smallest quarterly foreign fund inflows among government bond markets in the region that received net inflows in Q1 2021. Weak inflows in January and March plus outflows in February resulted in the modest quarterly figure. In April, foreign purchases of government bonds picked up to USD1.1 billion.

Indonesia and the Philippines saw foreign fund withdrawals from their government bond markets in Q1 2021. Risks to the economic outlook weighed on investor sentiment as the two economies accounted for the most COVID-19 cases in emerging East Asia. Together with the rise in US yields, investors may have reassessed their fund allocations and shifted to other markets in the region. A large fiscal deficit in Indonesia also contributed to investor worries.

Foreign investors in the Indonesian bond market sold USD1.6 billion of government bonds during the quarter, following a net purchase of USD2.8 billion in Q4 2020. Outflows in February and March wiped out the inflows in January. Foreign funds returned to Indonesia's government bond market in April with net inflows of USD0.9 billion. The Philippines saw foreign fund outflows in Q1 2021 of USD0.5 billion after a brief rebound in Q4 2020 that brought in USD1.9 billion. Net outflows were seen in each month of the quarter and again in April (USD0.6 billion). Only the Philippines among all economies in the region experienced a foreign sell-off in April, likely due to investor concerns over the surge in COVID-19 cases, a slow vaccine rollout, the reimposition of restrictions on movement in the National Capital Region and nearby provinces, and rising inflation.

LCY Bond Issuance

Issuance of LCY bonds in emerging East Asia slipped to USD1.9 trillion in Q1 2021 from USD2.0 trillion in Q4 2020.

LCY bond issuance in emerging East Asia tallied USD1.9 trillion in Q1 2021 versus USD2.0 trillion in Q4 2020 (**Table 3**). Issuance fell 1.7% q-o-q, although this was a much slower decline compared with the 14.7% drop posted in Q4 2020. The decline in issuance was largely due to high base effects in the prior 3 quarters of 2020 amid the COVID-19 outbreak, which resulted in increased borrowing by governments to finance stimulus and recovery measures. In nominal terms, issuance volumes

in Q1 2021 were larger than pre-COVID-19, highlighting the importance of LCY financing in supporting economic recovery.

Issuance of both central bank bonds and corporate bonds were down during the quarter, with only Treasury and other government bond issuance expanding marginally on a q-o-q basis. The overall regional issuance total was pulled down by decreased issuance from the PRC in Q1 2021. Other emerging East Asian markets that recorded a q-o-q decline in issuance were Hong Kong, China; Indonesia; Thailand; and Viet Nam. On the other hand, q-o-q increases in bond issuance were recorded in the Republic of Korea, Malaysia, the Philippines, and Singapore.

On a y-o-y basis, issuance growth moderated to 8.6% in Q1 2021 from 32.3% in Q4 2020. Issuance in six out of nine markets in the region increased compared with the same period a year earlier. The exceptions were the markets of the Republic of Korea, Thailand, and Viet Nam, where bond issuance contracted on an annual basis.

Government bonds continued to account for a higher share of the total issuance volume during the quarter with 55.8% of the total. This was slightly higher than a share of 54.8% in Q4 2020, which was due to the q-o-q contraction in corporate bond issuance. The region's aggregate government bond issuance during Q1 2021 tallied USD1,082.4 billion on marginal growth of 0.2% q-o-q, following a decline of 23.6% q-o-q in Q4 2020. On an annual basis, issuance grew at a slower pace of 10.8% y-o-y in Q1 2021 versus 47.5% y-o-y in Q4 2020.

Of the government issuance total, 68.2% comprised Treasury instruments and other government bonds. The issuance of which inched up 0.5% q-o-q, a reversal from the 31.3% q-o-q contraction in Q4 2020. Most of the region's bond markets posted slower q-o-q growth in issuance of Treasury and other government bonds during the review period on account of a higher base in the prior quarter. The only markets that recorded accelerated q-o-q issuance of Treasury and other government bonds were the Republic of Korea, Malaysia, the Philippines, and Thailand. Compared with the same period a year earlier, growth moderated to 12.7% y-o-y in Q1 2021 from 81.8% y-o-y in Q4 2020.

Table 3: Local-Currency–Denominated Bond Issuance (gross)

	Q1 2020		Q4 2020		Q1 2021		Growth Rate (LCY-base %)		Growth Rate (USD-base %)	
	Amount (USD billion)	% share	Amount (USD billion)	% share	Amount (USD billion)	% share	Q1 2021		Q1 2021	
							q-o-q	y-o-y	q-o-q	y-o-y
China, People's Rep. of										
Total	1,075	100.0	1,294	100.0	1,255	100.0	(2.6)	8.0	(3.0)	16.7
Government	491	45.7	590	45.6	575	45.8	(2.2)	8.3	(2.6)	17.0
Central Bank	0	0.0	0	0.0	0	0.0	–	–	–	–
Treasury and Other Govt.	491	45.7	590	45.6	575	45.8	(2.2)	8.3	(2.6)	17.0
Corporate	584	54.3	703	54.4	680	54.2	(3.0)	7.8	(3.3)	16.5
Hong Kong, China										
Total	136	100.0	146	100.0	143	100.0	(2.0)	5.9	(2.2)	5.6
Government	108	79.7	112	76.3	105	73.5	(5.6)	(2.3)	(5.8)	(2.6)
Central Bank	108	79.4	107	73.1	105	73.3	(1.7)	(2.4)	(2.0)	(2.6)
Treasury and Other Govt.	0.3	0.2	5	3.2	0.3	0.2	(92.6)	8.0	(92.6)	7.7
Corporate	28	20.3	35	23.7	38	26.5	9.6	38.1	9.3	37.6
Indonesia										
Total	19	100.0	47	100.0	34	100.0	(24.6)	61.0	(27.0)	80.8
Government	18	94.0	46	96.8	33	95.9	(25.2)	64.2	(27.7)	84.4
Central Bank	7	37.0	14	29.7	12	34.5	(12.4)	49.8	(15.3)	68.2
Treasury and Other Govt.	11	57.0	32	67.1	21	61.4	(30.9)	73.7	(33.2)	95.0
Corporate	1	6.0	2	3.2	1	4.1	(4.4)	10.7	(7.5)	24.3
Korea, Rep. of										
Total	197	100.0	210	100.0	205	100.0	1.6	(3.6)	(2.5)	3.8
Government	82	41.8	78	37.2	91	44.3	21.0	2.3	16.1	10.2
Central Bank	30	15.2	29	13.8	29	14.3	4.8	(9.7)	0.6	(2.8)
Treasury and Other Govt.	52	26.6	49	23.4	62	30.1	30.6	9.2	25.3	17.6
Corporate	115	58.2	132	62.8	114	55.7	(9.9)	(7.8)	(13.5)	(0.7)
Malaysia										
Total	21	100.0	22	100.0	24	100.0	11.7	8.2	8.3	12.8
Government	12	56.2	8	35.1	14	56.9	81.0	9.6	75.5	14.3
Central Bank	2	11.0	0	0.0	0	0.0	–	(100.0)	–	(100.0)
Treasury and Other Govt.	10	45.1	8	35.1	14	56.9	81.0	36.4	75.5	42.2
Corporate	9	43.8	14	64.9	10	43.1	(25.8)	6.3	(28.1)	10.8
Philippines										
Total	17	100.0	29	100.0	44	100.0	53.5	147.4	51.9	158.4
Government	14	83.0	28	95.8	43	97.3	55.8	190.0	54.2	202.9
Central Bank	0	0.0	17	60.2	23	51.2	30.5	–	29.2	–
Treasury and Other Govt.	14	83.0	10	35.6	20	46.0	98.7	37.3	96.6	43.4
Corporate	3	17.0	1	4.2	1	2.7	(0.2)	(60.0)	(1.3)	(58.2)
Singapore										
Total	125	100.0	164	100.0	169	100.0	4.7	27.5	2.9	34.8
Government	122	97.7	160	97.9	166	98.4	5.1	28.3	3.4	35.7
Central Bank	101	80.9	135	82.5	142	84.2	6.8	32.7	5.0	40.3
Treasury and Other Govt.	21	16.9	25	15.5	24	14.2	(3.9)	7.3	(5.5)	13.5
Corporate	3	2.3	3	2.1	3	1.6	(17.9)	(8.7)	(19.3)	(3.4)
Thailand										
Total	72	100.0	74	100.0	63	100.0	(11.1)	(16.3)	(14.8)	(12.2)
Government	62	85.9	65	87.6	54	85.1	(13.6)	(17.0)	(17.2)	(13.0)
Central Bank	56	77.8	49	66.4	34	53.1	(29.0)	(42.9)	(31.9)	(40.1)
Treasury and Other Govt.	6	8.1	16	21.2	20	32.0	34.5	233.0	29.0	249.0
Corporate	10	14.1	9	12.4	9	14.9	6.4	(11.7)	2.0	(7.4)

continued on next page

Table 3 *continued*

	Q1 2020		Q4 2020		Q1 2021		Growth Rate (LCY-base %)		Growth Rate (USD-base %)	
							Q1 2021		Q1 2021	
	Amount (USD billion)	% share	Amount (USD billion)	% share	Amount (USD billion)	% share	q-o-q	y-o-y	q-o-q	y-o-y
Viet Nam										
Total	8	100.0	8	100.0	3	100.0	(68.5)	(68.3)	(68.5)	(67.5)
Government	7	93.3	6	75.2	2	67.8	(71.6)	(76.9)	(71.5)	(76.4)
Central Bank	6	75.2	0	0.0	0	0.0	–	(100.0)	–	(100.0)
Treasury and Other Govt.	1	18.1	6	75.2	2	67.8	(71.6)	18.9	(71.5)	21.8
Corporate	0.5	6.7	2	24.8	1	32.2	(59.2)	53.0	(59.1)	56.8
Emerging East Asia										
Total	1,671	100.0	1,995	100.0	1,940	100.0	(1.7)	8.6	(2.8)	16.1
Government	918	54.9	1,093	54.8	1,082	55.8	0.2	10.8	(1.0)	18.0
Central Bank	310	18.6	352	17.6	344	17.7	(0.5)	6.9	(2.3)	10.9
Treasury and Other Govt.	607	36.3	741	37.2	738	38.1	0.5	12.7	(0.4)	21.6
Corporate	753	45.1	902	45.2	858	44.2	(3.9)	5.9	(4.9)	13.9
Japan										
Total	383	100.0	771	100.0	664	100.0	(7.7)	78.4	(13.9)	73.3
Government	356	92.9	718	93.2	640	96.4	(4.5)	85.2	(10.9)	79.8
Central Bank	0	0.0	0	0.0	0	0.0	–	–	–	–
Treasury and Other Govt.	356	92.9	718	93.2	640	96.4	(4.5)	85.2	(10.9)	79.8
Corporate	27	7.1	53	6.8	24	3.6	(51.2)	(9.5)	(54.5)	(12.1)

( ) = negative, – = not applicable, LCY = local currency, q-o-q = quarter-on-quarter, Q1 = first quarter, Q4 = fourth quarter, USD = United States dollar, y-o-y = year-on-year.
Notes:
1. Corporate bonds include issues by financial institutions.
2. Bloomberg LP end-of-period LCY–USD rates are used.
3. For LCY base, emerging East Asia growth figures are based on 31 March 2021 currency exchange rates and do not include currency effects.
Sources: People's Republic of China (CEIC); Hong Kong, China (Hong Kong Monetary Authority); Indonesia (Bank Indonesia; Directorate General of Budget Financing and Risk Management, Ministry of Finance; and Indonesia Stock Exchange); Republic of Korea (The Bank of Korea and KG Zeroin Corporation); Malaysia (Bank Negara Malaysia); Philippines (Bureau of the Treasury and Bloomberg LP); Singapore (Singapore Government Securities and Bloomberg LP); Thailand (Bank of Thailand and ThaiBMA); Viet Nam (Bloomberg LP, Hanoi Stock Exchange, and Vietnam Bond Market Association); and Japan (Japan Securities Dealers Association).

In Q1 2021, issuance of central bank bills and bonds declined 0.5% q-o-q, reversing the 0.3% q-o-q expansion in the previous quarter. The decline stemmed from tapered issuance from the Hong Kong Monetary Authority, Bank Indonesia, and the BOT during the quarter, and the cessation of issuance by Bank Negara Malaysia and the State Bank of Vietnam. On the other hand, the Bank of Korea, Bangko Sentral ng Pilipinas, and the MAS increased their respective sales of central bank instruments during the quarter in review. On an annual basis, central bank issuance was up 6.9% y-o-y in Q1 2021 versus 5.3% y-o-y in Q4 2020.

Similarly, corporate bond sales in the region slumped in Q1 2021, falling 3.9% q-o-q after a 0.8% q-o-q contraction in Q4 2020. The Republic of Korea and the PRC, two of the largest corporate bond markets in the region, had less issuance during the quarter, which pulled down the overall total for emerging East Asia. All other regional markets issued a smaller volume of corporate bonds in Q1 2021 than in Q4 2020 except for Thailand

and Hong Kong, China. Corporate bond issuance growth moderated to 5.9% y-o-y in Q1 2021 from 17.7% y-o-y in Q4 2020.

The PRC continued to account for the largest issuance volume among the region's bond markets. However, its share of the regional total slipped to 64.7% in Q1 2021 from 65.3% in Q4 2020. LCY bond issuance in the PRC totaled USD1,254.9 billion in Q1 2021, with issuance volume declining across all bond types. Government bond issuance dipped 2.2% q-o-q due to a slowdown in the issuance of Treasury bonds as the PRC's economy sustained its recovery. While the issuance of local government bonds increased during the quarter, the overall volume was relatively low at only CNY895.5 billion versus CNY1.6 trillion in Q1 2020. The government aims to scale back the issuance of such bonds this year to control risk in the financial system. This is contrary to what has happened in past years, when the government pushed for the acceleration and utilization of the local government bond quota at the start of the year to speed up infrastructure projects and development. During Q1 2021, the issuance of corporate bonds slipped 3.0% q-o-q amid heightened warnings by the government to ease borrowing and over-leveraging, particularly by property companies. The issuance of listed corporate bonds, commercial bank bonds, enterprise bonds, medium-term notes, and asset-backed securities slowed in Q1 2021. On an annual basis, LCY bond issuance in the PRC moderated to 8.0% y-o-y in Q1 2021 from 45.5% y-o-y in Q4 2020.

LCY bond sales in the Republic of Korea totaled USD204.9 billion, with growth slowing to 1.6% q-o-q in Q1 2021 from 3.2% q-o-q in Q4 2020. Overall growth was driven by the issuance of government bonds through a frontloading policy. Issuance of government bonds grew 21.0% q-o-q in Q1 2021 after a decline of 14.3% q-o-q in the preceding quarter. Increased government bond issuance is needed in 2021 to fund the government's budget worth KRW558 trillion. In addition, the Government of the Republic of Korea approved in late March a KRW15 trillion supplementary budget, with about two-thirds of the amount to be funded through bond issuance. To a lesser extent, issuance of central bank bills also contributed to overall growth, rising 4.8% q-o-q in a reversal from a decline of 12.0% in Q4 2020. In contrast, corporate bond issuance declined 9.9% q-o-q in Q1 2021 after rising 17.3% q-o-q in the previous quarter. On an annual basis, the Republic of Korea's LCY bond sales contracted 3.6% y-o-y in Q1 2021 after rising 0.7% y-o-y in Q4 2020.

In Hong Kong, China, LCY bond issuance reached USD143.1 billion, down 2.0% q-o-q in Q1 2021 from a 1.2% hike in the preceding quarter. The q-o-q decline was due mainly to less issuance of government bonds, particularly Treasury and other government bonds, following the large volume of issuance of iBonds and Silver Bonds in the last 2 months of 2020. In addition, the Hong Kong Monetary Authority issued a slightly reduced volume of Exchange Fund Bills and Exchange Fund Notes during the quarter. Issuance of corporate bonds increased in Q1 2021 on growth of 9.6% q-o-q, but this was slower than Q4 2020's 24.9% q-o-q hike. Compared with the same period in 2020, Hong Kong, China's LCY bond issuance grew 5.9% y-o-y in Q1 2021, down from a 13.4% y-o-y hike in Q4 2020.

LCY bond sales of ASEAN member economies totaled USD337.2 billion in Q1 2021, with its share of the regional total inching up to 17.4% from 17.1% in Q4 2020. Total LCY

bond issuance in ASEAN markets during the quarter was up marginally by 0.2% q-o-q after contracting 2.0% q-o-q in Q4 2020. On an individual market level, higher bond sales in Q1 2021 versus Q4 2020 were observed in Malaysia, the Philippines, and Singapore. In contrast, Indonesia, Thailand, and Viet Nam reduced their respective issuance volumes during the same period. Compared with the same period in the prior year, bond issuance of ASEAN economies was up 21.5% y-o-y in Q1 2021 but was lower than the 21.9% y-o-y uptick in Q4 2020. Among ASEAN peers, Singapore, Thailand, and the Philippines were the most active issuers of LCY bonds in Q1 2021.

New issuance in Singapore reached USD168.5 billion in Q1 2021, representing a 50.0% share of the aggregate total of ASEAN. Bond issuance climbed 4.7% q-o-q, driven largely by government bonds, in particular MAS bills and notes. In addition to issuing MAS bills, a 1-year floating rate note was issued beginning in March. The issuance of MAS bills and notes climbed 6.8% q-o-q in Q1 2021 and declined –3.9% q-o-q for SGS bills and bonds. Issuance by corporates further declined in Q1 2021, falling 17.9% q-o-q. On an annual basis, LCY bond issuance in Singapore surged to 27.5% y-o-y in Q1 2021 from 23.3% y-o-y in Q4 2020.

In Thailand, LCY bond sales tallied USD63.4 billion in Q1 2021, accounting for 18.8% of ASEAN's issuance total. The pace of issuance, however, slowed 11.1% q-o-q due to a decline in government bond issuance. Specifically, a decline in the issuance of BOT instruments exceeded the increased issuance of Treasury and other government bonds during the quarter. Issuance of BOT instruments slowed 29.0% q-o-q in Q1 2021 due to changes in BOT's issuance program for this year. The central bank will discontinue issuance of 2-week BOT bills, 6-month BOT bills, and 3-year BOT bonds this year. (The last issuance of 3-year BOT bonds was in January 2021). A new BOT floating-rate bond with a 6-month tenor that is indexed to the Thai Overnight Repurchase Rate was issued for the first time in March. Issuance of corporate bonds rebounded in Q1 2021, rising 6.4% q-o-q as more corporates tapped the bond market to lock in low interest rates. On an annual basis, issuance volume in Thailand declined 16.3% y-o-y in Q1 2021 after contracting 4.8% y-o-y in the prior quarter.

The Philippines saw increased issuance activity in Q1 2021 with total issuance climbing to USD44.1 billion. Overall growth surged 53.5% q-o-q, which was largely accounted for by the increased issuance of government bonds. The volume of Treasury and other government bond issuance almost doubled from the previous quarter, bolstered by the issuance of Retail Treasury Bonds in February and increased issuance during the weekly Treasury auctions that are needed to fund pandemic stimulus measures and the vaccine rollout program. Bangko Sentral ng Pilipinas issuance also contributed to the overall growth, rising 30.5% q-o-q in Q1 2021, while corporate bond issuance dropped a marginal 0.2% q-o-q. On a y-o-y basis, bond issuance growth moderated to 147.4% in Q1 2021 from 268.5% in Q4 2020.

In Indonesia, LCY bond issuance contracted across all bond types in Q1 2021 following a high volume of borrowing in 2020. Total issuance summed to USD34.4 billion, contracting 24.6% q-o-q. Government bond issuance, which accounted for 95.9% of total issuance, slumped 25.2% q-o-q due to declines in the issuance of Treasury bills and bonds, and central bank instruments. While the government normally adopts a frontloading policy at the start of the year, a high base effect from the previous quarter resulted in the quarterly decline in Q1 2021. Issuance volume was still high relative to pre-COVID-19 levels, as issuance of government bonds rose 64.2% y-o-y, led by Treasury bonds at 73.7% y-o-y. Corporate bond issuance fell 4.4% q-o-q during the quarter. On an annual basis, bond issuance in Indonesia rose 61.0% y-o-y in Q1 2021 after gaining 126.3% y-o-y in Q4 2020.

Malaysia recorded Q1 2021 issuance of USD24.2 billion, which was up 11.7% q-o-q after recording a 0.3% q-o-q decline in the previous quarter. The increase was due to a rise in government bond issuance of 81.0% q-o-q as the Government of Malaysia funded a 2021 budget that will be 8.5% higher than the 2020 budget. In addition, in March the government passed a supplemental budget of MYR20 billion, which will raise the 2021 deficit-to-GDP (forecast) share from 5.4% to 6.0%. On the other hand, corporate bond issuance fell 25.8% q-o-q in Q1 2021 after rising 51.8% q-o-q in the prior quarter. On a y-o-y basis, Malaysia's bond issuance rose 8.2% in Q1 2021, up from 7.2% in Q4 2020.

In Viet Nam, overall bond issuance fell 68.5% q-o-q in Q1 2021 to USD2.5 billion, which was much steeper than Q4 2020's 5.3% q-o-q drop. All bond categories recorded q-o-q declines, with government bond issuance contracting 71.6% q-o-q and corporate bonds declining

59.2% q-o-q. On an annual basis, bond issuance in Viet Nam fell 68.3% y-o-y, largely due to the 76.9% y-o-y contraction in government bonds.

Cross-Border Bond Issuance

Cross-border bond issuance in emerging East Asia totaled USD5.6 billion in Q1 2021.

Intraregional bond issuance in emerging East Asia reached USD5.6 billion in Q1 2021, an almost five-fold increase from the USD1.2 billion raised in Q4 2020 and almost double the volume from Q1 2020. Institutions from six economies issued cross-border bonds in Q1 2021, led by Hong Kong, China, which accounted for 68.3% of the regional aggregate (**Figure 4**). Other economies that issued cross-border bonds in Q1 2021 include Singapore, the Republic of Korea, Malaysia, Indonesia, and the PRC. Monthly issuance volumes amounted to USD1.1 billion, USD1.7 billion, and USD2.8 billion in January, February, and March, respectively.

In Q1 2021, Hong Kong, China dominated the region's cross-border issuance with a total of USD3.8 billion, a five-fold increase from the volume issued in the previous quarter. Fourteen institutions from Hong Kong, China issued cross-border bonds that were all denominated in Chinese yuan, except for one bond issued in Singapore dollars. The government-owned Hong Kong Mortgage Corporation led the market with total issuance of USD1.3 billion worth of

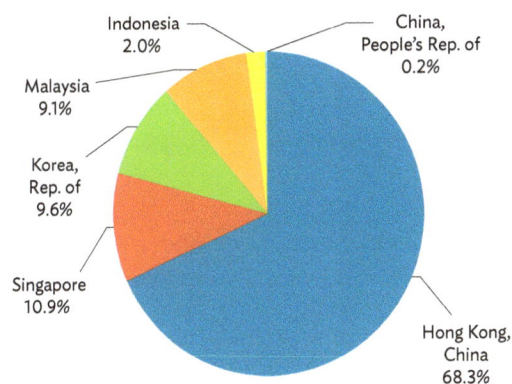

Figure 4: Origin Economies of Intra-Emerging East Asian Bond Issuance in the First Quarter of 2021

- Indonesia 2.0%
- China, People's Rep. of 0.2%
- Malaysia 9.1%
- Korea, Rep. of 9.6%
- Singapore 10.9%
- Hong Kong, China 68.3%

Source: *AsianBondsOnline* calculations based on Bloomberg LP data.

CNY-denominated bonds in various tenors. The largest of which was the CNY2.5 billion (USD381.5 million) 3-year bond offer in February as part of its USD12.0 billion medium-term note program. Another large issuer of cross-border bonds in Hong Kong, China was the majority state-owned public transportation company MTR Corporation, which raised USD366.3 million in March via 1-year and 3-year bonds.

Singapore had the second-largest, cross-border issuance volume in the region in Q1 2021 at USD605 million and a share of 10.9% of the regional total. Five institutions issued cross-border bonds, led by DBS Group Holdings, which raised USD244.2 million worth of CNY-denominated 10-year bonds. Asia Water Technology, a private industrial company in Singapore, issued USD228.9 million of 5-year bonds. Other issuing institutions in Q1 2021 included CMT MTN, Nomura International Fund, and DBS Bank, which issued CNY- and HKD-denominated bonds.

In the Republic of Korea, only two institutions issued intraregional bonds in Q1 2021 with a total issuance amount of USD533.2 million. The government-owned Export–Import Bank of Korea, the second-largest issuer of cross-border bonds in the region, raised USD369.9 million via issuance of multi-tenor bonds denominated in Chinese yuan and Philippine pesos. KEB Hana Bank issued 3-year CNY-denominated bonds worth USD163.3 million.

In Malaysia, total intraregional bond issuance amounted to USD508.3 million in Q1 2021. Malayan Banking, the fourth-largest issuer of cross-border bonds in the region, raised USD308.7 million via issuance of bonds denominated in Chinese yuan and Hong Kong dollars. Cagamas Global, a subsidiary of Malaysia's national mortgage corporation, Cagamas Berhad, issued a total of USD199.6 million of bonds denominated in Singapore dollars and Hong Kong dollars.

Property developer Ciputra Development was the sole issuer of intraregional bonds in Indonesia in Q1 2021, raising USD111.5 million via a 5-year bond denominated in Singapore dollars.

In the PRC, only two institutions issued cross-border bonds in Q1 2021 with a total amount of USD9.6 million. China Tontine Wines Group (USD5.1 million) and China Parenting Network (USD4.5 million) both issued in Hong Kong dollars.

The top 10 issuers of intraregional bonds in the region in Q1 2021 had an aggregate issuance volume of USD4.1 billion and comprised 73.2% of the regional total. The majority were firms from Hong Kong, China with combined issuance totaling USD3.4 billion. This included the Hong Kong Mortgage Corporation, which was the largest issuer in the region in Q1 2021 (USD1.3 billion), and MTR Corporation (USD366.3 million). The Export–Import Bank of Korea (USD369.9 million) and Malayan Banking (USD308.7 million) were the region's other large issuers of intraregional bonds in Q1 2021.

The Chinese yuan remained the predominant currency of cross-border bonds in emerging East Asia in Q1 2021 with an issuance volume equivalent to USD4.9 billion and a share of 88.6% of the regional total (**Figure 5**). Firms that issued in this currency were from Hong Kong, China; the Republic of Korea; Malaysia; and Singapore. Other issuance currencies included the Singapore dollar (USD356.9 million, 6.4%); Hong Kong dollar (USD231 million, 4.1%); and the Philippine peso (USD49.4 million, 0.9%).

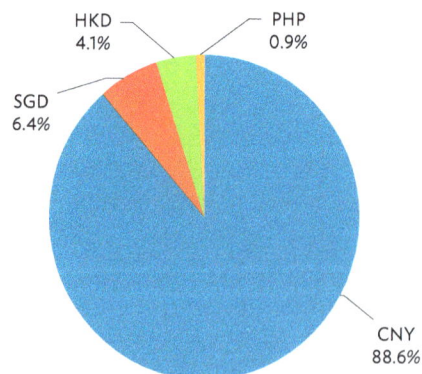

Figure 5: Currency Shares of Intra-Emerging East Asian Bond Issuance in the First Quarter of 2021

CNY = Chinese yuan, HKD = Hong Kong dollar, PHP = Philippine peso, SGD = Singapore dollar.
Source: *AsianBondsOnline* calculations based on Bloomberg LP data.

G3 Currency Issuance

In January–April, a total of USD139.6 billion in G3 currency bonds was issued in emerging East Asia.

In January–April, total G3 currency bonds issued in emerging East Asia reached USD139.6 billion, up 23.7% y-o-y from USD112.8 billion in January–April 2020 (**Table 4**).[5] The expansion can be attributed to increased G3 issuance in most of the region's economies compared to a year earlier. The first 4 months of 2021 saw companies and governments issuing amid a low-interest-rate environment, with several economies issuing sovereign bonds to fund their ongoing COVID-19 relief responses.

During the review period, 94.7% of all G3 currency bonds issued were denominated in US dollars, 4.8% in euros, and 0.5% in Japanese yen. A total of USD132.2 billion worth of bonds denominated in US dollars was issued in emerging East Asia in January–April, representing a jump of 27.8% y-o-y. EUR-denominated bond issuance totaled USD6.7 billion during the review period, a decrease of 21.3% y-o-y, as issuances from the Republic of Korea, the largest issuer of EUR-denominated bonds in January–April 2020, declined during the first 4 months of 2021. Bonds issued in Japanese yen totaled USD0.7 billion, a decline of 19.7% y-o-y.

The PRC dominated the region's G3 currency bond issuance, totaling USD75.1 billion in January–April. It was followed by the Republic of Korea with USD17.5 billion and Hong Kong, China with USD16.5 billion. US dollars were the main G3 currency of issuance in all three economies.

On a y-o-y basis, G3 currency bond issuance increased in the first 4 months of 2021 in Thailand (146.9%); Hong Kong, China (139.1%); the Republic of Korea (81.5%); Singapore (37.9%); the Philippines (33.0%); and the PRC (16.1%). Annual declines in G3 currency bond issuance were recorded in Malaysia (–10.9%) and Indonesia (–31.6%). Viet Nam issued G3 currency bonds during the January–April period after not issuing any during the same period in 2020.

Entities from the PRC accounted for 53.8% of all G3 currency issuance in emerging East Asia in January–April, issuing USD73.1 billion in US dollars and USD2.0 billion equivalent in euros. Technology company Alibaba Group raised USD5.0 billion in bonds denominated in US dollars in February. The four tranches of callable bonds had tenors ranging from 10 years to 40 years and will be used for general corporate purposes. In April, another technology company, Tencent Holdings, took advantage of the low-interest-rate environment by also issuing a four-tranche callable USD-denominated bond totaling USD4.2 billion with tenors ranging from 10 years to 40 years.

The Republic of Korea accounted for a 12.5% share of all G3 currency bond issuance during the review period: USD16.9 billion in US dollars and the equivalent of USD0.6 billion in euros. Every month during the first 4 months of 2021, the Korea Development Bank issued several USD-denominated bonds with tenors from 1 year to 10 years. Its most notable issuance was a 3-year floating-rate green bond, the bank's first issuance linked to the Secured Overnight Financing Rate.[6] Another prolific issuer in each of the first 4 months of the year was the Export–Import Bank of Korea with several issuances of USD-denominated bonds, the tenors of which ranged from 1 year to 10 years. The export credit agency's issuances included a bond with three tranches (3 years, 5 years, and 10 years) issued in February totaling USD1.5 billion.

Hong Kong, China accounted for an 11.8% share of G3 currency bond issuance in January–April 2021. By currency, USD16.3 billion was USD-denominated, while EUR-denominated and JPY-denominated bonds amounted to the equivalent of USD0.1 billion each. In January, the government issued USD2.5 billion worth of USD-denominated green bonds under its Government Green Bond Programme. The issuance comprised three tranches with tenors of 5 years, 10 years, and 30 years. The proceeds from the bond issue will be used for projects with environmental benefits and the economy's sustainable development.

ASEAN member economies' G3 currency bond issuance decreased 3.4% y-o-y to USD30.6 billion in January–April 2021 from USD31.6 billion in January–April 2020, driven

---

[5] G3 currency bonds are denominated in either euros, Japanese yen, or US dollars. For the discussion on G3 currency issuance, emerging East Asia comprises Cambodia; the People's Republic of China; Hong Kong, China; Indonesia; the Republic of Korea; the Lao People's Democratic Republic; Malaysia; the Philippines; Singapore; Thailand; and Viet Nam.

[6] The Secured Overnight Financing Rate is a benchmark reference rate for dollar-denominated loans established as an alternative to the London Interbank Offered Rate.

Table 4: G3 Currency Bond Issuance

2020			January–April 2021		
Issuer	**Amount (USD billion)**	**Issue Date**	**Issuer**	**Amount (USD billion)**	**Issue Date**
Cambodia	**0.4**		**Cambodia**	**0.0**	
China, People's Rep. of	**232.3**		**China, People's Rep. of**	**75.1**	
Industrial and Commercial Bank of China 3.58% Perpetual	2.9	23-Sep-20	Tencent Holdings 3.840% 2051	1.8	22-Apr-21
Bank of China 3.60% Perpetual	2.8	4-Mar-20	Alibaba Group 2.125% 2031	1.5	9-Feb-21
Bank of Communications 3.80% Perpetual	2.8	18-Nov-20	Alibaba Group 3.150% 2051	1.5	9-Feb-21
Others	223.8		Others	70.3	
Hong Kong, China	**34.8**		**Hong Kong, China**	**16.5**	
AIA Group 3.200% 2040	1.8	16-Sep-20	Hong Kong, China (Sovereign) 0.625% 2026	1.0	2-Feb-21
MTR Corporation 1.625% 2030	1.2	19-Aug-20	Hong Kong, China (Sovereign) 1.375% 2031	1.0	2-Feb-21
AIA Group 3.375% 2030	1.0	7-Apr-20	Airport Authority Hong Kong 1.625% 2031	0.9	4-Feb-21
Others	30.9		Others	13.6	
Indonesia	**27.9**		**Indonesia**	**9.4**	
Indonesia (Sovereign) 3.85% 2030	1.7	15-Apr-20	Indonesia (Sovereign) 1.85% 2031	1.3	12-Jan-21
Indonesia (Sovereign) 4.20% 2050	1.7	15-Apr-20	Indonesia (Sovereign) 3.05% 2051	1.3	12-Jan-21
Indonesia (Sovereign) 0.90% 2027	1.2	14-Jan-20	Indonesia (Sovereign) 1.10% 2033	1.2	12-Jan-21
Others	23.4		Others	5.7	
Korea, Rep. of	**30.0**		**Korea, Rep. of**	**17.5**	
Korea Housing Finance Corporation 0.010% 2025	1.2	5-Feb-20	SK Hynix 2.375% 2031	1.0	19-Jan-21
Korea Development Bank 1.250% 2025	1.0	3-Jun-20	SK Hynix 1.500% 2026	1.0	19-Jan-21
Export–Import Bank of Korea 0.829% 2025	0.9	27-Apr-20	SK Battery America 2.125% 2026	0.7	26-Jan-21
Others	26.9		Others	14.8	
Malaysia	**17.2**		**Malaysia**	**8.6**	
Petronas Capital 4.55% 2050	2.8	21-Apr-20	Malaysia (Sovereign) 2.070% 2031	0.8	28-Apr-21
Petronas Capital 3.50% 2030	2.3	21-Apr-20	Malaysia (Sovereign) 3.075% 2051	0.5	28-Apr-21
Others	12.2		Others	7.3	
Philippines	**15.5**		**Philippines**	**3.9**	
Philippines (Sovereign) 2.65% 2045	1.5	10-Dec-20	Philippines (Sovereign) 1.75% 2041	1.0	28-Apr-21
Philippines (Sovereign) 2.95% 2045	1.4	5-May-20	Philippines (Sovereign) 1.20% 2033	0.8	28-Apr-21
Others	12.6		Others	2.1	
Singapore	**14.7**		**Singapore**	**6.1**	
United Overseas Bank 0.010% 2027	1.2	1-Dec-20	BOC Aviation 1.625% 2024	0.8	29-Apr-21
Oversea-Chinese Banking Corporation 1.832% 2030	1.0	10-Sep-20	United Overseas Bank 2.000% 2031	0.8	14-Apr-21
Others	12.5		Others	4.6	
Thailand	**5.3**		**Thailand**	**2.0**	
Bangkok Bank in Hong Kong, China 5.0% Perpetual	0.8	23-Sep-20	GC Treasury Center 2.98% 2031	0.7	18-Mar-21
PTT Treasury 3.7% 2070	0.7	16-Jul-20	Krungthai Bank 4.40% Perpetual	0.6	25-Mar-21
Others	3.8		Others	0.7	
Viet Nam	**0.1**		**Viet Nam**	**0.5**	
Emerging East Asia Total	**378.1**		**Emerging East Asia Total**	**139.6**	
Memo Items:			Memo Items:		
India	**14.3**		**India**	**12.5**	
Vedanta Holdings Mauritius II 13.00% 2023	1.4	21-Aug-20	Vedanta Resources 8.95% 2025	1.2	11-Mar-21
Others	12.9		Others	11.3	
Sri Lanka	**0.4**		**Sri Lanka**	**0.04**	
Sri Lanka (Sovereign) 6.57% 2021	0.1	30-Jul-20	Sri Lanka (Sovereign) 6.89% 2022	0.04	22-Jan-21
Others	0.3		Others	0.004	

USD = United States dollar.
Notes:
1. Data exclude certificates of deposit.
2. G3 currency bonds are bonds denominated in either euros, Japanese yen, or US dollars.
3. Bloomberg LP end-of-period rates are used.
4. Emerging East Asia comprises Cambodia; the People's Republic of China; Hong Kong, China; Indonesia; the Republic of Korea; the Lao People's Democratic Republic; Malaysia; the Philippines; Singapore; Thailand; and Viet Nam.
5. Figures after the issuer name reflect the coupon rate and year of maturity of the bond.
Source: *AsianBondsOnline* calculations based on Bloomberg LP data.

by declining issuances from Indonesia and Malaysia.[7] As a share of emerging East Asia's total G3 currency bond issuance in the first 4 months of 2021, ASEAN issuance accounted for 21.9%, down from 28.1% in the same period in 2020. Despite a drop in each of their respective issuance volumes, Indonesia and Malaysia led all ASEAN members in G3 currency bond issuance, followed by Singapore, the Philippines, Thailand, and Viet Nam.

Indonesia's issuance of G3 currency bonds in January–April 2021 represented 6.8% of the total in emerging East Asia, comprising USD8.2 billion in US dollars and the equivalent of USD1.2 billion in euros. The Government of Indonesia raised the equivalent of USD4.2 billion in a dual-currency issuance in January in three tranches (10 years, 30 years, 50 years) denominated in US dollars, while one tranche (12 years) was in euros. Proceeds from the issuance will be used for general budgetary purposes including the funding of Indonesia's COVID-19 relief efforts.

G3 currency bond issuance by Malaysia accounted for 6.2% of the region's total in the first 4 months of the year. Issuance was solely denominated in USD amounting to USD8.6 billion. In April, the Government of Malaysia issued the first sovereign USD-denominated sustainability *sukuk* in the world. The issuance was a dual-tranche bond worth USD1.3 billion and with tenors of 10 years and 30 years. Proceeds from the issuance will be used for social and green projects to support achievement of the United Nations Sustainable Development Goals.

The Philippines' share of total G3 currency bond issuance in emerging East Asia during the January–April 2021 period was 2.8%, comprising bonds denominated in euros amounting to USD2.5 billion, USD0.9 billion in USD-denominated bonds, and JPY-denominated bonds worth USD0.5 billion. In April, the Government of the Philippines issued a zero-coupon, 3-year samurai bond worth USD0.5 billion. In the same month, the government also issued three tranches of a euro-denominated bond worth USD2.5 billion. Proceeds from both the issuances expanded the government's funding sources for its COVID-19 response and other priority programs that will help the economy rebound from the pandemic.

G3 currency bond issuance in Singapore was 4.4% of emerging East Asia's total in the first 4 months of 2021, comprising USD5.7 billion in US dollars, the equivalent of USD0.3 billion in euros, and USD0.1 billion in Japanese yen. In February, United Overseas Bank issued a USD0.3 billion zero-coupon, 30-year callable bond denominated in US dollars. In April, the Singapore bank issued a dual-tranche, USD-denominated bond worth USD1.5 billion. The issuance represented Singapore's first sustainable bond issuance, the proceeds of which may be used for projects such as green buildings and renewable energy, and also may extend to COVID-19-related loans to help businesses sustain employment and growth during the pandemic.

Entities from Thailand accounted for 1.4% of all G3 currency bonds issued in the region during the January–April period, comprising USD2.0 billion worth of USD-denominated bonds. In March, GC Treasury Center issued USD1.3 billion worth of callable USD-denominated bonds. The dual-tranche bond, with tenors of 10 years and 30 years, was issued under its parent company's global medium-term note program, the proceeds of which will be used for general corporate purposes. In the same month, Krung Thai Bank issued a USD0.6 billion perpetual callable bond denominated in US dollars with a coupon rate of 4.4%. Proceeds from the issuance will be used for funding and general corporate purposes.

During the review period, Viet Nam accounted for 0.4% of all G3 currency issuance in emerging East Asia with USD0.5 billion worth of USD-denominated bonds. In April, Viet Nam's largest conglomerate, Vingroup, issued a USD0.5 billion 5-year convertible bond with a coupon rate of 3.0%. Proceeds from the issuance will be used for refinancing existing facilities and funding capital expenditures and other general corporate purposes.

Monthly G3 currency issuance totals in emerging East Asia from April 2020 to April 2021 are presented in **Figure 6**. There was a high volume of G3 issuance in January 2021 as investors returned to the market after pandemic-related concerns led to declining issuances from September 2020 to December 2020. Issuances fell again in February and March 2021 as major issuers in the PRC, Indonesia, and the Republic of Korea reduced their issuances. In addition, rising US Treasury yields made borrowing in US dollars more costly for issuers.

---

[7] ASEAN G3 issuance data includes Cambodia, Indonesia, the Lao People's Democratic Republic, Malaysia, the Philippines, Singapore, Thailand, and Viet Nam.

Figure 6: G3 Currency Bond Issuance in Emerging East Asia

USD billion

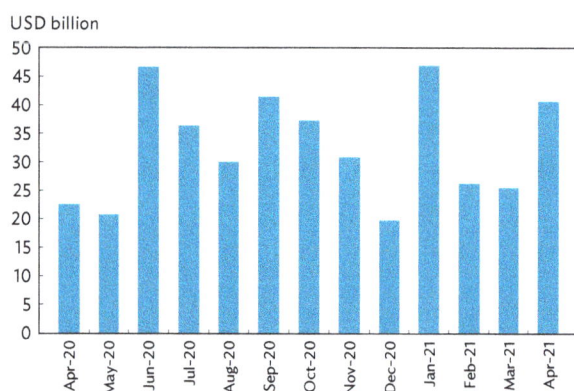

USD = United States dollar.

Notes:
1. Emerging East Asia comprises Cambodia; the People's Republic of China; Hong Kong, China; Indonesia; the Republic of Korea; the Lao People's Democratic Republic; Malaysia; the Philippines; Singapore; Thailand; and Viet Nam.
2. G3 currency bonds are bonds denominated in either euros, Japanese yen, or US dollars.
3. Figures were computed based on 30 April 2021 currency exchange rates and do not include currency effects.

Source: *AsianBondsOnline* calculations based on Bloomberg LP data.

Issuances picked up again in April, with most economies in emerging East Asia tapping international bond markets for their borrowing. Investors are cautiously optimistic about the global economic recovery due to successful vaccine rollouts in some places at the same time there are COVID-19 case resurgences and the emergence of new variants elsewhere.

Government Bond Yield Curves

Local currency government bond yield movements were mixed as the resurgence of COVID-19 cases and global inflation fears had varied effects on individual markets. Idiosyncratic factors also had an effect.

Uncertainty over the global economy rose in Q1 2021, largely due to the resurgence of COVID-19 cases in some economies, while financial markets were also affected by the potential for a liquidity withdrawal in response to global inflation fears.

The ongoing vaccination efforts and previous stimulus measures are expected to lead to a recovery in the global economy. However, the rise in COVID-19 cases and the emergence of new variants in some economies have

raised the possibility that economic recovery may be delayed in other markets. The pace of vaccine rollouts and the effectiveness of government responses also factor into the uncertain trajectory of economic recovery.

The US economy continued to have a rosy outlook. GDP in Q1 2021 expanded at an annualized rate of 6.4%, up from a 4.3% gain in Q4 2020. However, there are concerns of rising inflation risk leading to expectations that the Federal Reserve may tighten earlier than expected and reduce liquidity in the financial market. Consumer price inflation in the US accelerated to 5.0% y-o-y in May from 4.2% y-o-y in April and 2.6% y-o-y in March. While the Federal Reserve left monetary policy unchanged during its 15–16 June meeting, two rate hikes are expected in 2023.

In contrast, the euro area's GDP fell 1.3% y-o-y in Q1 2021 after falling 4.7% y-o-y in the previous quarter as a resurgence of COVID-19 led to additional containment measures. While the European Central Bank left monetary policy unchanged at its 22 April meeting, it announced that it would speed up the pace of its bond buying in Q2 2021. On 10 June, the European Central Bank affirmed its existing easy monetary stance. In Japan, annualized GDP fell 3.9% in Q1 2021 due to an extension of the state of emergency over the COVID-19 pandemic.

Similarly, the outlooks for emerging East Asia's economies are also mixed owing to market-specific factors. Between 28 February and 15 May, yield movements diverged across emerging East Asian economies. The 2-year yield trended upward in both the Republic of Korea and Singapore, largely due to positive economic outlooks as both markets have effectively managed the COVID-19 outbreak. Surprisingly, despite strong economic growth, the 2-year yield in the PRC trended downward during the review period (**Figure 7a**). This was largely the result of the government's focus on risk control as evidenced by the reduced issuance of government bonds compared to the same period in 2020 and less need for fiscal stimulus.

Positive economic sentiment also lifted the 2-year yield in Malaysia (**Figure 7b**). In the Philippines, the 2-year yield trended upward at the start of the year on rising inflation. After peaking in March, yields moved slightly downward over concerns that increased COVID-19 cases would delay economic recovery. The 2-year yield in Indonesia fell the most among its regional peers due to foreign

Figure 7a: 2-Year Local Currency Government Bond Yields

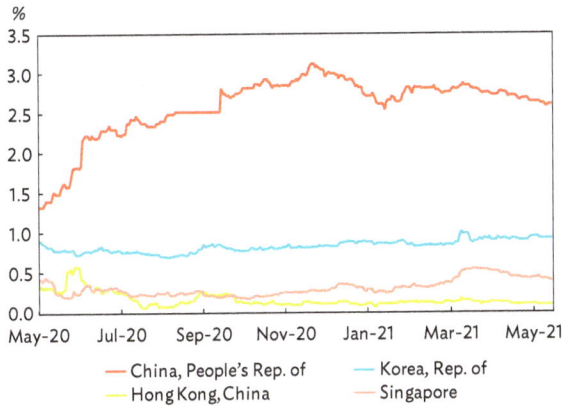

Note: Data coverage is from 2 May 2020 to 15 May 2021
Source: Based on data from Bloomberg LP.

Figure 7b: 2-Year Local Currency Government Bond Yields

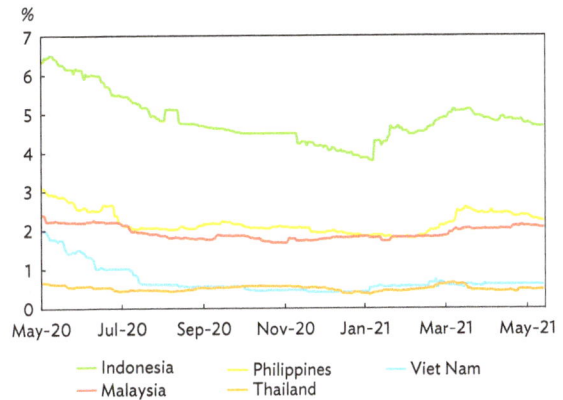

Note: Data coverage is from 2 May 2020 to 15 May 2021.
Source: Based on data from Bloomberg LP.

Figure 8a: 10-Year Local Currency Government Bond Yields

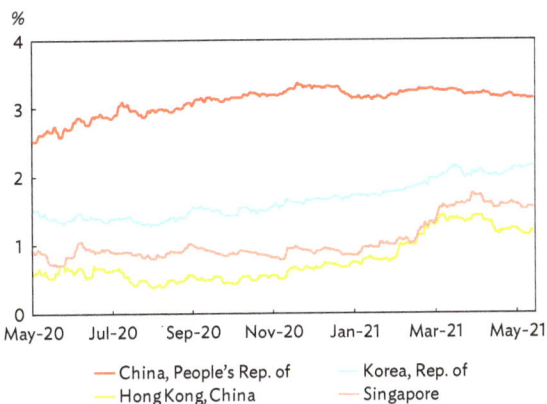

Note: Data coverage is from 2 May 2020 to 15 May 2021.
Source: Based on data from Bloomberg LP.

Figure 8b: 10-Year Local Currency Government Bond Yields

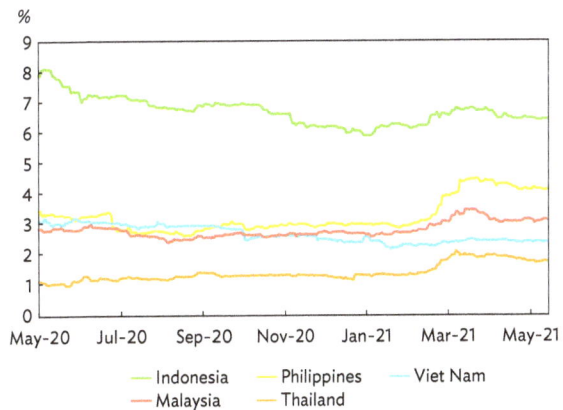

Note: Data coverage is from 2 May 2020 to 15 May 2021.
Source: Based on data from Bloomberg LP.

investor inflows and low inflation. In Thailand, 2-year yields trended downward starting in March on economic growth concerns over a rise in COVID-19 cases and the impact of the pandemic on Thailand's tourism industry. The 10-year yield in emerging East Asian markets largely followed the movement of the respective 2-year yield (**Figures 8a** and **8b**).

Between 28 February and 15 May, LCY government bond yield curves in emerging East Asia exhibited mixed trends (**Figure 9**). The PRC's yield curve shifted downward for all tenors except the 8-year, which was unchanged,

by an average of 18 bps over the tightening supply of government bonds. Indonesia's and Hong Kong, China's yield curves shifted downward for most tenors, as did Thailand's, over economic growth concerns. The yield curves of the Republic of Korea, Malaysia, and Singapore steepened during the review period, with most longer tenors rising on positive economic sentiment. While the Philippine yield curve shifted strongly upward for all tenors by an average of 25 bps, unlike other markets in the region, the rise was mostly due to rising inflation and the need for an increased bond supply to fund the budget deficit.

Figure 9: Benchmark Yield Curves—Local Currency Government Bonds

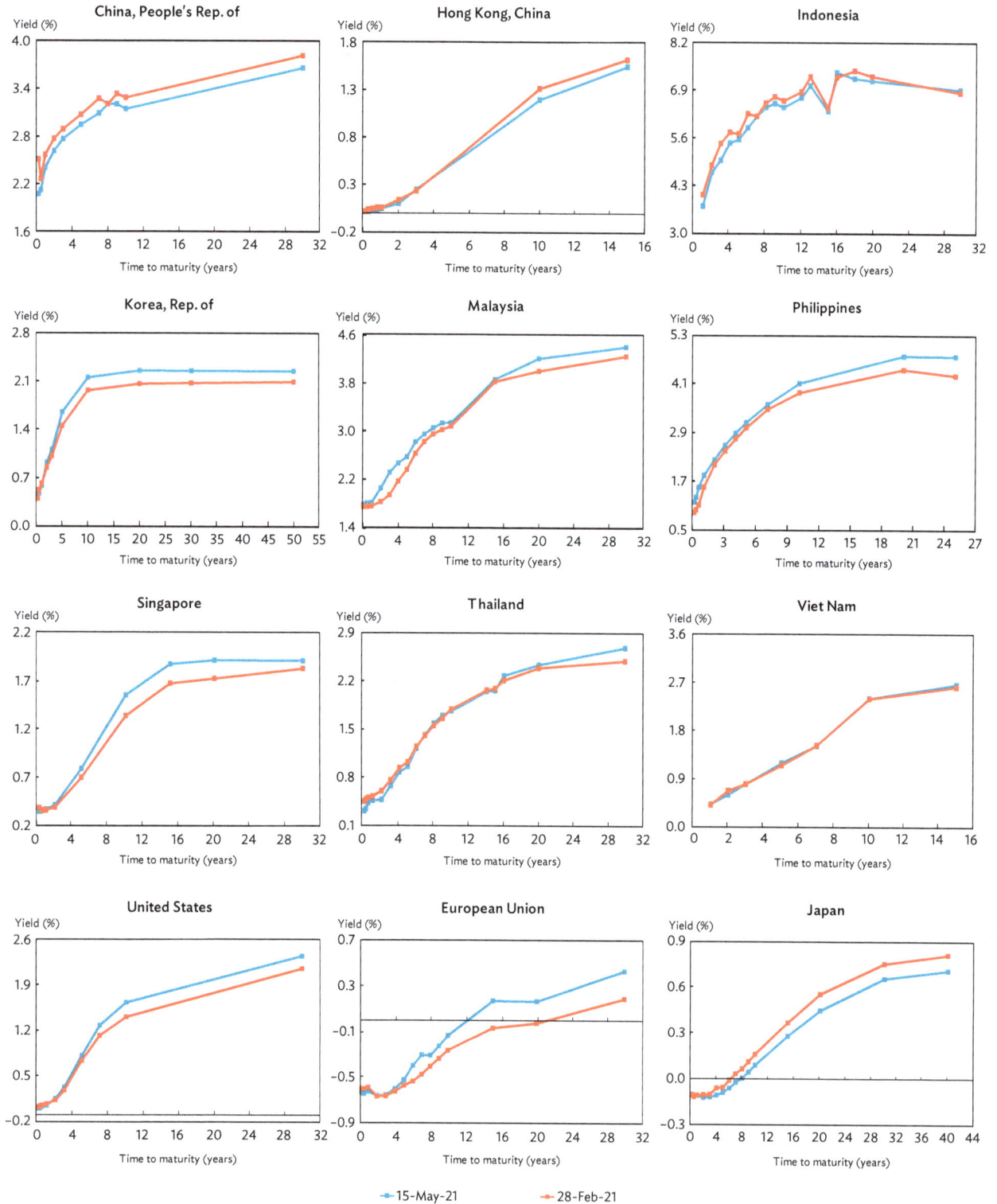

Sources: Based on data from Bloomberg LP and Thai Bond Market Association.

Between 28 February and 15 May, the 2-year versus 10-year yield spread largely widened in all emerging East Asian economies except for Malaysia and Hong Kong, China (**Figure 10**).

Economic performances in emerging East Asia improved in Q1 2021 versus Q4 2020. Both the PRC and Viet Nam continued to post positive economic growth rates. Economic recovery in the PRC was particularly strong, with GDP rising 18.3% y-o-y in Q1 2021. Viet Nam posted solid 4.5% y-o-y GDP growth in the same quarter, similar to the y-o-y expansion in Q4 2020. Hong Kong, China; the Republic of Korea; and Singapore each posted positive growth rates in Q1 2021 after their respective economies contracted in the previous quarter. Both Malaysia and Indonesia continued to post GDP contractions in Q1 2021, but the pace of contraction slowed to −0.5% y-o-y and −0.7% y-o-y, respectively, from −3.4% y-o-y and −2.2% y-o-y in Q4 2020. While GDP contractions in the Philippines and Thailand were also smaller in Q1 2021 than in the previous quarter, their negative growth rates remained relatively elevated at −4.2% y-o-y and −2.6% y-o-y, respectively.

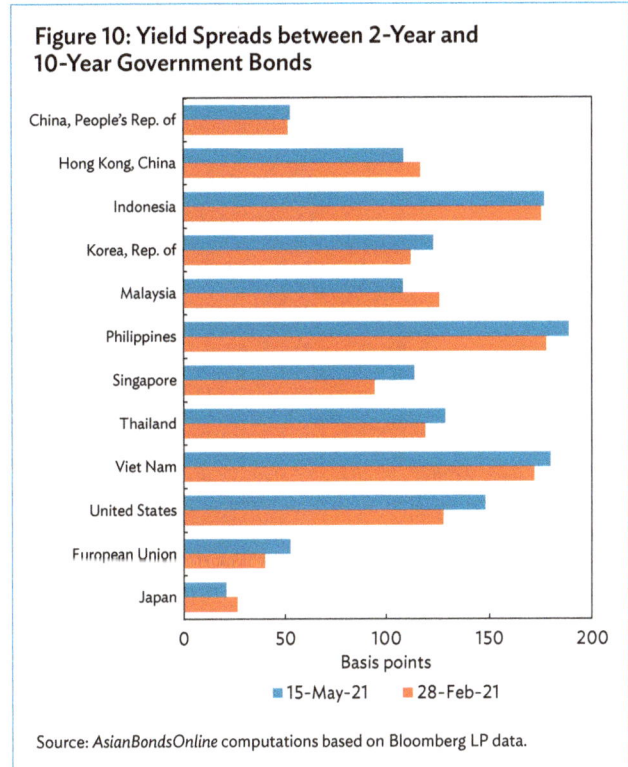

Figure 10: Yield Spreads between 2-Year and 10-Year Government Bonds

Source: *AsianBondsOnline* computations based on Bloomberg LP data.

With economic performance improving in some markets, inflation largely trended upward during the review period. The exception was Indonesia (**Figure 11a**), whose inflation rate either remained steady or dipped slightly. Inflation in Thailand rose to move the economy out of deflation, but this was largely due to base effects. The region's highest inflation during the review period occurred in Malaysia at 4.7% (**Figure 11b**). It was followed by the Philippines, with a rate of 4.5% y-o-y in April, owing to rising pork prices due to an outbreak of swine flu.

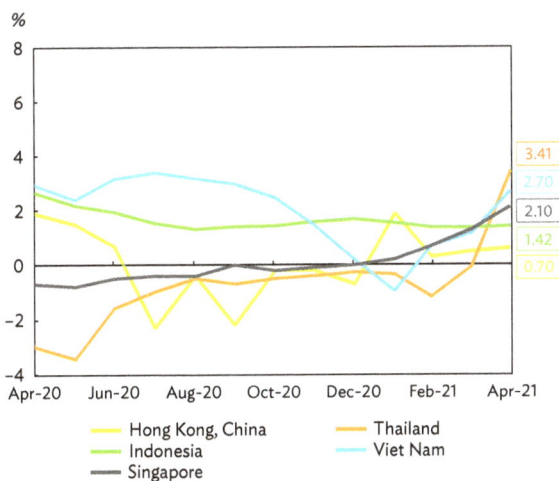

Figure 11a: Headline Inflation Rates

Note: Data coverage is from April 2020 to April 2021.
Source: Based on data from Bloomberg LP.

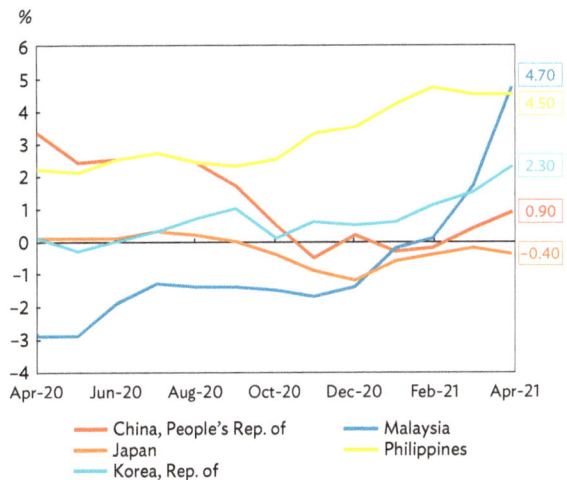

Figure 11b: Headline Inflation Rates

Note: Data coverage is from April 2020 to April 2021.
Source: Based on data from Bloomberg LP.

Figure 12a: Policy Rates

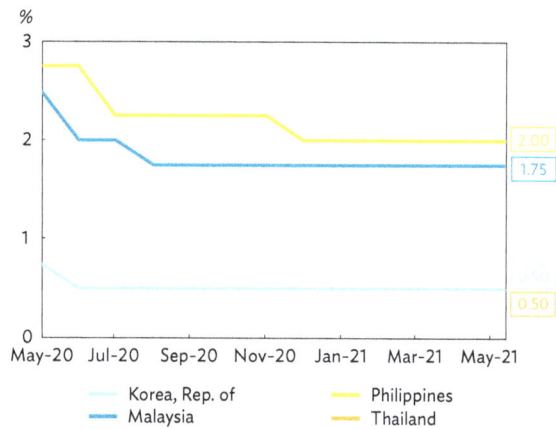

Notes:
1. Data coverage is from 2 May 2020 to 15 May 2021.
2. The Republic of Korea and Thailand have the same trend lines.
Source: Based on data from Bloomberg LP.

Figure 12b: Policy Rates

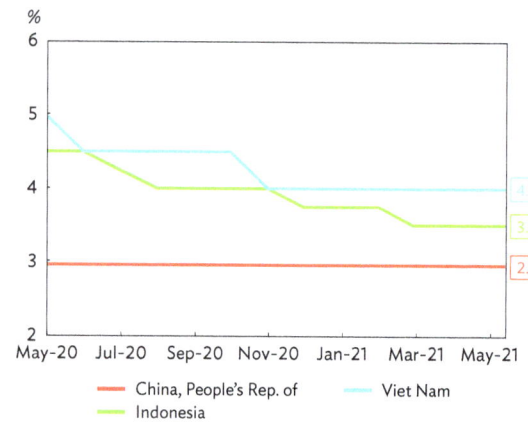

Notes:
1. Data coverage is from 2 May 2020 to 15 May 2021.
2. For the People's Republic of China, data used in the chart are the 1-year medium-term lending facility rate. While the 1-year benchmark lending rate is the official policy rate of the People's Bank of China, market players use the 1-year medium-term lending facility rate as a guide for the monetary policy direction of the People's Bank of China.
Source: Based on data from Bloomberg LP.

While inflation rates were rising, central banks in emerging East Asia largely left monetary policies unchanged, allowing the effects of past easing to work their way through the economy (**Figures 12a** and **12b**). Authorities also expected that growth would recover over the medium-term but rising COVID-19 cases in some markets have raised uncertainty. The exception to the regional trend was Indonesia, which reduced its policy rate by 25 bps in February.

AAA-rated corporate spreads rose in Malaysia and in the Republic of Korea and fell in Thailand.

The AAA-rated corporate versus government yield spread rose in the Republic of Korea and in Malaysia between 28 February and 15 May (**Figure 13a**), as the improved economic outlook led to increased risk-taking. The spread fell in Thailand, over increased demand for safer credit, and was largely unchanged in the PRC.

Lower-rated corporate spreads rose in the PRC and Thailand but fell in the Republic of Korea and Malaysia on demand for high-yield securities (**Figure 13b**).

Figure 13a: Credit Spreads—Local Currency Corporates Rated AAA vs. Government Bonds

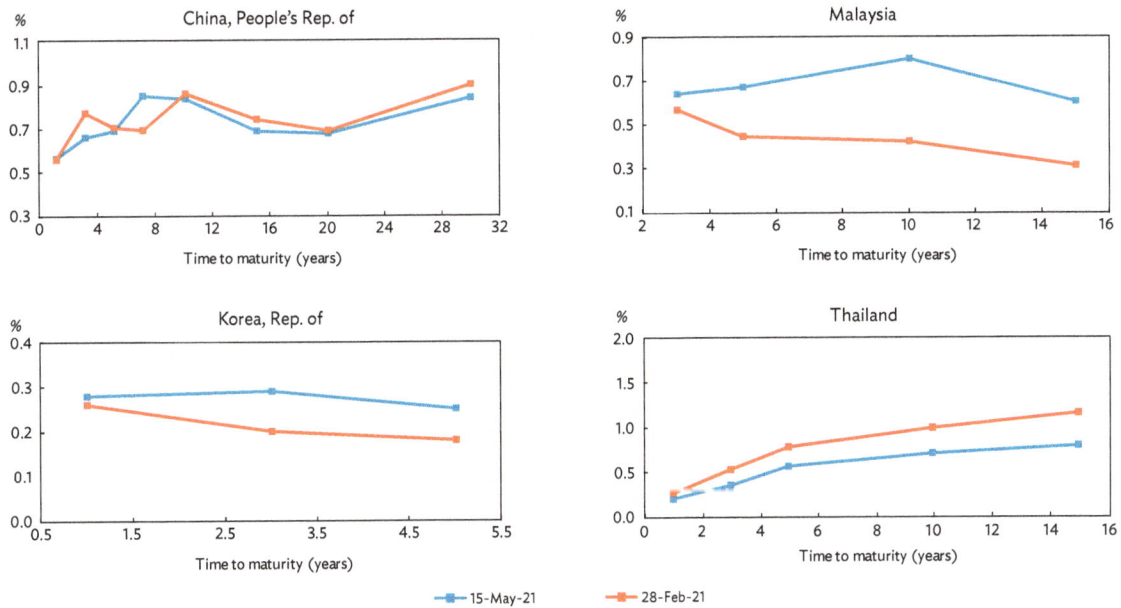

Notes:
1. Credit spreads are obtained by subtracting government yields from corporate indicative yields.
2. For the Republic of Korea, data on corporate bond yields are as of 26 February 2021 and 14 May 2021.
3. For Malaysia, data on corporate bonds yields are as of 26 February 2021 and 12 May 2021.
Sources: People's Republic of China (Bloomberg LP); Republic of Korea (KG Zeroin Corporation); Malaysia (Fully Automated System for Issuing/Tendering Bank Negara Malaysia); and Thailand (Bloomberg, LP).

Figure 13b: Credit Spreads—Lower-Rated Local Currency Corporates vs. AAA

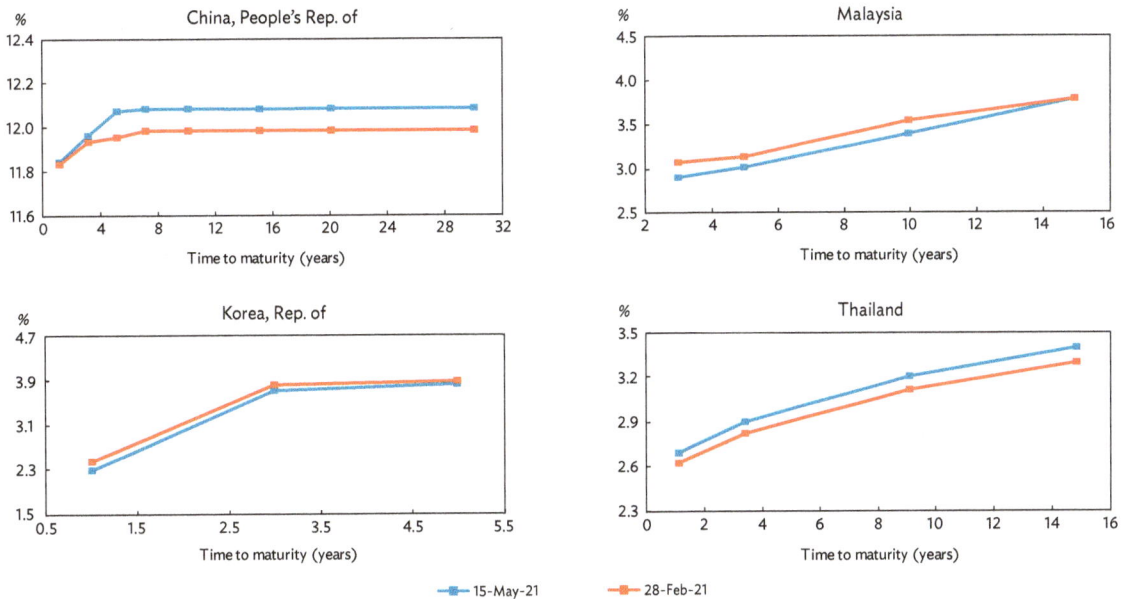

Notes:
1. Credit spreads are obtained by subtracting government yields from corporate indicative yields.
2. For the Republic of Korea, data on corporate bond yields are as of 26 February 2021 and 14 May 2021.
3. For Malaysia, data on corporate bonds yields are as of 26 February 2021 and 12 May 2021.
Sources: People's Republic of China (Bloomberg LP); Republic of Korea (KG Zeroin Corporation); Malaysia (Fully Automated System for Issuing/Tendering Bank Negara Malaysia); and Thailand (Bloomberg, LP).

Recent Developments in ASEAN+3 Sustainable Bond Markets

Sustainable bond markets continued to expand in ASEAN+3 in the first quarter (Q1) of 2021, with regional markets' aggregate growth quickening to 13.2% quarter-on-quarter (q-o-q) and 44.5% year-on-year (y-o-y) from 6.3% q-o-q and 34.9% y-o-y in the fourth quarter (Q4) of 2020 (**Figure 14**).[8] This growth was modest compared with the global sustainable bond market's expansion of about 20.0% q-o-q in Q1 2021. With an outstanding bond stock of USD301.3 billion, the sustainable bond market in ASEAN+3 continued to be a significant part of the global sustainable bond market, accounting for nearly 20.0% of the global total at the end of March. By bond type, the region's green bond market, social bond market, and sustainability bond market accounted for 20.4%, 12.6%, and 22.7% of the respective global totals.

Figure 14: Outstanding Amount of Green, Social, and Sustainability Bonds in ASEAN+3 Markets

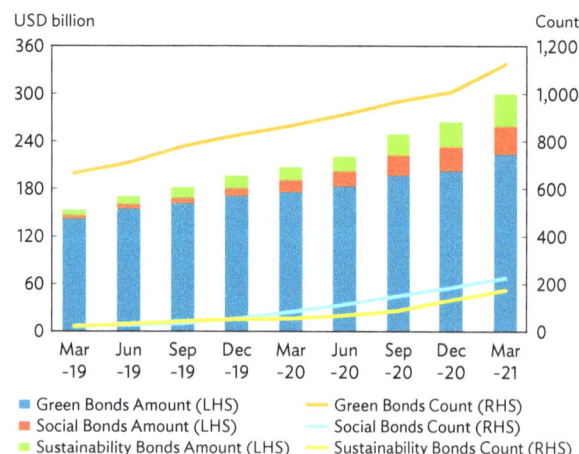

ASEAN = Association of Southeast Asian Nations, LHS = left-hand side, RHS = right-hand side, USD = United States dollar.
Notes:
1. ASEAN includes the markets of Indonesia, Malaysia, the Philippines, Singapore, and Thailand.
2. ASEAN+3 includes ASEAN members plus the People's Republic of China; Hong Kong, China; Japan; and the Republic of Korea.
Source: *AsianBondsOnline* computations based on Bloomberg LP data.

The majority of sustainable bonds outstanding continued to be green bonds in Q1 2021, with the outstanding amount reaching USD224.9 billion, equivalent to 74.6% of ASEAN+3's total sustainable bond stock at the end of March. Green bonds outstanding grew 10.5% q-o-q and 27.2% y-o-y in Q1 2021, compared to 2.8% q-o-q and 18.5% y-o-y in Q4 2020, reflecting the ongoing commitment from various stakeholders in the region to mitigate climate change risks. ASEAN markets accounted for 5.1% of the regional green bond outstanding stock at the end of March, while the PRC, Japan, and the Republic of Korea accounted for 70.0%, 10.8%, and 9.3%, respectively (**Figure 15**).

While green bonds continue to dominate the sustainable bond market, interest in social bonds and sustainability bonds has been rising, with both segments posting faster growth relative to green bonds in Q1 2021. Social bonds outstanding in ASEAN+3 markets gained 14.2% q-o-q to reach USD35.4 billion at the end of March, up from USD31.0 billion at the end of December, accounting for 11.7% of the region's total sustainable bond stock. Sustainability bonds grew the fastest at 29.2% q-o-q to reach USD41.1 billion at the end of March, up from USD31.8 billion at the end of December, accounting for a 13.6% share of the region's aggregate sustainable bond stock. At the end of Q1 2021, ASEAN markets accounted for 0.05% and 15.9% of the region's social and sustainability bonds, respectively. The PRC, the Republic of Korea, and Japan accounted for 2.5%, 57.4%, and 40.1% of regional social bonds, respectively, and 8.5%, 36.3%, and 39.3% of regional sustainability bonds, respectively.

Corporates continued to be major issuers of sustainable bonds in the region in Q1 2021 (**Figure 16**). Green corporate bonds accounted for an 88.1% share of the region's total green bonds at the end of March, slipping from 90.2% at the end of December, due to an uptick in government green bond issuance. Corporate issuers

---

[8] For the discussion on sustainable bonds, ASEAN+3 includes Association of Southeast Asian Nations (ASEAN) members Indonesia, Malaysia, the Philippines, Singapore, and Thailand, plus the People's Republic of China; Hong Kong, China; Japan; and the Republic of Korea.

Figure 15: Outstanding Green, Social, and Sustainability Bonds in ASEAN+3 by Economy (% share of total)

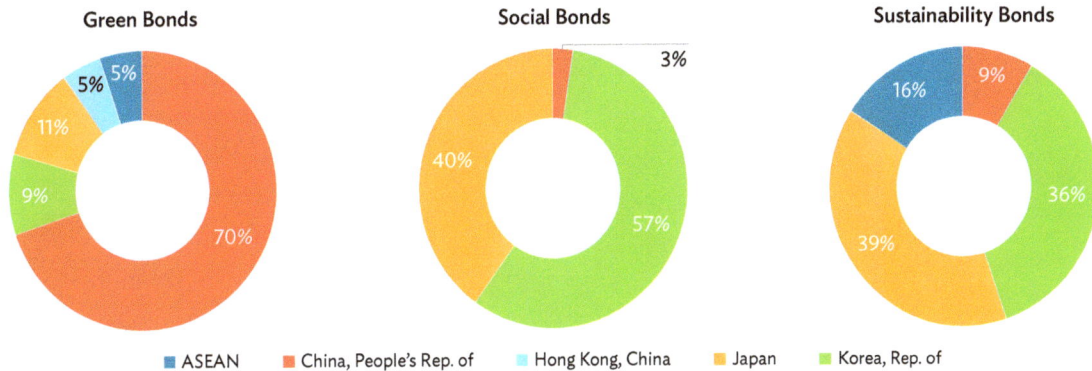

Green Bonds
Social Bonds
Sustainability Bonds

■ ASEAN   ■ China, People's Rep. of   ■ Hong Kong, China   ■ Japan   ■ Korea, Rep. of

ASEAN = Association of Southeast Asian Nations.
Notes:
1. Data as of 31 March 2021.
2. ASEAN includes the markets of Indonesia, Malaysia, the Philippines, Singapore, and Thailand.
3. ASEAN+3 includes ASEAN members plus the People's Republic of China; Hong Kong, China; Japan; and the Republic of Korea.
4. For social bonds, ASEAN share for 31 March 2021 is 0.05%.
Source: *AsianBondsOnline* computations based on Bloomberg LP data.

Figure 16: Outstanding Green, Social, and Sustainability Bonds in ASEAN+3 by Type of Bond

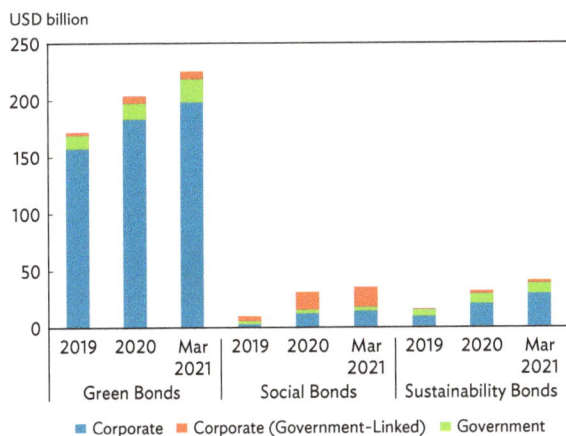

USD billion

■ Corporate   ■ Corporate (Government-Linked)   ■ Government

USD = United States dollar.
Notes: Corporate denotes bonds issued by private sector corporations.
Government bonds include bonds issued by sovereigns, regional governments,
and local governments. Corporate (Government-Linked) denotes corporations
with government affiliations.
Source: *AsianBondsOnline* computation based on Bloomberg LP data.

also continued to dominate the regional sustainability bond market, with their share of bonds outstanding rising to 72.5% at the end of March from 65.4% at the end of December. The public sector remained the major player in the regional social bond market, with governments and corporates with government links accounting for 59.2% of the region's total social bonds outstanding at the end of March.

By sector, financial firms were the largest issuers of sustainable bonds in ASEAN+3 markets, representing 37.7%, 61.4%, and 40.0% of the region's outstanding green bonds, social bonds, and sustainability bonds, respectively, at the end of March (**Figure 17**).

Green bonds and social bonds outstanding in ASEAN+3 markets were mostly issued in local currency, while sustainability bonds, which have both green and social impacts, were largely issued in foreign currency such as US dollars and euros (**Figure 18**).

Figure 17: Outstanding Green, Social, and Sustainability Bonds in ASEAN+3 by Sector of Issuer (% share of total)

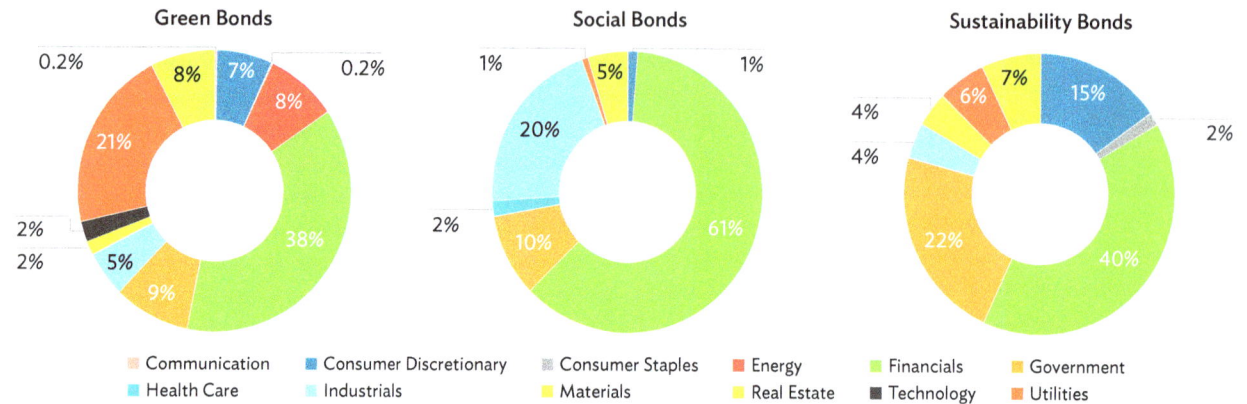

Green Bonds

Social Bonds

Sustainability Bonds

Legend: Communication, Consumer Discretionary, Consumer Staples, Energy, Financials, Government, Health Care, Industrials, Materials, Real Estate, Technology, Utilities

ASEAN = Association of Southeast Asian Nations.
Notes:
1. Data as of 31 March 2021.
2. ASEAN includes the markets of Indonesia, Malaysia, the Philippines, Singapore, and Thailand.
3. ASEAN+3 includes ASEAN members plus the People's Republic of China; Hong Kong, China; Japan; and the Republic of Korea.
Source: *AsianBondsOnline* computations based on Bloomberg LP data.

Figure 18: Outstanding Green, Social, and Sustainability Bonds in ASEAN+3 by Type of Currency (% share of total)

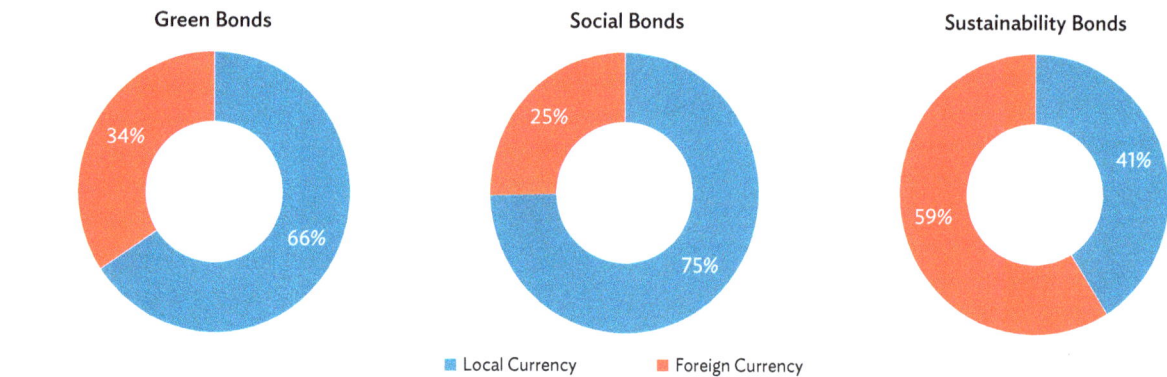

Green Bonds

Social Bonds

Sustainability Bonds

Legend: Local Currency, Foreign Currency

ASEAN = Association of Southeast Asian Nations.
Notes:
1. Data as of 31 March 2021.
2. ASEAN includes the markets of Indonesia, Malaysia, the Philippines, Singapore, and Thailand.
3. ASEAN+3 includes ASEAN members plus the People's Republic of China; Hong Kong, China; Japan; and the Republic of Korea.
Source: *AsianBondsOnline* computations based on Bloomberg LP data.

Policy and Regulatory Developments

People's Republic of China

The People's Bank of China and the State Administration of Foreign Exchange Implement Cross-Border Pilot Program for Multinational Corporations

In March, the People's Bank of China and the State Administration of Foreign Exchange launched a pilot program to allow multinational corporations with good credit standing to enjoy a more streamlined process for cross-border fund transfers. The pilot program is meant to integrate multinational corporations' transfers of both Chinese yuan and foreign currencies. The benefits of the pilot program for the companies include a unified policy on Chinese yuan and other foreign currencies, the relaxation of quotas on external debt and overseas loans, and the easier cross-border transfer of currencies and purchases of foreign currencies subject to quota.

The People's Bank of China Adjusts Foreign Exchange Reserve Requirement Ratio

Effective 15 June, the foreign exchange reserve requirement ratio of financial institutions was raised to 7.0% from 5.0%, as previously announced by the People's Bank of China in May.

Hong Kong, China

Hong Kong Monetary Authority and Bank of Japan Launch a Cross-Border Delivery-Versus-Payment Link

On 1 April, the Hong Kong Monetary Authority and the Bank of Japan (BOJ) launched a delivery-versus-payment link for cross-currency securities transactions between the Hong Kong Dollar Clearing House Automated Transfer System and the BOJ Financial Network System for Japanese Government Bond (JGB) Services. The delivery-versus-payment link provides settlement infrastructure for Hong Kong dollar sale and repurchase transactions using JGBs as collateral. It helps reduce settlement risk by guaranteeing simultaneous delivery of Hong Kong dollars in Hong Kong, China and JGBs in Japan. The link is operated by the BOJ in Japan and the Hong Kong Interbank Clearing Limited in Hong Kong, China.

Hong Kong Monetary Authority Launches Green and Sustainable Finance Grant Scheme

On 10 May, the Hong Kong Monetary Authority launched the Green and Sustainable Finance Grant Scheme, which will provide subsidies for eligible bond issuers and loan borrowers to cover expenses related to bond issuance and external review services. The scheme, which will last for 3 years, aims to strengthen Hong Kong, China's position as a regional green and sustainable finance hub, and help enrich its green and sustainable finance ecosystem. Eligible green and sustainable loans are those issued in Hong Kong, China with a size of at least HKD200 million, or the equivalent in a foreign currency, and have procured pre-issuance external review services by a recognized provider.

Indonesia

Indonesia Expands Economic Stimulus Program

In January, Indonesia raised its National Economic Recovery budget to IDR553 trillion from the previously approved IDR372 trillion budget. The program includes programs for health spending and social support.

Bank Indonesia Revises Regulation for Monitoring Foreign Exchange Transactions

In June, a new Bank Indonesia regulation came into effect to strengthen the monitoring of foreign exchange transactions. Under the new regulation, banks must include in the foreign exchange transaction monitoring system those client transactions with a transaction value of at least USD250,000 and derivative transactions with a minimum value of USD1 million.

Republic of Korea

National Assembly Passes KRW14.9 Trillion Supplementary Budget

On 25 March, the National Assembly passed the KRW14.9 trillion supplementary budget, which was slightly less than the proposed KRW15.0 trillion. The additional budget will mostly be used to fund COVID-19 relief programs, support for small businesses hit by the pandemic, and job retention and creation programs. The supplementary budget brought the total 2021 budget to KRW572.9 trillion and increased the fiscal deficit to 4.5% of GDP.

Malaysia

FTSE Russell Removes Malaysia from Its Watch List

On 29 March, FTSE Russell announced that it had removed Malaysia from its fixed-income watch list and retained Malaysia in its FTSE World Government Bond Index. The decision was made in consideration of regulatory enhancements in Malaysia's financial market. When Malaysia was included in FTSE Russell's watch list in 2019, Bank Negara Malaysia (BNM) introduced regulations that made its government bond market more accessible to foreign investors by improving secondary market liquidity and facilitating foreign exchange transactions.

Bank Negara Malaysia Liberalizes Foreign Exchange Policy

On 31 March, BNM introduced regulations that provide greater flexibility to export-oriented industries. Effective 15 April, resident exporters can (i) manage the conversion of their export proceeds based on their foreign currency needs, (ii) settle their domestic trades in foreign currency with other residents, (iii) extend the repatriation of their export proceeds without seeking approval from BNM, and (iv) net-off their export proceeds against permitted foreign currency liabilities without seeking approval from BNM. Resident corporates can engage in commodity derivatives hedging with nonresident counterparties. These new regulations aim to attract foreign direct investments to support Malaysia's economic recovery.

Philippines

Bangko Sentral ng Pilipinas Increases Net Open Foreign Exchange Limit

In June, the Monetary Board of the Bangko Sentral ng Pilipinas approved an increase in the net open foreign exchange position (NOP) limit for banks in response to rising demand for foreign exchange that is underpinned by the increased volume of trade transactions and investments. The NOP limit was raised to either 25% of qualifying capital or USD150 million, whichever is lower. The previous limit was 20% of unimpaired capital or USD50 million. According to the Bangko Sentral ng Pilipinas, the increase in the NOP limit is part of a larger set of amendments to the framework for the management of banks' open foreign exchange positions, which aim to make the calculation and measurement of a bank's NOP more risk-based. The amendments will take effect on 1 August 2021.

Bureau of the Treasury Plans to Borrow PHP555 Billion in the Second Quarter of 2021

The Bureau of the Treasury (BTr) is set to borrow PHP555 billion from the domestic debt market in the second quarter of 2021. For April and May, the monthly programmed Treasury bill offerings were PHP100 billion, while Treasury bond offerings were PHP70 billion. In June, the BTr increased its issuance plan by holding more auctions and shifting to a higher offer volume of Treasury bonds. The BTr is seeking to raise PHP215 billion from the market in June, comprising PHP75 billion of Treasury bills and P140 billion of Treasury bonds, through its weekly auctions.

Singapore

Bilateral Investment Treaty with Indonesia Begins

On 9 March, the bilateral investment treaty signed in 2018 by Singapore and Indonesia entered into force. The treaty establishes rules and additional protections for investors and investments in each other's economies. The establishment of the bilateral investment treaty aims to foster a better economic relationship and increase investment flows between Singapore and Indonesia.

Singapore and Japan Renew Bilateral Swap Arrangement

On 21 May, Monetary Authority of Singapore and the BOJ renewed the existing bilateral swap arrangement between Singapore and Japan. Singapore can swap Singapore dollars up to the equivalent of USD3 billion in Japanese yen. Japan can swap Japanese yen up to the equivalent of USD1 billion in Singapore dollars. With the renewal of the arrangement, the two economies will be able to continue to exchange their local currency for United States dollars from each other. This gives flexibility to both economies in meeting their liquidity needs, while also promoting financial stability and better economic ties between Singapore and Japan.

Thailand

Bank of Thailand Adjusts Bond Issuance Program for 2021

The Bank of Thailand (BOT) adjusted its bond issuance program for 2021 to accommodate changes in market demand and support the government's financing needs for COVID-19 relief measures. The BOT and the Public Debt Management Office continued to coordinate so that BOT and government bonds would be issued at different sections of the yield curve. In particular, the BOT discontinued the issuance of 6-month bills and 3-year bonds in line with the Public Debt Management Office's plan to issue 6-month Treasury bills and 3-year government bonds in 2021. The BOT also terminated the issuance of 2-week bills as the need for these short-term bills had declined in recent years. Furthermore, the BOT replaced the Bangkok Interbank Offered Rate-linked floating rate bonds with Thai Overnight Repurchase Rate-linked floating rate bonds to promote the development of the new reference rate.

Viet Nam

Ministry of Finance Lists Market Makers

Viet Nam's Ministry of Finance released Decision No. 2290/QD-BTC, which lists market makers for the debt market effective 1 January–31 December 2021. The market markers for 2021 comprise 17 commercial banks and securities firms, up from only 13 in 2020. The entities have the right to participate in the bidding of government bonds, act as the main guarantor organization for the issuance of government bonds, and provide inputs for drafting new policies for the bond market. The Ministry of Finance will evaluate the entities toward the end of the year if they can maintain their status as market makers.

State Bank of Vietnam Issues Regulation to Control Credit Quality in Risky Sectors

In May, the State Bank of Vietnam issued Official Dispatch No. 3029/NHNN-TTGSNH to credit institutions and foreign bank branches, instructing them to implement strict control over the quality of credit in sectors with potential risks such as real estate and securities. High-risk credit areas include investments in corporate bonds, securities credit, real estate, build-operate-transfer, and consumer loans. For corporate bonds, issuance from the real estate sector has rapidly increased in volume, with almost none having any collateral. This risks the formation of a property bubble that could inflict huge losses on investors when the bubble bursts.

Governing Sustainable Finance

Environmental challenges—such as climate change; biodiversity loss; and soil, water, and air pollution—are threatening human well-being and sustainable livelihoods.[9] It is now widely recognized that climate change and environmental degradation pose serious dangers to economic activity and threaten macrofinancial stability. Financial supervisors and market participants have come to realize the financial risks related to climate change and other environmental challenges, and that these risks need to be mitigated.

Vast financial resources need to be mobilized for investment in sustainable infrastructure—including energy, transportation, waste management, and health—to deliver better and more inclusive economic, social, and environmental conditions, and to achieve the Sustainable Development Goals (SDGs) and the objectives of the Paris Agreement. These investment needs will not be met until sustainability considerations are mainstreamed in financial markets. To achieve the climate goals, it will be imperative to align financial flows with a pathway toward low greenhouse gas emissions and climate-resilient development, as stipulated in Article 2.1c of the Paris Agreement.

Recent years have seen an intensifying discourse on the role of financial governance in addressing climate and other sustainability risks and in scaling up sustainable finance. The COVID-19 crisis has further highlighted the need for greater social resilience, which is now becoming a key issue for financial decision makers. To align finance with sustainability goals and to mitigate financial risk, it is crucial to incorporate environmental, social, and governance (ESG) criteria into financial decision making.

Sustainability risks can pose financial risks both to individual financial institutions and the financial system at large. As recently pointed out by the International Monetary Fund, "ESG issues may have material impacts on corporate performance and may give rise to financial stability risks via exposure of banks and insurers and large losses from climate change" (International Monetary Fund 2019). Governance failures at financial and nonfinancial institutions have historically contributed to financial crises, including the 1997/98 Asian financial crisis. Social inequality and stagnant income among lower-income groups, as well as attempts by policymakers to address these problems through easier access to credit, contributed to the subprime mortgage crisis in the United States (Rajan 2010). With respect to environmental risk, the focus has been primarily on the physical and transition risks related to climate change (e.g., Bank of England 2015, Network of Central Banks and Supervisors for Greening the Financial System [NGFS] 2019a, Bolton et al. 2020), but issues like biodiversity loss are getting more attention recently (e.g., van Toor et al. 2020, World Bank 2020a).

Rating agencies and financial markets are increasingly paying attention to these risks. Empirical evidence shows that climate vulnerability raises the cost of capital for countries (Buhr et al. 2018; Beirne, Renzhi, and Volz 2020) and that macrofinancial risks from climate change may also amplify sovereign risk (Volz et al. 2020). Moreover, climate vulnerability is also affecting firms' cost of capital and access to finance (Kling et al. 2021).

Recent years have seen multiple public and private policies and initiatives aimed at developing standards, practices, and governance frameworks for sustainable finance, both at the national and global levels. This theme chapter presents an overview of the emerging practice of embedding sustainable development into the financial system. It first reviews initiatives aimed at enhancing market practice—through standards, taxonomies, and disclosure—before examining the efforts of central banks and supervisors to integrate sustainability factors into monetary and prudential frameworks.

---

[9] This theme chapter was written by Ulrich Volz, director of the Centre for Sustainable Finance at SOAS University of London and senior research fellow at the German Development Institute.

Standards, Taxonomies, and Disclosure

A lack of clarity in definitions and standards is one of the major obstacles to scaling up green and sustainable financing (Berensmann et al. 2017). The lack of commonly agreed definitions of what constitutes sustainable lending and investment practices contributes to the fragmentation of sustainable finance markets and holds back their development. A standardization of green finance practices also helps to impede greenwashing, i.e., making misleading claims about environmental impact or the performance of financial products.

To provide clarity on what financial products should be labeled "green" or "sustainable," various industry standards and initiatives have emerged, often with support from international organizations. Public–private initiatives—including the United Nations (UN) Principles for Responsible Investment (PRI), the UN Principles for Responsible Banking, and the UN Principles for Sustainable Insurance Initiative—have tried to establish sustainability standards in different areas of the financial system. Such international initiatives have been complemented by guidelines and recommendations from national finance industry associations. For instance, the Association of Banks in Singapore released Guidelines on Responsible Financing in 2015. That same year, the Indian Banking Association introduced the National Voluntary Guidelines for Responsible Finance.

The segment of sustainable finance that has received the most attention is the green bond market. Green bonds are debt securities whose proceeds are used to finance green projects and assets. The International Capital Market Association (ICMA), a self-regulatory body for participants in capital markets, has emerged as a key player for standard setting in this market with voluntary best practice guidelines, including the Green Bond Principles, the Social Bond Principles, and the Sustainability Bond Principles. These guidelines set out criteria regarding the definition, disclosure, and impact reporting for green, social, and sustainability themed bonds, and are widely recognized as the main international standards in this area. A number of countries have issued their own standards for green or sustainable bonds, including the People's Republic of China (PRC) in 2015 as the first country globally to do so, India in 2016, and Indonesia and Japan in 2017. In 2017, the Association of Southeast Asian Nations (ASEAN) Capital Markets

Forum, which comprises capital market regulators from all 10 jurisdictions of ASEAN, issued the ASEAN Green Bonds Standards as an effort to nurture this market and facilitate green investments. The ASEAN Green Bond Standards are based on ICMA's Green Bond Principles. In 2018, the ASEAN Capital Markets Forum published the ASEAN Social Bond Standards and the ASEAN Sustainability Bond Standards.

To provide greater transparency and address problems of greenwashing, several governments and financial authorities have taken steps to develop or implement sustainable finance taxonomies. A sustainable finance taxonomy is "a classification system identifying activities, assets, and/or project categories that deliver on key climate, green, social or sustainable objectives with reference to identified thresholds and/or targets" (ICMA 2020). Well-defined and structured green taxonomies can facilitate better investment decisions and help economic policymaking in achieving national environmental objectives (World Bank 2020b). Several jurisdictions across Asia have introduced green or sustainable taxonomies, or are in the process of implementing them, including the PRC (2015), Bangladesh (2017), Mongolia (2019), Malaysia (2021), and Singapore (2021). In March 2021, the ASEAN finance ministers and central bank governors announced their support for an ASEAN Taxonomy of Sustainable Finance. The European Union's (EU) sustainable finance taxonomy regulation, which entered into force in July 2020, has emerged as the de facto global standard: not only must all EU-based financial institutions comply with the taxonomy, but also all international financial firms that wish to offer sustainable finance products to EU entities.

To enhance transparency and facilitate the analysis of climate- and environment-related risks, disclosure has become a key issue for sustainable finance. The Financial Stability Board's Task Force on Climate-Related Financial Disclosures (TCFD) has emerged as a focal point for promoting disclosure. The TCFD (2017) highlighted the importance of transparency in pricing risk, including risk related to climate change, to support informed and efficient decisions on capital allocation. The TCFD recommendations have been endorsed by many financial supervisors, some of which are planning to integrate disclosure in prudential requirements. Acknowledging the importance of environment-related financial risks beyond climate, a new Taskforce on Nature-Related Financial

Disclosure was announced in July 2020 by a coalition of nongovernmental and UN organizations to broaden the scope of disclosure.

Across Asia, several governments, supervisors, stock exchanges, and financial associations have introduced sustainability disclosure guidance in recent years (Volz 2019). The Shanghai Stock Exchange introduced Guidelines on Listed Companies' Environmental Information Disclosure in 2008. In 2010, the Singapore Stock Exchange released a Guide to Sustainability Reporting for Listed Companies. In 2016, the Singapore Stock Exchange made it mandatory for all listed companies to publish sustainability reports, effective December 2017. In 2012, the Hong Kong Exchanges and Clearing Limited introduced voluntary ESG reporting guidelines. Since 2012, the Securities and Exchange Board of India has required the 100-largest listed enterprises to publish annual business responsibility reports, while the Indian Ministry of Corporate Affairs' imposed corporate social responsibility reporting requirements under the Companies Act, 2013. In 2015, the Securities and Exchange Board of India established a "comply or explain" reporting system for corporate governance under which the top 500 companies were asked to report, among other issues, their environmental and social risk assessment standards and how they are addressing climate change and global warming. The Philippines Securities Exchange Commission has requested an annual corporate governance report from listed firms since 2013. In Viet Nam, the State Securities Commission introduced a Sustainability Reporting Handbook for Vietnamese Companies in 2013. In 2020, the National Bank of Georgia published ESG reporting and disclosure principles.

The EU has adopted the most comprehensive, and arguably most influential, disclosure framework. As part of its Action Plan for Financing Sustainable Growth, the EU introduced a Sustainable Finance Disclosure Regulation (SFDR). The SFDR, which came into effect in March 2021, sets out "harmonised rules for financial market participants and financial advisers on transparency with regards to the integration of sustainability risks and the consideration of adverse sustainability impacts in their processes and the provision of sustainability-related information with respect to financial products" (EU 2019). While the SFDR is directly effective in the EU only, it is likely to have a global impact as all financial firms that are selling products or services in the EU must meet these disclosure standards.

Upgrading Monetary and Prudential frameworks

A growing number of central banks and supervisors are adopting sustainable finance policies or guidelines, or have started to incorporate climate risks into micro-prudential or macroprudential frameworks (Dikau and Volz 2019). Through their regulatory oversight of money, credit, and the financial system, monetary and financial authorities are in a powerful position to support the development of sustainable finance approaches and enforce an adequate pricing of sustainability risks by financial institutions (Volz 2017). Several fora have emerged aimed at enhancing regulatory practices, including the Sustainable Banking Network, which was launched in 2012 and now comprises members from 43 emerging markets (including from 19 countries in Asia and the Pacific), and the NGFS, which was established by eight central banks and supervisors in 2017 and has grown to a membership of 90 institutions, including 17 members from Asia and the Pacific. The NGFS has become the leading platform for international cooperation to advance sustainable finance and promote best practice.

Central banks in developing Asia were among the first to introduce sustainable finance policies and incorporate environmental risk into prudential frameworks (Volz 2019). Monetary and financial authorities in the PRC started in 2007 to develop green credit policies and have since been among the most active in promoting green finance. Bangladesh Bank issued Policy Guidelines for Green Banking and Guidelines on Environmental Risk Management in 2011, requiring environmental risk management from bank and nonbank financial institutions.

Central banks and supervisors in Asia and beyond have sought to promote sustainable finance through engagement with the financial industry, e.g., through multistakeholder dialogues, capacity building efforts, and sustainable finance roadmaps. For instance, the People's Bank of China established a Green Finance Committee in 2015 to develop green finance practices, environmental stress testing for the banking sector, and guidelines on greening the PRC's overseas investments. The same year, Indonesia's Financial Services Authority (Otoritas Jasa Keuangan) established a multistakeholder task force to promote and further develop its Roadmap for Sustainable Finance through dialogue and to develop the sustainability skills of professionals (Volz 2015). Other central banks, including the State Bank of Vietnam and the Reserve Bank of India, have also developed policies to boost green lending.

A growing number of monetary and financial authorities have developed initiatives aimed at promoting market development. For instance, the Monetary Authority of Singapore established in 2017 a Green Bond Grant Scheme for issuances that comply with internationally recognized green bond standards such as ICMA's Green Bond Principles and the ASEAN Green Bond Standards. In 2018, the Hong Kong Quality Assurance Agency launched a similar Green Finance Certification Scheme. Since 2020, the Monetary Authority of Singapore has also sought to promote the potential of digital finance in accelerating the development of green finance in Singapore and the region through a Global FinTech Hackcelerator.

The NGFS has forged a consensus among central banks and supervisors that it is necessary to integrate climate-related risks into micro-supervision and develop macroprudential approaches to address environmental (and especially climate) risks. In December 2020, the ASEAN central banks and monetary authorities jointly published the *Report on the Roles of ASEAN Central Banks in Managing Climate and Environment-Related Risks*, which emphasized that "[c]entral banks should be in a state of readiness to manage the risks stemming from climate change and environment-related events more proactively to ensure ASEAN continues to grow and prosper in a sustainable manner, into the far future and for the generations to come" (Anwar et al. 2020). Several central banks in the region have already started to adjust their prudential policies. Already in 2015, the State Bank of Vietnam issued a directive on managing environmental and social risks in credit extension. The Bangko Sentral ng Pilipinas launched a Sustainable Finance Framework in April 2020, setting out expectations for banks to develop transition plans and integrate these into their corporate governance and risk management frameworks. The Bangko Sentral ng Pilipinas is currently amending this framework to direct banks and other financial institutions to integrate climate change and other environmental and social risks in their enterprise-wide risk management frameworks. In December 2020, the Monetary Authority of Singapore published three guidelines on environmental risk management for financial institutions to formulate expectations of environmental risk management for all banks, insurers, and asset managers. And Bank Negara

Malaysia issued guidance for the financial sector for enhancing risk management as part of its Climate Change and Principle-Based Taxonomy in May 2021.

Building on the pioneering work of the Bank of England (2019) and De Nederlandsche Bank (Vermeulen et al. 2018), numerous central banks have started to work on climate stress-testing that considers multiple scenarios associated with different low-carbon transition pathways. In 2020, De Nederlandsche Bank was the first central bank to carry out an analysis of biodiversity risks for the financial sector (van Toor et al. 2020). Such climate and environment stress tests can be used for both micro- and macroprudential supervision.

Last but not least, central banks have also started to integrate sustainability factors into their own portfolio management. The NGFS (2019b) has recommended that central banks adopt sustainable and responsible investment principles such as the PRI for portfolio management, including policy portfolios, and commit to following the recommendations of the TCFD. In 2019, the DNB was the first central bank to sign the PRI. In 2020, the Bank of England was the first central bank to publicly disclose the climate-related financial risks in its portfolio, building on the TCFD recommendations.

Challenges and Outlook

In the face of significant macrofinancial risks stemming from climate change and other sustainability risks, monetary and financial authorities have started to develop policies and frameworks for mitigating and managing these risks and for scaling up sustainable finance. Financial markets are also starting to integrate sustainability risks in investment and lending decisions.

However, major challenges remain. Despite rapid growth, sustainable lending and investment still account only for a small fraction of the total. Financial markets continue to finance investments that undermine the achievement of the Paris Agreement's objectives and the SDGs. Financial markets still predominantly focus on short-term returns and ignore long-term risks to nature and society. The timeframe to prevent catastrophic global warming and reverse biodiversity loss is short. It will be crucial to rapidly align financial markets with sustainable development goals to enable a green recovery from the economic impacts of the COVID-19 pandemic.

Despite laudable private sector initiatives, it is clear that public policies are needed to mainstream sustainable finance and ensure that sustainability risks are disclosed and fully incorporated in risk analysis. A key step is to make the disclosure of climate risks mandatory, building on the TCFD recommendations. Moreover, supervisors need to set clear expectations regarding risk management by financial institutions. Methodologies for environmental risk analysis and stress testing have improved significantly and are easily available (Ma, Caldecott, and Volz 2020). Financial supervisors must ensure that these are widely adopted. Furthermore, central banks and supervisors need to calibrate their monetary and prudential instruments to take account of sustainability risks. Importantly, policy efforts need to go beyond addressing the climate challenge and not forget other environmental challenges (Northrop et al. 2020, World Bank 2020a).

International cooperation among monetary and financial authorities through fora such as the NGFS and the Sustainable Banking Network will help advance best practice for sustainable finance policies. Governments and supervisors can also support sustainable lending and investment by developing a taxonomy of economic activities. To facilitate cross-border comparability, international cooperation will be important. Public financial institutions can play an important role in enhancing sustainable finance not only through their own balance sheets but also by promoting best practice.

While financial policies can go a long way in mainstreaming sustainable finance, governments also need to set conducive framework conditions and work on overcoming bottlenecks to sustainable investment in the real economy. Without the right fiscal, energy, and infrastructure policies in place, we are unlikely to see investment in renewable energy and sustainable infrastructure to the scale needed to achieve the objectives of the Paris Agreement and the SDGs.

References

Anwar, R.S., M. Mohamed, S.M. Hamzan, N.S.A. Malek, M.H.M. Zain, M.H. Jaafar, S. Sani, R.M. Brazil-De Vera, M.C.T. Desquitado, V. Praneeprachachon, D. Wong, B.A. Lim, G. Goh, W. Tan, and J. Hong. 2020. *Report on the Roles of ASEAN Central Banks in Managing Climate and Environment-Related Risks*. Kuala Lumpur: ASEAN Central Banks and Monetary Authorities. https://asean.org/storage/2020-11-17-ASEAN-Task-Force-Report_for-publication.pdf. p. 8.

Bank of England. 2015. *The Impact of Climate Change on the UK Insurance Sector: A Climate Change Adaptation Report by The Prudential Regulation Authority*. London.

———. 2019. *Financial Stability Report, December*. London.

Beirne, J., N. Renzhi, and U. Volz. 2020. Feeling the Heat: Climate Risks and the Cost of Sovereign Borrowing. *ADBI Working Paper*. No. 1160. Tokyo: Asian Development Bank Institute.

Berensmann, K., U. Volz, I. Alloisio, C. Bak, A. Bhattacharya, G. Leipold, H. Schindler, L. MacDonald, T. Huifang, and Q. Yang. 2017. Fostering Sustainable Global Growth through Green Finance–What Role for the G20? *G20 Insights*. https://www.g20-insights.org/wp-content/uploads/2017/04/Climate_Green-Finance_V2.pdf.

Bolton, P., M. Despres, L.A. Pereira Da Silva, F. Samama, and R. Svartzman. 2020. *The Green Swan. Central Banking and Financial Stability in the Age of Climate Change*. Basel and Paris: Bank for International Settlements and Banque de France.

Buhr, B., U. Volz, C. Donovan, G. Kling, Y. Lo, V. Murinde, and N. Pullin. 2018. *Climate Change and the Cost of Capital in Developing Countries*. London and Geneva: Imperial College London, SOAS University of London, and UN Environment.

Dikau, S. and U. Volz. 2019. Central Banking, Climate Change and Green Finance. In J. Sachs, W.T. Woo, N. Yoshino, and F. Taghizadeh-Hesary, eds. *Springer Handbook of Green Finance: Energy Security and Sustainable Development*, pp. 81–102. Heidelberg and New York: Springer.

European Union. 2019. Regulation (EU) 2019/2088 of the European Parliament and of the Council of 27 November 2019 on Sustainability-related Disclosures in the Financial Services Sector. https://eur-lex.europa.eu/legal-content/EN/TXT/HTML/?uri=CELEX:02019R2088-20200712&from=EN. p. 4.

International Capital Market Association. 2020. Sustainable Finance High-level Definitions. https://www.icmagroup.org/assets/documents/Regulatory/Green-Bonds/Sustainable-Finance-High-Level-Definitions-May-2020-110520v4.pdf. p. 5

International Monetary Fund. 2019. *Global Financial Stability Report: Lower for Longer*. Washington, DC. p. 81.

Kling, G., U. Volz, V. Murinde, and S. Ayas. 2021. The Impact of Climate Vulnerability on Firms' Cost of Capital and Access to Finance. *World Development* 137. pp. 105–31.

Ma, J., B. Caldecott, and U. Volz, eds. 2020. Case Studies of Environmental Risk Analysis Methodologies. *NGFS Occasional Paper*. Paris: Network of Central Banks and Supervisors for Greening the Financial System.

Network of Central Banks and Supervisors for Greening the Financial System. 2019a. *A Call for Action. Climate Change as a Source of Financial Risk*. Paris.

———. 2019b. *A Sustainable and Responsible Investment Guide for Central Banks' Portfolio Management*. Paris.

Northrop, E., M. Konar, N. Frost, and E. Hollaway. 2020. *A Sustainable and Equitable Blue Recovery to the COVID-19 Crisis*. Secretariat of the High Level Panel for a Sustainable Ocean Economy. Washington, DC: World Resources Institute.

Rajan, R. 2010. *Fault Lines: How Hidden Fractures Still Threaten the World Economy*. Princeton: Princeton University Press.

Task Force on Climate-Related Financial Disclosures. 2017. *Recommendations of the Task Force on Climate-Related Financial Disclosures*. Basel.

van Toor, J., D. Piljic, G. Schellekens, M. van Oorschot, and M. Kok. 2020. *Indebted to Nature. Exploring Biodiversity Risks for the Dutch Financial Sector*. Amsterdam: De Nederlandsche Bank and Netherlands Environmental Assessment Agency.

Vermeulen, R., E. Schets, M. Lohuis, B. Kölbl, D.-J. Jansen, and W. Heeringa. 2018. *An Energy Transition Risk Stress Test for the Financial System of the Netherlands*. Amsterdam: De Nederlandsche Bank.

Volz, U. 2015. *Towards a Sustainable Financial System in Indonesia*. Geneva and Washington, DC: UNEP Inquiry into the Design of a Sustainable Financial System and International Finance Corporation.

———. 2017. On the Role of Central Banks in Enhancing Green Finance. *UN Inquiry Working Paper 17/01*. Geneva: UN Environment Inquiry into the Design of a Sustainable Financial System.

———. 2019. Fostering Green Finance for Sustainable Development in Asia. In U. Volz, P. Morgan, and N. Yoshino, eds. *Routledge Handbook of Banking and Finance in Asia*, pp. 488–504. London and New York: Routledge.

Volz, U., J. Beirne, N. Ambrosio Preudhomme, A. Fenton, E. Mazzacurati, N. Renzhi, and J. Stampe. 2020. *Climate Change and Sovereign Risk*. London, Tokyo, Singapore, Berkeley: SOAS University of London, Asian Development Bank Institute, WWF Singapore, and Four Twenty Seven.

World Bank. 2020a. Mobilizing Private Finance for Nature. *World Bank Group Paper on Private Finance for Biodiversity and Ecosystem Services*. Washington, DC.

———. 2020b. *Developing a National Green Taxonomy: A World Bank Guide*. Washington, DC.

Market Summaries

People's Republic of China

Yield Movements

Between 28 February and 15 May, the local currency (LCY) government bond yield curve of the People's Republic of China (PRC) shifted downward for all tenors except the 8-year bond, which was unchanged (**Figure 1**). The largest decline was seen for the 3-month tenor, which fell 44 basis points (bps), followed by the 7-year tenor, which fell 18 bps. All other maturities fell between 12 bps and 16 bps. As a result, the 2-year versus 10-year yield spread moved upward only 1 bp during the review period.

While bond yields in the PRC fell, the economy continued to post strong gains as it recovered from the COVID-19 pandemic. The declines in the PRC's bond yields despite strong economic gains were largely due to expectations that the Government of the PRC would reduce the supply of government bonds outstanding given the domestic economic recovery, which has reduced the need for additional fiscal stimulus. The PRC is also focusing on mitigating credit risk in financial markets, and investors expect the government to rein in the issuance of local government bonds.

The PRC's GDP expanded rapidly in the first quarter (Q1) of 2021, growing 18.1% year-on-year (y-o-y) after gaining 6.5% y-o-y in the fourth quarter (Q4) of 2020. While all major sectors showed accelerated growth, the gains were particularly notable in the secondary and tertiary industries. The secondary industry's growth rate rose to 24.4% y-o-y in Q1 2021 from 2.6% y-o-y in the prior quarter, while the tertiary industry's growth increased to 15.6% y-o-y from 2.1% y-o-y in the same period. Primary industry grew 8.1% y-o-y in Q1 2021 versus 3.0% y-o-y in Q4 2020.

Industrial production also sustained its momentum but at a slower pace. In April, industrial production grew 9.8% y-o-y, which was lower than March's 14.1% y-o-y gain and the 35.1% y-o-y growth reported in January–February.

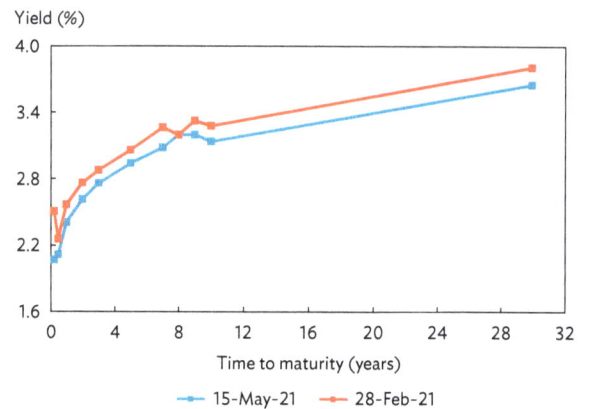

Figure 1: The People's Republic of China's Benchmark Yield Curve—Local Currency Government Bonds

Source: Based on data from Bloomberg LP.

Despite the PRC's sustained economic recovery, inflation in the PRC remained manageable. Consumer price inflation rose to 0.9% y-oy in April, which was higher than the rate of 0.4% y-o-y recorded in March.

Size and Composition

LCY bonds outstanding in the PRC grew 2.1% quarter-on-quarter (q-o-q) in Q1 2021 after rising 3.3% q-o-q in Q4 2020 to CNY103.5 trillion (USD15.8 trillion) (**Table 1**). Bond growth also slowed on a y-o-y basis to 17.3% from 20.5% in the same period. The slower growth rate was largely due to a decline in government bond issuance in Q1 2021.

Government bonds. Government bonds outstanding in the PRC grew 1.6% q-o-q in Q1 2021, slower than Q4 2020's growth of 3.8% q-o-q. The slowdown was due to a decline in the issuance of Treasury bonds of 37.8% q-o-q in Q1 2021 due to reduced fiscal stimulus needs amid the economy's sustained recovery. In addition, the government shifted its policies toward risk control, leading Treasury bonds and other government bonds outstanding to grow only 0.5% q-o-q in Q1 2021 versus 8.3% q-o-q in the previous quarter.

Table 1: Size and Composition of the Local Currency Bond Market in the People's Republic of China

| | Outstanding Amount (billion) | | | | | | Growth Rates (%) | | | |
| | Q1 2020 | | Q4 2020 | | Q1 2021 | | Q1 2020 | | Q1 2021 | |
	CNY	USD	CNY	USD	CNY	USD	q-o-q	y-o-y	q-o-q	y-o-y
Total	88,270	12,464	101,413	15,537	103,528	15,799	4.9	16.1	2.1	17.3
Government	55,852	7,886	65,130	9,978	66,198	10,102	3.5	13.8	1.6	18.5
Treasury Bonds and Other Government Bonds	16,850	2,379	20,933	3,207	21,032	3,210	0.9	13.2	0.5	24.8
Central Bank Bonds	19	3	15	2	15	2	(15.9)	1,133.3	0.0	(18.9)
Policy Bank Bonds	15,985	2,257	18,040	2,764	18,382	2,805	1.8	8.2	1.9	15.0
Local Government Bonds	22,999	3,247	26,142	4,005	26,769	4,085	6.6	18.5	2.4	16.4
Corporate	32,418	4,577	36,283	5,559	37,329	5,697	7.3	20.3	2.9	15.2

CNY = Chinese yuan, q-o-q = quarter-on-quarter, Q1 = first quarter, Q4 = fourth quarter, USD = United States dollar, y-o-y = year-on-year.
Notes:
1. Calculated using data from national sources.
2. Treasury bonds include savings bonds and local government bonds.
3. Bloomberg LP end-of-period local currency–USD rates are used.
4. Growth rates are calculated from local currency base and do not include currency effects.
Sources: CEIC and Bloomberg LP.

Local government bonds, which used to be the major driver of bond market growth in the PRC, grew only 2.4% q-o-q in Q1 2021 after rising 0.8% q-o-q in Q4 2020, largely due to base effects. In Q4 2020, local governments hardly issued bonds after having mostly completed their annual quotas for special bonds. However, in Q1 2020, despite the renewal of the quotas at the start of the year, local government bond issuance rose only 16.9% q-o-q and fell 44.5% y-o-y. The central government is slowing the issuance of local government bonds unlike in previous years when it had pushed for the utilization of the quotas early in the year. The government also reduced the local government bond quota to CNY3.65 trillion in 2021 from CNY3.75 trillion in 2020.

Policy bank bonds, however, posted a moderate growth of 1.9% q-o-q in Q1 2021 after gaining 0.9% in Q4 2020.

Corporate bonds. The PRC's corporate bond market's growth rate inched up to 2.9% q-o-q in Q1 2021 from 2.4% q-o-q in Q4 2020. Issuance of corporate bonds declined 3.0% q-o-q in Q1 2021 due to government directives on overleveraging as well as investor concerns regarding credit risks.

Commercial paper outstanding rose 8.9% q-o-q in Q1 2021 as companies used short-term borrowing in anticipation of lower interest rates (**Table 2**). State-owned enterprise bonds and medium-term notes outstanding were roughly unchanged owing to a reduction in issuance due to risk controls. Financial bonds gained 4.3% q-o-q as commercial banks beefed up their funding in anticipation of increased economic activity.

Credit risk concerns also led to a decline in nearly all major corporate bond issuance categories (**Figure 2**). The exceptions were commercial paper, with issuance

Table 2: Corporate Bonds Outstanding in Key Categories

| | Amount (CNY billion) | | | Growth Rate (%) | | | |
| | | | | Q1 2020 | | Q1 2021 | |
	Q1 2020	Q4 2020	Q1 2021	q-o-q	y-o-y	q-o-q	y-o-y
Financial Bonds	6,364	7,427	7,746	1.1	34.2	4.3	21.7
Enterprise Bonds	3,707	3,880	3,860	1.0	(4.3)	(0.5)	4.1
Listed Corporate Bonds	8,328	10,223	10,603	1.1	26.0	3.7	27.3
Commercial Paper	2,671	2,152	2,344	1.3	19.2	8.9	(12.2)
Medium-Term Notes	6,829	7,381	7,382	1.1	17.5	0.03	8.1
Asset-Backed Securities	2,388	2,883	2,942	1.0	38.2	2.0	23.2

( ) = negative, CNY = Chinese yuan, q-o-q = quarter-on-quarter, Q1 = first quarter, Q4 = fourth quarter, y-o-y = year-on-year.
Source: CEIC.

Figure 2: Corporate Bond Issuance in Key Sectors

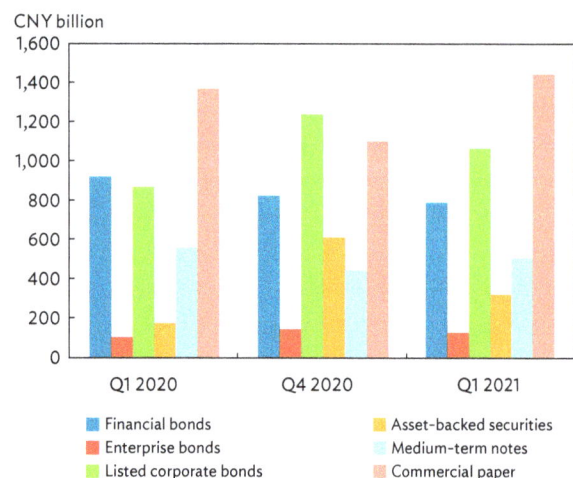

CNY = Chinese yuan, Q1 = first quarter, Q4 = fourth quarter.
Source: CEIC.

rising 31.3% q-o-q, and medium-term notes, which rose 13.8% q-o-q. Financial bond issuance was roughly unchanged, declining 4.3% q-o-q.

The top 30 issuers' share of total LCY corporate bonds outstanding remained roughly unchanged at 28.7% in Q1 2021 (**Table 3**). By the end of March, the bonds outstanding of the top 30 issuers reached CNY10.7 trillion. Of the top 30, the 10 largest issuers accounted for an aggregate CNY7.0 trillion. China Railway remained the largest issuer, accounting for 24.8% of the total bonds outstanding of the top 30 issuers. The top 30 issuers included 14 banks.

Table 4 lists the largest corporate bond issuances in Q1 2021. Of the five top issuers, four are financial institutions that sought to increase their liquidity and funding during the quarter. The largest issuer in the PRC has consistently been China Railway, which again issued bonds for infrastructure development in Q1 2021. The firm raised a total of CNY70 billion during the quarter through bonds with various maturities.

Investor Profile

Government bonds. Banks remained the majority investor group in the government bond market in Q1 2021 (**Figure 3**). However, with strong inflows from other types of investors, banks' holding share fell somewhat from a year earlier. At the end of March, banks

held 65.5% of outstanding Treasury bonds (down from 67.5% at the end of March 2020), 55.9% of outstanding policy bank bonds (down from 57.4%), and 87.6% of outstanding local government bonds.

In contrast, the Treasury bond holdings share of foreign investors increased during the review period, rising to 10.9% at the end of March from 9.0% a year earlier, while their share of policy bank bonds rose to 5.4% from 3.4%.

Liquidity

The volume of interest rate swaps rose 6.4% q-o-q in Q1 2021 (**Table 5**). Demand for interest rate swaps was lower given the decline in interest rates. The 7-day repo rate remained the most used interest rate swap with an 85.7% share of all transactions.

Policy, Institutional, and Regulatory Developments

The People's Bank of China and the State Administration of Foreign Exchange Implement Cross-Border Pilot Program for Multinational Corporations

In March, the People's Bank of China and the State Administration of Foreign Exchange launched a pilot program to allow multinational corporations with good credit standing to enjoy a more streamlined process for cross-border fund transfers. The pilot program is meant to integrate multinational corporations' transfers of both Chinese yuan and foreign currencies. The benefits of the pilot program for the companies include a unified policy on Chinese yuan and other foreign currencies, the relaxation of quotas on external debt and overseas loans, and the easier cross-border transfer of currencies and purchases of foreign currencies subject to quota.

The People's Bank of China Adjusts Foreign Exchange Reserve Requirement Ratio

Effective 15 June, the foreign exchange reserve requirement ratio of financial institutions was raised to 7.0% from 5.0%, as previously announced by the People's Bank of China in May.

Table 3: Top 30 Issuers of Local Currency Corporate Bonds in the People's Republic of China

	Issuers	Outstanding Amount		State-Owned	Listed Company	Type of Industry
		LCY Bonds (CNY billion)	LCY Bonds (USD billion)			
1.	China Railway	2,648.5	404.2	Yes	No	Transportation
2.	Agricultural Bank of China	680.3	103.8	Yes	Yes	Banking
3.	Bank of China	641.4	97.9	Yes	Yes	Banking
4.	Industrial and Commercial Bank of China	640.1	97.7	Yes	Yes	Banking
5.	Shanghai Pudong Development Bank	485.9	74.2	No	Yes	Banking
6.	Bank of Communications	462.1	70.5	No	Yes	Banking
7.	Central Huijin Investment	456.0	69.6	Yes	No	Asset Management
8.	China Construction Bank	388.1	59.2	Yes	Yes	Banking
9.	Industrial Bank	326.3	49.8	No	Yes	Banking
10.	State Grid Corporation of China	291.0	44.4	Yes	No	Public Utilities
11.	China National Petroleum	274.9	42.0	Yes	No	Energy
12.	China Securities Finance	264.0	40.3	Yes	No	Financial Services
13.	China Minsheng Banking	260.0	39.7	No	Yes	Banking
14.	China CITIC Bank	255.0	38.9	No	Yes	Banking
15.	State Power Investment	253.8	38.7	Yes	No	Energy
16.	China Everbright Bank	215.9	32.9	Yes	Yes	Banking
17.	China Merchants Bank	209.2	31.9	Yes	Yes	Banking
18.	Ping An Bank	198.7	30.3	No	Yes	Banking
19.	Huaxia Bank	198.0	30.2	Yes	No	Banking
20.	China Southern Power Grid	182.5	27.9	Yes	No	Energy
21.	CITIC Securities	168.8	25.8	Yes	Yes	Brokerage
22.	Tianjin Infrastructure Construction and Investment Group	160.6	24.5	Yes	No	Industrial
23.	Postal Savings Bank of China	160.0	24.4	Yes	Yes	Banking
24.	Shaanxi Coal and Chemical Industry Group	144.0	22.0	Yes	No	Energy
25.	China Merchants Securities	136.0	20.8	Yes	No	Brokerage
26.	Huatai Securities	131.8	20.1	Yes	Yes	Brokerage
27.	PetroChina	119.0	18.2	Yes	Yes	Energy
28.	Jinneng Holding Coal Group	118.2	18.0	Yes	Yes	Coal
29.	Datong Coal Mine Group	114.2	17.4	Yes	No	Coal
30.	China Three Gorges Corporation	114.0	17.4	Yes	No	Power
	Total Top 30 LCY Corporate Issuers	**10,698.1**	**1,632.6**			
	Total LCY Corporate Bonds	**37,329.5**	**5,696.7**			
	Top 30 as % of Total LCY Corporate Bonds	**28.7%**	**28.7%**			

CNY = Chinese yuan, LCY = local currency, USD = United States dollar.
Notes:
1. Data as of 31 March 2021.
2. State-owned firms are defined as those in which the government has more than a 50% ownership stake.
Source: *AsianBondsOnline* calculations based on Bloomberg LP data.

Table 4: Notable Local Currency Corporate Bond Issuances in the First Quarter of 2021

Corporate Issuers	Coupon Rate (%)	Issued Amount (CNY billion)
China Railway[a]		
5-year bond	3.40	20.0
5-year bond	3.53	20.0
10-year bond	3.65	15.0
10-year bond	3.56	7.0
20-year bond	3.82	8.0
Shanghai Pudong Development Bank		
3-year bond	2.48	60.0
China Merchants Securities[a]		
3-month bond	2.49	4.0
3-month bond	3.03	3.0
3-month bond	3.25	4.2
1-year bond	3.55	6.0
2-year bond	3.85	6.0
2-year bond	3.24	1.5
3-year bond	3.95	6.0
3-year bond	3.95	4.8
3-year bond	3.53	4.5
3-year bond	3.58	1.4
China Everbright Bank		
3-year bond	3.45	40.0
Bank of China		
3-year bond	3.36	10.0
10-year bond	4.15	15.0
15-year bond	4.38	10.0

CNY = Chinese yuan.
[a] Multiple issuance of the same tenor indicates issuance on different dates.
Source: Based on data from Bloomberg LP.

Figure 3: Local Currency Treasury Bonds and Policy Bank Bonds Investor Profile

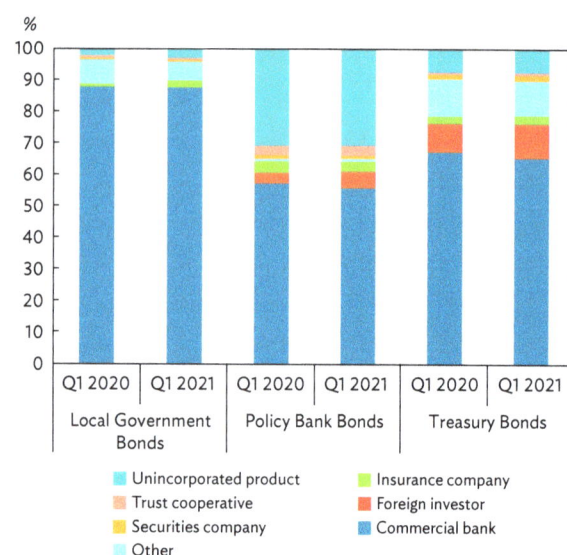

Q1 = first quarter.
Source: CEIC.

Table 5: Notional Values of the People's Republic of China's Interest Rate Swap Market in the First Quarter of 2021

Interest Rate Swap Benchmarks	Notional Amount (CNY billion)	Share of Total Notional Amount (%)	Growth Rate (%)
	Q1 2021		q-o-q
1-Day Repo Rate (Deposit Institutions)	0.2	0.004	0.0
7-Day Repo Rate	4,594.3	85.7	1.0
7-day Repo Rate (Deposit Institutions)	0.3	0.005	0.4
Overnight SHIBOR	21.3	0.4	2.1
3-Month SHIBOR	685.1	12.8	1.2
1-Year Lending Rate	23.0	0.4	2.1
5-Year Lending Rate	5.8	0.1	9.7
10-Year Treasury Yield	10.5	0.2	0.5
3-Year AAA Short-Term Notes/ Government Debt	0.1	0.001	0.3
China Development Bank 10-Year Bond Yield	11.0	0.2	0.5
10-Year Bond Yield/10-Year Government Bond Yield	10.5	0.2	0.5
Total	5,362.1	100.0	6.4

CNY = Chinese yuan, q-o-q = quarter-on-quarter, Q1 = first quarter, Repo = repurchase, SHIBOR = Shanghai Interbank Offered Rate.
Note: Growth rate computed based on notional amounts.
Sources: *AsianBondsOnline* and *ChinaMoney*.

Hong Kong, China

Yield Movements

Between 28 February and 15 May, the local currency (LCY) government bond yield curve in Hong Kong, China shifted downward for all tenors except the 3-year, which gained 1 basis point (bp), and the 1-month, which was unchanged (**Figure 1**). Yields fell 3 bps on average, with the 10-year tenor showing the steepest drop at 12 bps. The spread between the 2-year and 10-year bonds narrowed from 117 bps to 109 bps from 28 February to 15 May.

The drop in yields for Hong Kong, China's LCY government bonds with maturities of 1 year or less broadly tracked the movements of short-dated United States (US) Treasury yields. Low yields also reflected strong liquidity in the domestic financial system. Due to several interventions by the Hong Kong Monetary Authority (HKMA) to maintain the Hong Kong dollar's peg to the US dollar amid seasonal and equity-related demand in 2020, the Aggregate Balance remained elevated during the review period. The Aggregate Balance, an indicator of liquidity in the financial system, totaled HKD457.5 billion on 15 May.

For bonds with maturities longer than 1 year, yield movements diverged from those of US Treasuries, whose rise reflected expectations that inflation in the US would quicken along with the pace of the domestic economic recovery. In contrast, inflation expectations in Hong Kong, China were subdued as economic activities remained below pre-recession levels. Consumer price inflation inched up to 0.7% year-on-year (y-o-y) in April from 0.5% y-o-y in March, mainly driven by a rise in local transport costs and motor fuel prices. The government's latest inflation outlook predicted headline and underlying consumer price inflation for full-year 2021 of 1.6% and 1.0%, respectively.

Hong Kong, China's GDP expanded 7.9% y-o-y in the first quarter (Q1) of 2021, ending 6 straight quarters of contraction. Nonetheless, the recovery was uneven. The growth was mainly driven by merchandise exports, which rose 30.2% y-o-y as economic recovery gained momentum in the People's Republic of China and the US. Consumption and investment remained muted as social distancing measures continued to limit tourism and other economic activities. The establishment of a travel bubble

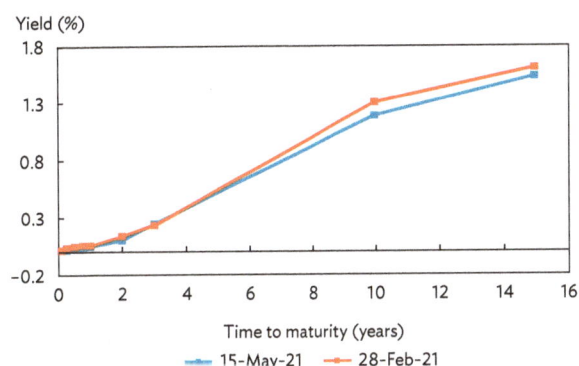

Figure 1: Hong Kong, China's Benchmark Yield Curve—Exchange Fund Bills and Notes

Source: Based on data from Bloomberg LP.

with Singapore was postponed again due to a resurgence of COVID-19 cases. Private consumption inched up 1.6% y-o-y, while investment expanded moderately at 4.5% y-o-y in Q1 2021. Hong Kong, China's unemployment rate reached a 16-year high of 6.8% in January–March before easing slightly to 6.4% in February–April.

Despite the initial economic recovery, uncertainties linger stemming from several domestic and global factors. Hong Kong, China's vaccination rate trails that of other Asian financial hubs despite having an ample supply of vaccines. Geopolitical tension between the People's Republic of China and the US continues to pose downside risks to the domestic growth outlook. Finally, Hong Kong, China's path to recovery remains highly reliant on the global trajectory of the pandemic, particularly the speed and efficacy of vaccine rollouts.

Size and Composition

Hong Kong, China's LCY bonds outstanding expanded 1.7% quarter-on-quarter (q-o-q) in Q1 2021 to reach HKD2,445.7 billion (USD314.6 billion) at the end of March (**Table 1**). The growth in the LCY bond market stemmed primarily from the corporate bond segment, which grew 3.1% q-o-q in Q1 2021. The government bond segment showed tepid growth of 0.2% q-o-q during the review period. Government bonds accounted for 48.6% of total LCY bonds outstanding at the end of March. On a y-o-y basis, the LCY bond market expanded 8.4% in Q1 2021, up from 6.1% in the fourth quarter of 2020.

Table 1: Size and Composition of the Local Currency Bond Market in Hong Kong, China

	Outstanding Amount (billion)						Growth Rate (%)			
	Q1 2020		Q4 2020		Q1 2021		Q1 2020		Q1 2021	
	HKD	USD	HKD	USD	HKD	USD	q-o-q	y-o-y	q-o-q	y-o-y
Total	2,255	291	2,405	310	2,446	315	(0.5)	0.3	1.7	8.4
Government	1,170	151	1,185	153	1,187	153	(1.1)	0.7	0.2	1.5
Exchange Fund Bills	1,060	137	1,043	135	1,043	134	0.4	2.4	0.02	(1.5)
Exchange Fund Notes	27	3	25	3	25	3	0.0	(14.7)	0.0	(6.0)
HKSAR Bonds	83	11	117	15	119	15	(16.9)	(12.2)	2.3	43.2
Corporate	1,086	140	1,220	157	1,258	162	0.2	(0.2)	3.1	15.9

( ) = negative, HKD = Hong Kong dollar, HKSAR = Hong Kong Special Administrative Region, q-o-q = quarter-on-quarter, Q1 = first quarter, Q4 = fourth quarter, USD = United States dollar, y-o-y = year-on-year.
Notes:
1. Calculated using data from national sources.
2. Bloomberg LP end-of-period local currency–USD rates are used.
3. Growth rates are calculated from local currency base and do not include currency effects.
Source: Hong Kong Monetary Authority.

Government bonds. LCY government bonds outstanding reached HKD1,187.5 billion at the end of March on growth of 0.2% q-o-q. The growth was driven solely by a 2.3% q-o-q expansion of Hong Kong Special Administrative Region (HKSAR) bonds. The stock of Exchange Fund Bills (EFBs) and Exchange Fund Notes (EFNs) held steady during the review period. On a y-o-y basis, the stock of LCY government bonds rose 1.5% in Q1 2021. Government issuance declined 5.6% q-o-q in Q1 2021 as issuance of EFBs and HKSAR bonds contracted during the quarter.

Exchange Fund Bills. Due to maturities and a decline in issuance, outstanding EFBs barely grew in Q1 2021, amounting to HKD1,043.3 billion at the end of March. On a y-o-y basis, EFBs outstanding contracted 1.5% in Q1 2021. Issuance of EFBs amounted to HKD814.1 billion in Q1 2021, contracting 1.7% q-o-q.

Exchange Fund Notes. Since 2015, the HKMA has limited its issuance of EFNs to 2-year tenors. In February, the HKMA issued a 2-year EFN worth HKD1.2 billion. Due to maturities, outstanding EFNs remained steady at HKD25.0 billion in Q1 2021.

HKSAR bonds. HKSAR bonds outstanding amounted to HKD119.2 billion at the end of March on growth of 2.3% q-o-q and 43.2% y-o-y. The government issued a 10-year HKSAR bond worth HKD1.7 billion in February and a 15-year HKSAR bond worth HKD1.0 billion in March under the Institutional Bond Issuance Programme.

Corporate bonds. Corporate bonds outstanding reached HKD1,258.2 billion at the end of March on growth of 3.1% q-o-q and 15.9% y-o-y. The growth was driven by strong issuance as corporates tapped the bond market to meet their funding needs amid the low-interest-rate environment.

Hong Kong, China's top 30 nonbank issuers had a combined HKD283.6 billion of bonds outstanding at the end of March, accounting for 22.5% of the total LCY corporate bond market (**Table 2**). The government-owned Hong Kong Mortgage Corporation remained the top issuer with HKD60.7 billion of bonds outstanding at the end of Q1 2021. Sun Hung Kai & Co. maintained its position as second-largest issuer with HKD18.8 billion of bonds outstanding. The third-largest issuer was utilities provider Hong Kong and China Gas Company, with HKD17.3 billion of outstanding debt. The top 30 issuers were predominantly finance and real estate companies. A majority of the top 30 issuers were listed on the Hong Kong Stock Exchange; only four were government-owned corporations.

Corporate bond issuance totaled HKD294.8 billion in Q1 2021 on growth of 9.6% q-o-q and 38.1% y-o-y. Among the top nonbank issuers in Q1 2021, the Hong Kong Mortgage Corporation was the largest issuer with an aggregate HKD26.2 billion from 47 issuances, the largest of which was a 2-year bond with a 0.5% coupon worth HKD7.0 billion (**Table 3**). The next top issuer was Cathay Pacific, which raised HKD6.7 billion from a 5-year

Table 2: Top 30 Nonbank Corporate Issuers of Local Currency Corporate Bonds in Hong Kong, China

	Issuers	Outstanding Amount LCY Bonds (HKD billion)	LCY Bonds (USD billion)	State-Owned	Listed Company	Type of Industry
1.	Hong Kong Mortgage Corporation	60.7	7.8	Yes	No	Finance
2.	Sun Hung Kai & Co.	18.8	2.4	No	Yes	Finance
3.	The Hong Kong and China Gas Company	17.3	2.2	No	Yes	Utilities
4.	New World Development	14.2	1.8	No	Yes	Diversified
5.	Link Holdings	12.9	1.7	No	Yes	Finance
6.	Hong Kong Land	12.5	1.6	No	No	Real Estate
7.	Hang Lung Properties	12.4	1.6	No	Yes	Real Estate
8.	Henderson Land Development	12.3	1.6	No	Yes	Real Estate
9.	MTR	12.2	1.6	Yes	Yes	Transportation
10.	Swire Pacific	11.6	1.5	No	Yes	Diversified
11.	Cathay Pacific	9.3	1.2	No	Yes	Transportation
12.	Airport Authority Hong Kong	8.9	1.1	Yes	No	Transportation
13.	Hongkong Electric	8.5	1.1	No	No	Utilities
14.	Wharf Real Estate Investment	8.2	1.1	No	Yes	Real Estate
15.	CLP Power Hong Kong Financing	7.7	1.0	No	No	Finance
16.	Guotai Junan International Holdings	7.6	1.0	No	Yes	Finance
17.	Swire Properties	7.6	1.0	No	Yes	Diversified
18.	Smart Edge	6.5	0.8	No	No	Finance
19.	AIA Group	6.3	0.8	No	Yes	Insurance
20.	Hysan Development Corporation	5.7	0.7	No	Yes	Real Estate
21.	Future Days	4.2	0.5	No	No	Transportation
22.	Lerthai Group	3.0	0.4	No	Yes	Real Estate
23.	China Dynamics Holdings	2.4	0.3	No	Yes	Automotive
24.	Champion REIT	2.3	0.3	No	Yes	Real Estate
25.	South Shore Holdings	2.2	0.3	No	Yes	Industrial
26.	IFC Development	2.0	0.3	No	No	Finance
27.	Nan Fung	1.8	0.2	No	No	Real Estate
28.	Kowloon-Canton Railway	1.7	0.2	Yes	No	Transportation
29.	Haitong International	1.4	0.2	No	Yes	Finance
30.	Emperor Capital	1.4	0.2	No	Yes	Finance
	Total Top 30 Nonbank LCY Corporate Issuers	283.6	36.5			
	Total LCY Corporate Bonds	1,258.2	161.8			
	Top 30 as % of Total LCY Corporate Bonds	22.5%	22.5%			

HKD = Hong Kong dollar, LCY = local currency, REIT = real estate investment trust, USD = United States dollar.
Notes:
1. Data as of 31 March 2021.
2. State-owned firms are defined as those in which the government has more than a 50% ownership stake.
Source: *AsianBondsOnline* calculations based on Bloomberg LP data.

Table 3: Notable Local Currency Corporate Bond Issuances in the First Quarter of 2021

Corporate Issuers	Coupon Rate (%)	Issued Amount (HKD billion)
Hong Kong Mortgage Corporation		
2-year bond	0.50	7.00
Cathay Pacific		
5-year bond	2.75	6.74
New World Development		
10-year bond	3.50	1.50
Guotai Junan International Holdings		
1-year bond	1.00	0.56
Hang Lung Properties		
7-year bond	2.35	0.56
Swire Pacific		
10-year bond	2.35	0.30

HKD = Hong Kong dollar.
Source: Bloomberg LP.

bond with a 2.75% coupon. Other notable issuers during the quarter include New World Development, Guotai Junan International Holdings, Hang Lung Properties, and Swire Pacific. The longest tenor issued during the quarter were 10-year bonds from two issuers. New World Development raised HKD1.5 with its 10-year bond carrying a 3.50% coupon, while Swire Pacific raised a relatively smaller amount of HKD0.3 billion with its 10-year bond carrying a 2.35% coupon. Finance company Guotai Junan was another large issuer during the quarter. It raised a total of HKD2.7 billion from 10 issuances, the largest of which was a 1-year bond worth HKD0.6 billion and with a 1.0% coupon. Hang Lung Properties, another finance company, also raised a total of HKD2.7 billion. Its largest issue was a 7-year bond with a 2.35% coupon worth HKD0.56 billion.

Policy, Institutional, and Regulatory Developments

Hong Kong Monetary Authority and Bank of Japan Launch a Cross-Border Delivery-Versus-Payment Link

On 1 April, the HKMA and the Bank of Japan (BOJ) launched a delivery-versus-payment link for cross-currency securities transactions between the Hong Kong Dollar Clearing House Automated Transfer System and BOJ Financial Network System for Japanese Government Bond (JGB) Services. The delivery-versus-payment link provides settlement infrastructure for Hong Kong dollar sale and repurchase transactions using

JGBs as collateral. It helps reduce settlement risk by guaranteeing simultaneous delivery of Hong Kong dollars in Hong Kong, China and JGBs in Japan. The link is operated by BOJ in Japan and the Hong Kong Interbank Clearing Limited in Hong Kong, China.

Hong Kong Monetary Authority Launches Green and Sustainable Finance Grant Scheme

On 10 May, the HKMA launched the Green and Sustainable Finance Grant Scheme, which will provide subsidies for eligible bond issuers and loan borrowers to cover expenses related to bond issuance and external review services. The scheme, which will last for 3 years, aims to strengthen Hong Kong, China's position as a regional green and sustainable finance hub, and help enrich its green and sustainable finance ecosystem. Eligible green and sustainable loans are those issued in Hong Kong, China with a size of at least HKD200 million, or the equivalent in a foreign currency, and have procured pre-issuance external review services by a recognized provider.

Hong Kong Monetary Authority Holds Countercyclical Capital Buffer at 1.0%

On 17 May, the HKMA announced that the countercyclical buffer (CCyB) would remain unchanged at 1.0%. The HKMA noted that while there have been initial signs of recovery, the economy continued to face uncertainties driven by the global pandemic. Thus, holding the CCyB steady and monitoring the economic situation for a few more quarters was deemed more appropriate. The CCyB is an integral part of the Basel III regulatory capital framework designed to increase the resilience of the banking sector during periods of excess credit growth.

Indonesia

Yield Movements

Between 28 February and 15 May, local currency (LCY) government bond yields in Indonesia fell for most tenors (**Figure 1**). Bond yields across the curve declined an average of 21 basis points (bps), while yields for the 16-year and 30-year maturities gained 13 bps and 8 bps, respectively. Yields fell the most for the 3-year tenor, shedding 47 bps during the review period. The spread between the 2-year and 10-year maturities slightly widened from 175 bps on 28 February to 177 bps on 15 May.

The decline in yields across the curve was influenced by the 25-bps rate cut by Bank Indonesia on 18 February, which brought the 7-day reverse repo rate to 3.50%, the deposit facility rate to 2.75%, and the lending facility rate to 4.25%. From January to May, Bank Indonesia was the sole central bank in emerging East Asia to ease policy rates. The policy rate has been held steady since then. In its latest meeting on 24–25 May, Bank Indonesia left rates unchanged at their current levels to support growth and manage the stability of the Indonesian rupiah amid the absence of inflationary pressure.

Contributing to the decline in yields during the review period, particularly at the shorter-end of the curve, was Indonesia's low and managed inflation rate. Consumer price inflation rose slightly to 1.7% year-on-year (y-o-y) in May from 1.4% y-o-y in April. The rise was due to the Muslim holidays of Ramadan and Idul Fitri, but the gain was considered manageable compared to the 2.2% y-o-y rise in May 2020. The government noted that an adequate supply of food products from the harvest season more than offset increased demand for goods during the Ramadan festivities. The uptick in May inflation was also capped as consumer sentiment was affected by some restrictions limiting travel and social gatherings during the Muslim holidays. The inflation rate also remained below Bank Indonesia's full-year 2021 inflation rate target of 2.0%–4.0%.

The drop in yields was also fueled by the recovery in foreign fund inflows from 1 April through 15 May. In February and March, the bond market was struck by a market sell-off over concerns that the United States (US) Federal Reserve would tighten monetary policy sooner than expected due to rising inflation. Market conditions normalized somewhat

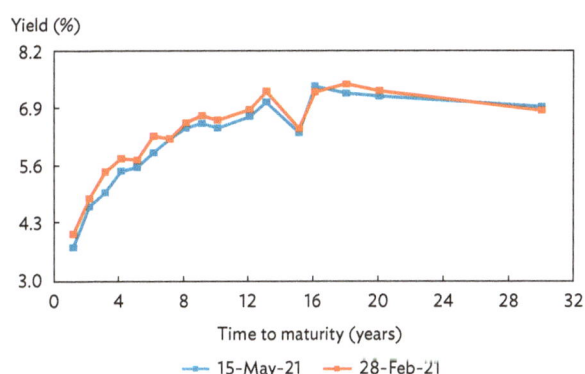

Figure 1: Indonesia's Benchmark Yield Curve— Local Currency Government Bonds

Yield (%)

Time to maturity (years)

— 15-May-21   — 28-Feb-21

Source: Based on data from Bloomberg LP.

beginning in April as the Federal Reserve noted that the inflation spike was likely to be transitory.

Economic performance remained muted, with GDP declining for 4 quarters in a row. The pace of contraction slowed, however, indicating the economic activity was slowly picking up. GDP declined 0.7% y-o-y in the first quarter (Q1) of 2021, following contractions of 2.2% y-o-y in the fourth quarter (Q4) of 2020, 3.5% y-o-y in the third quarter of 2020, and 5.3% y-o-y in the second quarter of 2020. The Finance Ministry expects full-year GDP growth for 2021 of between 4.5% and 5.3%.

During the review period, the Indonesian rupiah was broadly stable, rising a marginal 0.3% versus the US dollar. The slight uptick was fueled by the recovery in foreign fund inflows in April.

Size and Composition

The outstanding size of Indonesia's LCY bond market expanded to IDR4,799.4 trillion (USD330.4 billion) at the end of March (**Table 1**). Bond market growth moderated to 6.2% quarter-on-quarter (q-o-q) in Q1 2021 from 10.0% q-o-q in Q4 2020. Government bonds continued to drive much of the growth, stemming largely from increases in the stock of central government bonds, which comprised both Treasury bills and bonds. The stocks of central bank bonds and nontradable bonds declined at the end of March. Corporate bonds also contributed

Table 1: Size and Composition of the Local Currency Bond Market in Indonesia

| | Outstanding Amount (billion) | | | | | | Growth Rate (%) | | | |
| | Q1 2020 | | Q4 2020 | | Q1 2021 | | Q1 2020 | | Q1 2021 | |
	IDR	USD	IDR	USD	IDR	USD	q-o-q	y-o-y	q-o-q	y-o-y
Total	3,528,670	216	4,517,251	322	4,799,432	330	0.6	6.4	6.2	36.0
Government	3,085,761	189	4,091,542	291	4,366,500	301	0.7	6.7	6.7	41.5
Central Govt. Bonds	2,833,359	174	3,870,757	275	4,155,596	286	2.9	12.1	7.4	46.7
of which: *Sukuk*	478,152	29	686,561	49	765,420	53	(1.5)	11.9	11.5	60.1
Central Bank Bonds	48,423	3	55,421	4	54,927	4	(52.7)	(63.2)	(0.9)	13.4
of which: *Sukuk*	36,173	2	55,421	4	54,927	4	16.0	45.2	(0.9)	51.8
Nontradable Bonds	203,978	13	165,365	12	155,977	11	(2.2)	(12.5)	(5.7)	(23.5)
of which: *Sukuk*	38,805	2	38,778	3	35,684	2	(11.4)	0.1	(8.0)	(8.0)
Corporate	442,909	27	425,709	30	432,931	30	(0.5)	4.4	1.7	(2.3)
of which: *Sukuk*	30,200	2	30,341	2	31,172	2	0.3	22.7	2.7	3.2

( ) = negative, IDR = Indonesian rupiah, q-o-q = quarter-on-quarter, Q1 = first quarter, Q4 = fourth quarter, USD = United States dollar, y-o-y = year-on-year.
Notes:
1. Calculated using data from national sources.
2. Bloomberg LP end-of-period local currency–USD rates are used.
3. Growth rates are calculated from local currency base and do not include currency effects.
4. *Sukuk* refers to Islamic bonds.
Sources: Bank Indonesia; Directorate General of Budget Financing and Risk Management, Ministry of Finance; Indonesia Stock Exchange; and Bloomberg LP.

to the growth but to a lesser extent. Compared with the same period a year earlier, the LCY bond market of Indonesia expanded 36.0% y-o-y in Q1 2021, up from 28.7% y-o-y in Q4 2020.

Government bonds continued to account for a majority share of Indonesia's LCY bond market, representing 91.0% of the aggregate bond stock at the end of March. Indonesia has the largest share of government bonds to total bonds among its emerging East Asian peers. This reflects the importance of LCY bond financing to Indonesia's economy, as it supports capital-intensive infrastructure and economic development. The bond market has also helped to raise funds for COVID-19 stimulus measures and recovery efforts.

At the end of March, conventional bonds accounted for over 80.0% of Indonesia's LCY bond market. While smaller, the share of *sukuk* (Islamic bonds) inched up to 18.5% of total bonds outstanding at the end of March from 18.0% at the end of December 2020 and 16.5% at the end of March 2020.

Government bonds. The outstanding stock of government bonds reached IDR4,366.5 trillion at the end of March. Growth, however, eased to 6.7% q-o-q in Q1 2021 following an 11.6% uptick in Q4 2020. On a y-o-y basis, government bond market growth accelerated to 41.5% in Q1 2021 from 33.6% in Q4 2020.

Central government bonds. At the end of March, the outstanding amount of central government bonds stood at IDR4,155.6 trillion, representing 95.2% of the aggregate government bond total. While positive, overall growth slowed amid a sharp decline in the issuance of Treasury bills and bonds during the quarter. Growth decelerated to 7.4% q-o-q in Q1 2021 from 11.8% q-o-q in Q4 2020. The stock of central government bonds posted strong growth of 46.7% y-o-y in Q1 2021 versus a 40.6% y-o-y uptick in the previous quarter.

The stock of central government bonds continued to expand in Q1 2021 despite a slowdown in issuance caused by a rise in market volatility, especially in February and March. During the period, investors sought higher interest rates during the weekly government bond auctions. However, the government still had ample reserves from previous fundraising efforts.

In Q1 2021, new issuance of Treasury bills and Treasury bonds tallied IDR307.0 trillion, down from IDR444.4 trillion in the preceding quarter. More borrowing in the prior quarter led to a high base effect, resulting in a q-o-q decline in Q1 2021. However, issuance activities in Q1 2021 were still above pre-COVID-19 levels, indicating the government's need for ongoing stimulus measures. The government continued to issue in relatively large volumes during its weekly auctions in Q1 2021, making use of the "green shoe

Table 2: Top 30 Issuers of Local Currency Corporate Bonds in Indonesia

	Issuers	Outstanding Amount		State-Owned	Listed Company	Type of Industry
		LCY Bonds (IDR billion)	LCY Bonds (USD billion)			
1.	Perusahaan Listrik Negara	35,986	2.48	Yes	No	Energy
2.	Indonesia Eximbank	26,657	1.84	Yes	No	Banking
3.	Sarana Multi Infrastruktur	20,513	1.41	Yes	No	Finance
4.	Bank Rakyat Indonesia	17,320	1.19	Yes	Yes	Banking
5.	Sarana Multigriya Finansial	16,592	1.14	Yes	No	Finance
6.	Bank Tabungan Negara	15,975	1.10	Yes	Yes	Banking
7.	Bank Mandiri	14,000	0.96	Yes	Yes	Banking
8.	Bank Pan Indonesia	13,427	0.92	No	Yes	Banking
9.	Indosat	11,779	0.81	No	Yes	Telecommunications
10.	Permodalan Nasional Madani	10,089	0.69	Yes	No	Finance
11.	Indah Kiat Pulp & Paper	10,000	0.69	No	Yes	Pulp and Paper
12.	Waskita Karya	9,402	0.65	Yes	Yes	Building Construction
13.	Pegadaian	9,255	0.64	Yes	No	Finance
14.	Pupuk Indonesia	9,046	0.62	Yes	No	Chemical Manufacturing
15.	Astra Sedaya Finance	7,313	0.50	No	No	Finance
16.	Semen Indonesia	7,078	0.49	Yes	Yes	Cement Manufacturing
17.	Telekomunikasi Indonesia	7,000	0.48	Yes	Yes	Telecommunications
18.	Bank CIMB Niaga	6,806	0.47	No	Yes	Banking
19.	Tower Bersama Infrastructure	6,703	0.46	No	Yes	Telecommunications Infrastructure Provider
20.	Hutama Karya	6,500	0.45	Yes	No	Nonbuilding Construction
21.	Adira Dinamika Multi Finance	6,328	0.44	No	Yes	Finance
22.	Federal International Finance	5,981	0.41	No	No	Finance
23.	Bank Pembangunan Daerah Jawa Barat Dan Banten	5,248	0.36	Yes	Yes	Banking
24.	Angkasa Pura II	5,000	0.34	Yes	No	Airport Management Services
25.	Wijaya Karya	5,000	0.34	Yes	Yes	Building Construction
26.	Mandiri Tunas Finance	4,878	0.34	No	No	Finance
27.	Bank Maybank Indonesia	4,849	0.33	No	Yes	Banking
28.	Chandra Asri Petrochemical	4,489	0.31	No	Yes	Petrochemicals
29.	Adhi Karya	4,316	0.30	Yes	Yes	Building Construction
30.	Kereta Api Indonesia	4,000	0.28	Yes	No	Transportation
	Total Top 30 LCY Corporate Issuers	**311,528**	**21.45**			
	Total LCY Corporate Bonds	**432,931**	**29.81**			
	Top 30 as % of Total LCY Corporate Bonds	**72.0%**	**72.0%**			

IDR = Indonesian rupiah, LCY = local currency, USD = United States dollar.
Notes:
1. Data as of 31 March 2021.
2. State-owned firms are defined as those in which the government has more than a 50% ownership stake.
Source: *AsianBondsOnline* calculations based on Indonesia Stock Exchange data.

option" as a strategy when investor bids were above its acceptable rate. Aside from the weekly Treasury auctions, the government also raised IDR26.0 trillion from the sale of retail Treasury bonds in February.

Central bank bonds. The stock of central bank bills and bonds slipped to IDR54.9 trillion at the end of March, contracting 0.9% q-o-q but rising 13.4% y-o-y. Issuance of central bank instruments totaled IDR172.2 trillion in Q1 2021, representing a 12.4% q-o-q decline. The reduced issuance stemmed from efforts to boost liquidity amid the market sell-off in February and March.

Corporate bonds. The stock of corporate bonds inched up to IDR432.9 trillion on growth of 1.7% q-o-q in Q1 2021, rebounding from a decline of 3.4% q-o-q in Q4 2020. On a y-o-y basis, a contraction of 2.3% was recorded in Q1 2021 versus a decline of 4.4% in the prior quarter. The weak growth in Q1 2021 was influenced by uncertainties in the trajectory of economic recovery.

Table 2 presents the 30 largest issuers of corporate bonds in Indonesia at the end of March. Collectively, their bonds outstanding summed to IDR311.5 trillion, slightly higher than the IDR309.7 trillion recorded at the end of December. However, their share of total corporate bonds slightly dipped to 72.0% at the end of March from 72.7% in the preceding quarter.

Among the 30 firms on the list, 16 came from the banking and financial sectors. Some firms from capital-intensive sectors—such as energy, telecommunications, and building and construction—also made the list. Nearly two-thirds of the firms on the list were state-owned entities, with eight

of them ranking in the top 10. A majority (17) of the issuers are listed on the Indonesia Stock Exchange.

State-owned energy firm Perusahaan Listrik Negara continued to lead the list of top 30 issuers at the end of March, with outstanding bonds amounting to IDR36.0 trillion and representing 8.3% of the aggregate corporate bond total during the period. In the second spot was Indonesia Eximbank (IDR26.7 trillion), followed by Sarana Multi Infrastruktur (IDR20.5 trillion), Bank Rakyat Indonesia (IDR17.3 trillion), and Sarana Multigriya (IDR16.6 trillion). The composition of top five firms was the same as in the previous quarter.

New corporate bond issuance tallied IDR20.6 trillion in Q1 2021, representing a decline of 4.4% q-o-q. This, however, was an improvement over the 42.5% q-o-q contraction recorded in Q4 2020. Despite the low-interest-rate environment and the fiscal stimulus measures of the government, some corporates remained reluctant to issue and have reconsidered their borrowing plans in light of uncertainties brought about by the COVID-19 pandemic.

Only 16 firms tapped the bond market for funding during the quarter, adding 41 bond series to the corporate bond stock. Of the 41 new bond series issued, four were structured as *sukuk mudharabah* (Islamic bonds backed by a profit-sharing scheme from a business venture or partnership) and two were structured as *sukuk ijarah* (Islamic bonds backed by lease agreements).

The largest new corporate bonds issued in Q1 2021 are presented in **Table 3**. Leading the list was Indah

Table 3: Notable Local Currency Corporate Bond Issuances in the First Quarter of 2021

Corporate Issuers	Coupon Rate (%)	Issued Amount (IDR billion)	Corporate Issuers	Coupon Rate (%)	Issued Amount (IDR billion)
Indah Kiat Pulp & Paper			Tower Bersama Infrastructure		
370-day bond	7.25	1,081	370-day bond	5.50	1,898
3-year bond	9.50	1,895	3-year bond	6.75	1,017
5-year bond	10.50	277	Pupuk Indonesia		
Wijaya Karya			3-year bond	5.60	350
3-year bond	8.50	495	5-year bond	6.20	1,600
3-year *sukuk mudharabah*	8.50	134	7-year bond	7.20	800
5-year bond	9.10	746	Sarana Multigriya Finansial		
5-year *sukuk mudharabah*	9.10	212	370-day bond	4.75	1,500
7-year bond	9.75	1,260	370 day *sukuk mudharabah*	4.75	100
7-year *sukuk mudharabah*	9.75	154	3-year bond	5.75	401

IDR = Indonesian rupiah.
Note: *Sukuk mudharabah* are Islamic bonds backed by a profit-sharing scheme from a business venture or partnership.
Source: Indonesia Stock Exchange.

Kiat Pulp & Paper, which issued three tranches of bonds in March totaling IDR3,253.1 billion. Next was state-owned Wijaya Karya with issuance amounting to IDR3,000 billion in both conventional bonds and *sukuk*. In the third spot was Tower Bersama Infrastructure with total bond issuance of IDR2,915.0 billion via a dual-tranche issuance.

Investor Profile

The Indonesian bond market saw net foreign bond outflows of USD1.6 billion in Q1 2021, reversing the USD2.8 billion of inflows posted in Q4 2020. Outflows were recorded in February and March following a rise in US Treasury rates, leading foreign investors to reallocate funds to safe-haven assets. This resulted in the further decline of the foreign holdings share in the Indonesian LCY government bond market.

At the end of March, the holdings of offshore investors shrank to 22.9% from 25.2% at the end of December 2020 and from 32.7% at the end of March 2020 (**Figure 2**). The accelerated decline in the foreign holdings share was also fueled by the rapid growth of government bonds since last year to support stimulus and relief measures.

Most foreign investors that stayed in the bond market remained invested in longer-dated maturities, reflecting their confidence in Indonesia's growth potential and sound fundamentals (**Figure 3**). About 70% of foreign funds were placed in bonds with maturities of more than 5 years, while only 7.0% were invested in bonds with maturities of 2 years or less.

At the end of March, banking institutions were the largest investor group in Indonesia's government bond market. Ample market liquidity, brought about by the series of policy rate cuts since 2020, and the slowdown in economic activity led banks to allocate more funds to the

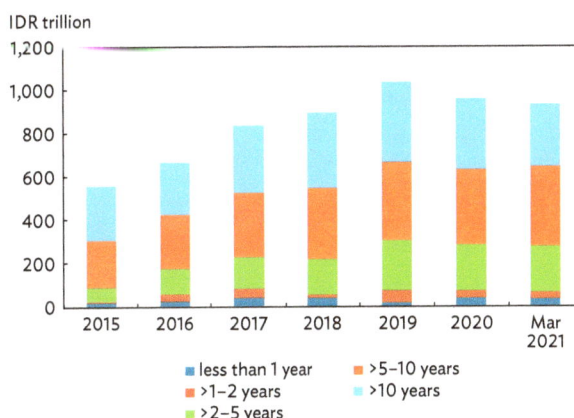

Figure 3: Foreign Holdings of Local Currency Central Government Bonds by Maturity

IDR = Indonesian rupiah.
Source: Directorate General of Budget Financing and Risk Management, Ministry of Finance.

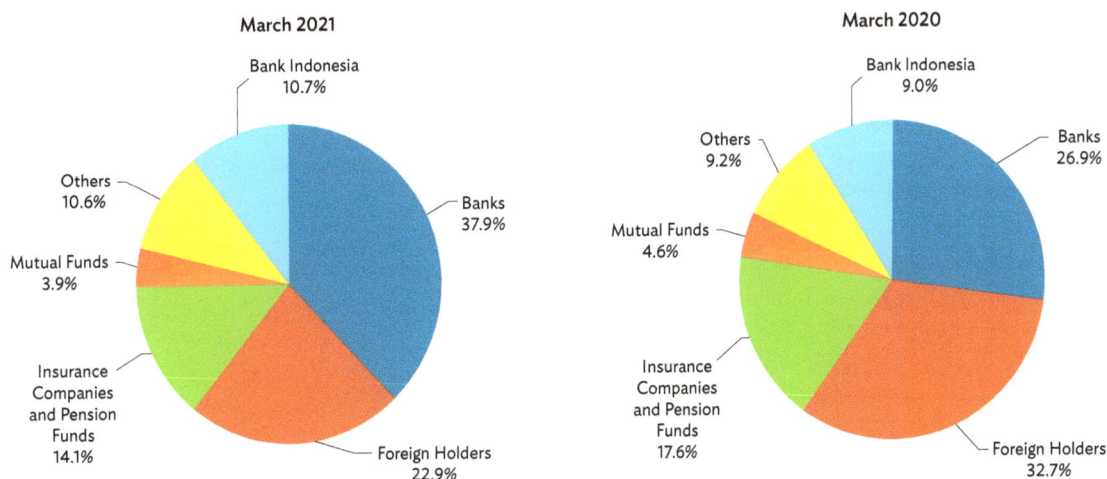

Figure 2: Local Currency Central Government Bonds Investor Profile

March 2021

- Bank Indonesia 10.7%
- Others 10.6%
- Mutual Funds 3.9%
- Insurance Companies and Pension Funds 14.1%
- Banks 37.9%
- Foreign Holders 22.9%

March 2020

- Bank Indonesia 9.0%
- Others 9.2%
- Mutual Funds 4.6%
- Insurance Companies and Pension Funds 17.6%
- Banks 26.9%
- Foreign Holders 32.7%

Source: Directorate General of Budget Financing and Risk Management, Ministry of Finance.

government bond market. Bank holdings of government bonds climbed to a 37.9% share at the end of March from 26.9% a year earlier.

Bank Indonesia also increased its holdings of government bonds as it continued to support the bond market. The central bank's holdings of government bonds rose from a share of 9.0% at the end of March 2020 to 10.7% at the end of March 2021. Other investors, comprising individuals and securities firms among others, also increased their holdings share of government bonds during the review period.

On the other hand, institutional investors, especially insurance companies and pension funds, reduced holdings of government bonds. Their holdings slipped from 17.6% in March 2020 to 14.1% in March 2021. Similarly, mutual funds saw a slight drop in their share of holdings of government bonds.

Ratings Update

On 22 March, Fitch Ratings affirmed Indonesia's BBB sovereign credit rating. The rating was given a stable outlook. In its decision, Fitch Ratings cited Indonesia's positive economic outlook over the medium-term and a low (but rising) government-debt-to-GDP ratio. The rating agency, however, raised concerns over Indonesia's external borrowing, weak government revenues, and lagging structural reforms (as evidenced by low governance indicators and GDP per capita relative to other BBB-rated sovereigns).

On 22 April, Rating and Investment Information, Inc. affirmed Indonesia's BBB+ investment grade rating. The rating was given a stable outlook. In its assessment, the rating agency took note of the following: (i) an expected rebound to pre-COVID-19 levels in 1–2 years for Indonesia's economy, (ii) a low government debt ratio, and (iii) an economic resilience to external shocks.

Also on 22 April, S&P Global Ratings (S&P) affirmed Indonesia's sovereign credit rating at BBB. In contrast to other rating agencies, it gave a negative outlook, citing sustained fiscal and external pressures in the next 12 to 24 months. According to S&P, the ratings affirmation reflected solid economic growth prospects and judicious policies. S&P expects Indonesia's economy to gain traction in 2022 amid its vaccination rollout and as economic activities gradually normalize.

Policy, Institutional, and Regulatory Developments

Indonesia Expands Economic Stimulus Program

In January, Indonesia raised its National Economic Recovery budget to IDR553 trillion from the previously approved IDR372 trillion budget. The program includes programs for health spending and social support.

Bank Indonesia Revises Regulation for Monitoring Foreign Exchange Transactions

In June, a new Bank Indonesia regulation came into effect to strengthen the monitoring of foreign exchange transactions. Under the new regulation, banks must include in the foreign exchange transaction monitoring system those client transactions with a transaction value of at least USD250,000 and derivative transactions with a minimum value of USD1 million.

Republic of Korea

Yield Movements

The Republic of Korea's local currency (LCY) government bond yields rose for most tenors between 28 February and 15 May (**Figure 1**). The yield for the 3-month tenor rose 6 basis points (bps), while yields for the 6-month and 1-year tenor fell 5 bps and 3 bps, respectively. Yields for the 2-year and 3-year tenors rose 8 bps on average, while the 5-year tenor rose the most with a 20-bps increase. Yields for long-term tenors of 10–50 years rose 18 bps on average. The spread between 2-year and 10-year yields widened to 123 bps from 112 bps during the review period.

Domestic bond yields in the Republic of Korea largely tracked the upward trend in United States (US) Treasury yields. Yields increased in the US on rising inflation expectations and speculation that the Federal Reserve would tighten monetary policy earlier than expected. On the domestic front, increased bond issuance arising from the passage of a supplementary budget contributed to the rise in yields in the Republic of Korea, albeit to a lesser extent. On 25 March, the National Assembly passed the KRW14.9 trillion supplementary budget, bringing the 2021 budget to KRW572.9 trillion. Despite the Bank of Korea's announcement of its bond purchase program to address oversupply concerns and stabilize the market, yield volatility remained high. As a result of volatility from the middle to the long-end of the yield curve, investors demand for short-term paper rose, which resulted in declining yields.

The Bank of Korea on both its 15 April and 27 May monetary policy meetings decided to leave the base rate unchanged at 0.50%. The Bank of Korea noted that global economic growth had strengthened on the back of economic stimulus and accelerated vaccine distribution. Domestic economic growth was also deemed to have strengthened, supported by the continued recovery in exports and investments. Economic growth for 2021 was projected to be around 4.0%, compared with the February forecast of 3.0%.

The Republic of Korea's economic growth accelerated to 1.7% quarter-on-quarter (q-o-q) in the first quarter (Q1) of 2021 from 1.1% q-o-q in the fourth quarter

Figure 1: The Republic of Korea's Benchmark Yield Curve—Local Currency Government Bonds

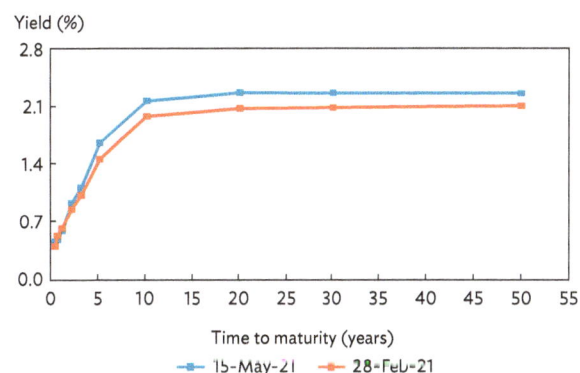

Source: Based on data from Bloomberg LP.

(Q4) of 2020. The higher growth was mainly driven by the recovery in consumption, which rose 1.3% q-o-q in Q1 2021 after a 1.1% q-o-q contraction in the previous quarter. Growth in gross fixed capital formation also accelerated to 2.5% q-o-q in Q1 2021 from 1.8% q-o-q in Q4 2020. Meanwhile, exports posted a lower growth rate of 2.0% q-o-q from 5.3% q-o-q. The Republic of Korea's economy grew 1.9% year-on-year (y-o-y) in Q1 2020, reversing a 1.1% y-o-y contraction in Q4 2020. Inflation continued to accelerate in the first 4 months of 2021, rising from 0.6% y-o-y in January to 2.3% y-o-y in April, driven by increased prices for agricultural and livestock products, and the impact of rising crude oil prices on industrial goods.

The LCY bond market has attracted a massive amount of net foreign inflows in Q1 2021, particularly in the months of February and March, with net inflows reaching KRW8,988 billion and KRW9,164 billion, respectively. This was a rebound from the KRW899 of net outflows registered in Q4 2020, and a large increase from the KRW1,158 billion of net inflows in January. The net inflows trend continued in April, albeit at a smaller amount of KRW3,346 billion.

The Korean won strengthened in March and April; its performance was closely tied to that of the domestic equities market. However, the gain was reversed as the won weakened in early May amid volatility in the equities market, which was partly due to the lifting of the ban on short selling. As a result, the Korean won registered a slight depreciation of 0.4% from 28 February to 15 May, settling at KRW1,128.54 per US dollar.

Size and Composition

The Republic of Korea's LCY bonds outstanding posted growth of 2.4% q-o-q in Q1 2021 to reach KRW2,695.5 trillion (USD2,381.6 billion) at the end of March (**Table 1**). This was higher than the 1.2% q-o-q growth registered in Q4 2020. Growth in Q1 2021 was largely driven by the surge in issuance of central government bonds during the quarter. Corporate bonds also posted an increase, albeit at a slower pace. On a y-o-y basis, the Republic of Korea's LCY bond market expanded 8.9%, which was slightly lower than the 9.4% growth registered in Q4 2020.

Government bonds. The Republic of Korea's LCY government bond market expanded 4.0% q-o-q and 13.1% y-o-y to reach a size of KRW1,122.4 trillion at the end of Q1 2021. This was largely driven by the 5.9% q-o-q growth in central government bonds, which amounted to KRW769.3 trillion at the end of March. Issuance of central government bonds surged 33.6% q-o-q in Q1 2021, reaching KRW50.4 billion as a result of the government's frontloading policy. In December, the Ministry of Economy and Finance announced plans to spend 72.4% of the original 2021 budget in the first half of the year as part of its support for economic recovery. Increased

bond issuance is expected to continue in the succeeding quarter as the government subsequently passed a KRW14.9 trillion supplementary budget in March, with partial spending also expected to be in the second quarter of the year.

Government agency bonds outstanding increased 1.5% q-o-q to KRW195.8 trillion at the end of March. Meanwhile, the stock of Monetary Stabilization Bonds issued by the Bank of Korea fell 1.3% q-o-q to KRW157.2 trillion as the volume of maturities exceeded new issuance. The Bank of Korea reduced its issuance of 1-year and 2-year bonds in March in an effort to ease the yield volatility caused by the sharp rise in US Treasury yields.

Corporate bonds. The Republic of Korea's LCY corporate bond market posted marginal growth of 1.2% q-o-q to reach a size of KRW1,573.2 trillion at the end of March, as issuance slowed during the quarter. **Table 2** lists the top 30 LCY corporate bond issuers in the Republic of Korea at the end of Q1 2021, with aggregate bonds outstanding amounting to KRW949.4 trillion and accounting for 60.3% of the total LCY corporate bond market. Financial institutions involved in securities trading continued to comprise the largest share of the top 30 list at 40.5%, followed by banks with a share of 24.2%. State-owned Korea Housing Finance Corporation remained the largest issuer with bonds outstanding valued at KRW146.8 trillion at the end of March.

Table 1: Size and Composition of the Local Currency Bond Market in the Republic of Korea

	Outstanding Amount (billion)						Growth Rate (%)			
	Q1 2020		Q4 2020		Q1 2021		Q1 2020		Q1 2021	
	KRW	USD	KRW	USD	KRW	USD	q-o-q	y-o-y	q-o-q	y-o-y
Total	2,476,170	2,032	2,633,219	2,424	2,695,546	2,382	2.8	8.7	2.4	8.9
Government	992,346	814	1,078,982	993	1,122,368	992	4.2	6.6	4.0	13.1
Central Government Bonds	645,928	530	726,766	669	769,339	680	5.6	10.6	5.9	19.1
Central Bank Bonds	165,710	136	159,260	147	157,230	139	1.0	(3.2)	(1.3)	(5.1)
Others	180,708	148	192,956	178	195,799	173	2.5	2.8	1.5	8.4
Corporate	1,483,824	1,218	1,554,237	1,430	1,573,178	1,390	1.9	10.2	1.2	6.0

( ) = negative, KRW = Korean won, q-o-q = quarter-on-quarter, Q1 = first quarter, Q4 = fourth quarter, USD = United States dollar, y-o-y = year-on-year.
Notes:
1. Calculated using data from national sources.
2. Bloomberg LP end-of-period local currency–USD rates are used.
3. Growth rates are calculated from local currency base and do not include currency effects.
4. "Others" comprise Korea Development Bank Bonds, National Housing Bonds, and Seoul Metro Bonds.
5. Corporate bonds include equity-linked securities and derivatives-linked securities.
Sources: The Bank of Korea and KG Zeroin Corporation.

Table 2: Top 30 Issuers of Local Currency Corporate Bonds in the Republic of Korea

| | Issuers | Outstanding Amount | | State-Owned | Listed on | | Type of Industry |
		LCY Bonds (KRW billion)	LCY Bonds (USD billion)		KOSPI	KOSDAQ	
1.	Korea Housing Finance Corporation	146,844	129.7	Yes	No	No	Housing Finance
2.	Industrial Bank of Korea	73,020	64.5	Yes	Yes	No	Banking
3.	Mirae Asset Securities Co.	65,508	57.9	No	Yes	No	Securities
4.	Korea Investment and Securities	59,758	52.8	No	No	No	Securities
5.	KB Securities	51,641	45.6	No	No	No	Securities
6.	Hana Financial Investment	51,288	45.3	No	No	No	Securities
7.	NH Investment & Securities	36,826	32.5	Yes	Yes	No	Securities
8.	Samsung Securities	31,243	27.6	No	Yes	No	Securities
9.	Korea Land & Housing Corporation	30,406	26.9	Yes	No	No	Real Estate
10.	Shinhan Investment Corporation	30,074	26.6	No	No	No	Securities
11.	Shinhan Bank	28,132	24.9	No	No	No	Banking
12.	Korea Electric Power Corporation	27,410	24.2	Yes	Yes	No	Electricity, Energy, and Power
13.	Korea Expressway	24,940	22.0	Yes	No	No	Transport Infrastructure
14.	The Export–Import Bank of Korea	22,635	20.0	Yes	No	No	Banking
15.	Meritz Securities Co.	21,107	18.6	No	Yes	No	Securities
16.	Kookmin Bank	20,864	18.4	No	No	No	Banking
17.	KEB Hana Bank	19,930	17.6	No	No	No	Banking
18.	Woori Bank	19,580	17.3	Yes	Yes	No	Banking
19.	Korea National Railway	19,210	17.0	Yes	No	No	Transport Infrastructure
20.	NongHyup Bank	19,190	17.0	Yes	No	No	Banking
21.	Shinyoung Securities	18,981	16.8	No	Yes	No	Securities
22.	Hanwha Investment and Securities	18,330	16.2	No	No	No	Securities
23.	Korea SMEs and Startups Agency	17,588	15.5	Yes	No	No	SME Development
24.	Shinhan Card	16,605	14.7	No	No	No	Credit Card
25.	KB Kookmin Bank Card	14,550	12.9	No	No	No	Consumer Finance
26.	Hyundai Capital Services	14,385	12.7	No	No	No	Consumer Finance
27.	NongHyup	13,200	11.7	Yes	No	No	Banking
28.	Standard Chartered Bank Korea	13,100	11.6	No	No	No	Banking
29.	Samsung Card Co.	11,558	10.2	No	Yes	No	Credit Card
30.	Korea Gas Corporation	11,469	10.1	Yes	Yes	No	Gas Utility
	Total Top 30 LCY Corporate Issuers	**949,370**	**838.8**				
	Total LCY Corporate Bonds	**1,573,178**	**1,389.9**				
	Top 30 as % of Total LCY Corporate Bonds	**60.3%**	**60.3%**				

KOSDAQ = Korean Securities Dealers Automated Quotations, KOSPI = Korea Composite Stock Price Index, KRW = Korean won, LCY = local currency, SMEs = small and medium-sized enterprises, USD = United States dollar.
Notes:
1. Data as of 31 March 2021.
2. State-owned firms are defined as those in which the government has more than a 50% ownership stake.
3. Corporate bonds include equity-linked securities and derivatives-linked securities.
Sources: *AsianBondsOnline* calculations based on Bloomberg LP and KG Zeroin Corporation data.

Table 3: Notable Local Currency Corporate Bond Issuances in the First Quarter of 2021

Corporate Issuers	Coupon Rate (%)	Issued Amount (KRW billion)	Corporate Issuers	Coupon Rate (%)	Issued Amount (KRW billion)
Shinhan Bank[a]			Kookmin Bank[a]		
1-year bond	0.92	200	1-year bond	0.85	300
1-year bond	0.90	300	2-year bond	0.99	300
1-year bond	0.88	330	2-year bond	0.99	350
1-year bond	0.91	510	10-year bond	2.26	500
1-year bond	0.89	550	NongHyup Bank[a]		
2-year bond	0.99	530	1-year bond	0.91	230
2-year bond	1.02	620	1-year bond	0.88	500
Woori Bank[a]			2-year bond	0.92	200
1-year bond	0.88	250	3-year bond	1.31	400
1-year bond	0.96	270	LG Chem		
1-year bond	0.99	400	3-year bond	1.14	350
2-year bond	1.05	300	5-year bond	1.51	270
2-year bond	1.02	300	7-year bond	1.76	200
2-year bond	0.99	450	10-year bond	2.14	260
			Naver Corporation		
			3-year bond	1.24	250
			5-year bond	1.60	450

KRW = Korean won.
[a] Multiple issuance of the same tenor indicates issuance on different dates.
Source: Based on data from Bloomberg LP.

Issuance of corporate bonds in the Republic of Korea declined 9.9% q-o-q in Q1 2021 to KRW129.1 trillion. However, the large quarterly decline came from a high base in Q4 2020 after a surge in issuance during the last quarter of the year. **Table 3** lists notable corporate bond issuances in Q1 2021, which remain dominated by financial institutions such as Shinhan Bank, Woori Bank, and Kookmin Bank.

Investor Profile

Insurance companies and pension funds remained the largest holders of LCY government bonds in the Republic of Korea at the end of December 2020 with a share of 35.7%, slightly lower than their share of 36.2% in December 2019 (**Figure 2**). Banks were the second-largest investor group, but their share declined to 16.7% from 17.6% during the review period. The same trend was registered for the holdings of the general government, with its share falling to 16.3% from 17.8%. Meanwhile, the share of other financial institutions rose to 15.7% from 12.6%. Foreign holdings of LCY government bonds also increased to 13.6% from 12.5% during the review period. Nonfinancial corporations and households continued to register negligible shares of 0.4% and 1.7%, respectively.

The Republic of Korea's LCY corporate bond market continued to be dominated by insurance companies and pension funds with a share of 37.3% at the end of December 2020; other financial institutions comprised a 36.7% share (**Figure 3**). Both investor groups registered an increase in their respective shares of 37.1% and 35.8% in December 2019. The share of the general government was only slightly changed at 13.7% in December 2020 versus 13.6% a year earlier, while banks' share increased to 9.6% from 8.5% during the review period. Foreign holdings of Korean LCY corporate bonds remained negligible at 0.1%.

Foreign investor demand for the Republic of Korea's LCY bonds rebounded in the first 4 months of 2021, posting net inflows of KRW1,158 billion in January following an aggregate of KRW899 of net outflows in Q4 2020 (**Figure 4**). Net foreign inflows peaked in February and March at KRW8,988 billion and KRW9,164 billion, respectively. The Republic of Korea continued to be a safe haven relative to other bond markets in the region for which data are available, some of which recorded net outflows in the previous months amid rising US Treasury yields. Moreover, foreign institutions reinvested in short-term LCY bonds following a high volume of maturities in Q4 2020. The net inflows trend continued in April, albeit at a smaller amount of KRW3,346 billion.

Figure 2: Local Currency Government Bonds Investor Profile

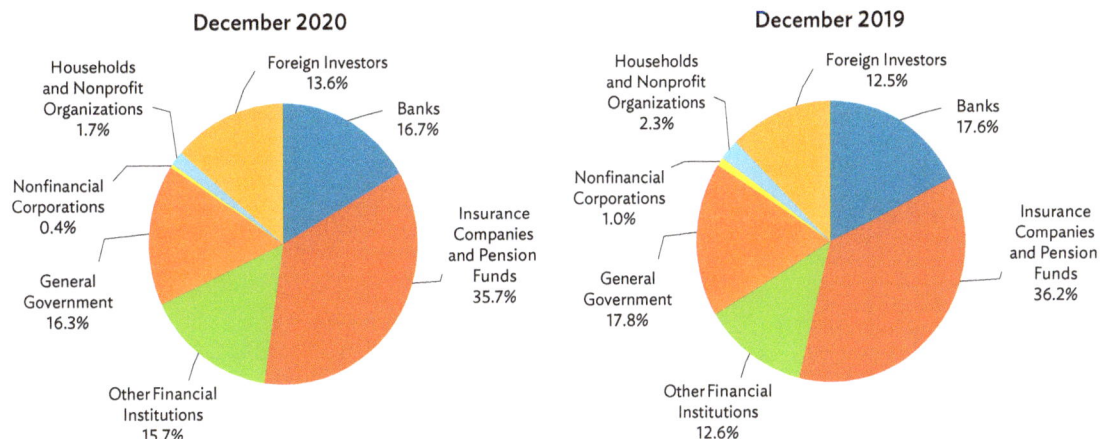

December 2020

Households and Nonprofit Organizations 1.7%
Foreign Investors 13.6%
Banks 16.7%
Nonfinancial Corporations 0.4%
General Government 16.3%
Insurance Companies and Pension Funds 35.7%
Other Financial Institutions 15.7%

December 2019

Households and Nonprofit Organizations 2.3%
Foreign Investors 12.5%
Banks 17.6%
Nonfinancial Corporations 1.0%
General Government 17.8%
Insurance Companies and Pension Funds 36.2%
Other Financial Institutions 12.6%

Source: AsianBondsOnline and The Bank of Korea.

Figure 3: Local Currency Corporate Bonds Investor Profile

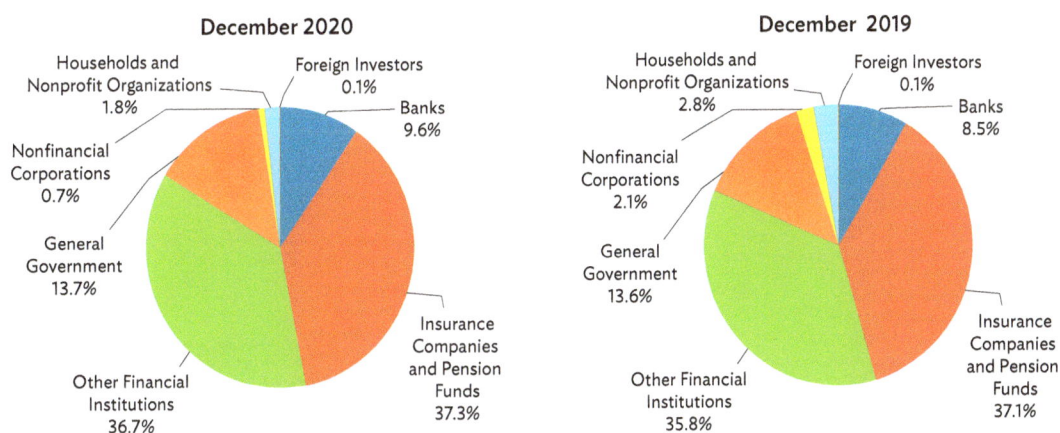

December 2020

Households and Nonprofit Organizations 1.8%
Foreign Investors 0.1%
Banks 9.6%
Nonfinancial Corporations 0.7%
General Government 13.7%
Insurance Companies and Pension Funds 37.3%
Other Financial Institutions 36.7%

December 2019

Households and Nonprofit Organizations 2.8%
Foreign Investors 0.1%
Banks 8.5%
Nonfinancial Corporations 2.1%
General Government 13.6%
Insurance Companies and Pension Funds 37.1%
Other Financial Institutions 35.8%

Source: AsianBondsOnline and The Bank of Korea.

Ratings Update

On 28 April, S&P Global Ratings affirmed the Republic of Korea's sovereign credit rating at AA with a stable outlook. The rating agency cited the Republic of Korea's strong economic growth prospects relative to other developed countries, sound fiscal position, and robust net external creditor position as some of the reasons behind the rating affirmation. The stable outlook is supported by expectations that the economy will post growth higher than most other high-income economies in the coming years and the government's budget will return to a surplus in 2023. The rating agency also forecasts annual real GDP growth to be 3.6% and 3.1% in 2021 and 2022, respectively.

Figure 4: Net Foreign Investment in Local Currency Bonds in the Republic of Korea

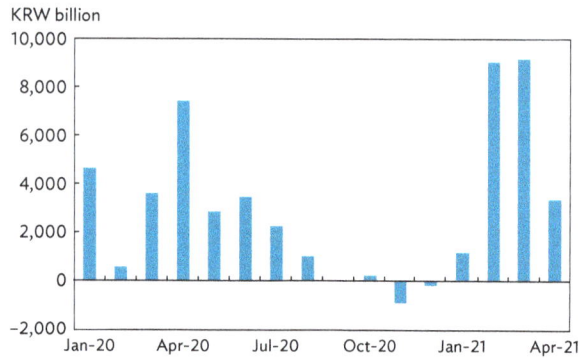

KRW = Korean won.
Source: Financial Supervisory Service.

Policy, Institutional, and Regulatory Developments

National Assembly Passes KRW14.9 Trillion Supplementary Budget

On 25 March, the National Assembly passed the KRW14.9 trillion supplementary budget, which was slightly less than the proposed KRW15.0 trillion. The additional budget will mostly be used to fund COVID-19 relief programs, support for small businesses hit by the pandemic, and job retention and creation programs. The supplementary budget brought the total 2021 budget to KRW572.9 trillion and increased the fiscal deficit to 4.5% of GDP.

Malaysia

Yield Movements

Between 28 February and 15 May, Malaysia's local currency (LCY) government bond yields increased across all tenors (**Figure 1**). Yields of tenors from 1 month to 1 year jumped an average of 4 basis points (bps). The belly of the curve (2–9 years) went up an average of 20 bps. At the longer-end of the yield curve, 20-year and 30-year bonds increased an average of 18 bps, while 10-year and 15-year bonds increased an average of only 5 bps. The yield spread between 2-year and 10-year government bonds contracted from 126 bps to 108 bps during the review period.

The increase in yields tracked the increase in long-term United States Treasury yields as consumer price inflation in the United States was expected to rise, due to base effects, supply shortages, and recent stimulus packages. Low demand for Malaysia's long-term securities can also be attributed to investor cautiousness due to the uncertainty of the path of the COVID-19 pandemic. Events that pose challenges to the economy are potential vaccine rollout complications and a resurgence of cases necessitating a Movement Control Order once again.

On 6 May, Bank Negara Malaysia's (BNM) monetary policy committee kept its policy rate unchanged at 1.75% as the global and domestic economic outlooks remained positive. Consumer price inflation in Malaysia is also expected to trend upward in 2021. The overnight policy rate has been at 1.75% since July 2020.

Malaysia's economy contracted 0.5% year-on-year (y-o-y) in the first quarter (Q1) of 2021, an improvement from a decline of 3.4% y-o-y in the fourth quarter (Q4) of 2020. On a quarter-on-quarter (q-o-q) seasonally adjusted basis, Malaysia's economy rebounded to expand 2.7% after contracting 1.5% in the previous quarter. The improved performance of the economy in Q1 2021 can be attributed to the gradual resumption of economic activities after the Movement Control Order restricted business operations last year. Various stimulus packages also contributed to Malaysia's economic recovery. BNM forecasts full-year economic growth of 6.0%–7.5% in 2021.

The prices of basic goods and services in Malaysia increased 4.7% y-o-y in April from a low base. Consumer

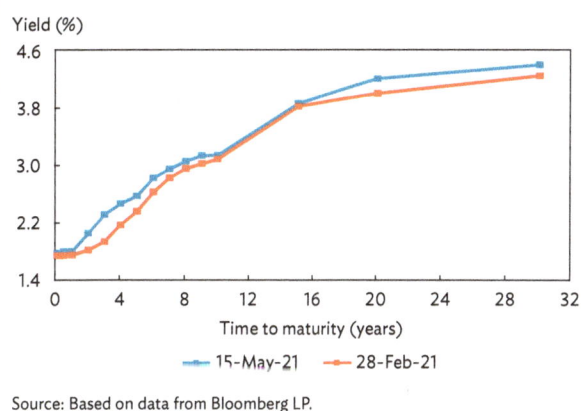

Figure 1: Malaysia's Benchmark Yield Curve—Local Currency Government Bonds

Source: Based on data from Bloomberg LP.

price inflation rebounded to 0.1% y-o-y in February after a decline of 0.2% y-o-y in January. The increase in inflation in the transport segment contributed to the rise in consumer price inflation as oil prices rose. Higher prices of housing, water, electricity, gas and other fuels, and food and nonalcoholic beverages also helped push consumer prices upward. BNM expects consumer price inflation for full-year 2021 to be between 2.5% and 4.0%, driven by higher global oil prices.

On 12 May, Malaysia reverted to a Movement Control Order due to a resurgence of COVID-19 cases. Economic activities will continue, however, while social activities were limited. BNM noted that the reimposition of containment measures will have less severe effects on the economy than in 2020 as businesses will be allowed to operate.

Size and Composition

Malaysia's LCY bond market expanded 2.8% q-o-q in Q1 2021 to reach a size of MYR1,648.9 billion (USD397.8 billion) at the end of March, up from MYR1,604.5 billion at the end of Q4 2020 (**Table 1**). The growth corresponds to a 7.9% y-o-y jump from MYR1,527.8 billion at the end of Q1 2020. The growth in the LCY bond market in Q1 2021 was supported by expansions in both LCY government and corporate bonds, which accounted for 54.0% and 46.0%, respectively, of total LCY bonds outstanding at the end of March. Total

Table 1: Size and Composition of the Local Currency Bond Market in Malaysia

| | Outstanding Amount (billion) | | | | | | Growth Rate (%) | | | |
| | Q1 2020 | | Q4 2020 | | Q1 2021 | | Q1 2020 | | Q1 2021 | |
	MYR	USD	MYR	USD	MYR	USD	q-o-q	y-o-y	q-o-q	y-o-y
Total	1,528	354	1,604	399	1,649	398	2.9	6.0	2.8	7.9
Government	804	186	853	212	890	215	3.9	4.9	4.3	10.7
Central Government Bonds	767	177	827	206	865	209	4.0	6.4	4.6	12.8
of which: *Sukuk*	362	84	384	95	403	97	5.9	10.6	5.1	11.5
Central Bank Bills	10	2	2	0	1	0	11.1	(42.2)	(50.0)	(90.0)
of which: *Sukuk*	2	0	0	0	0	0	50.0	(71.2)	–	(100.0)
Sukuk Perumahan Kerajaan	27	6	24	6	24	6	0.0	(3.9)	0.0	(10.1)
Corporate	724	168	752	187	759	183	1.7	7.3	1.0	4.8
of which: *Sukuk*	577	133	609	151	614	148	1.5	11.0	0.9	6.5

( ) = negative, – = not applicable, MYR = Malaysian ringgit, q-o-q = quarter-on-quarter, Q1 = first quarter, Q4 = fourth quarter, USD = United States dollar, y-o-y = year-on-year.
Notes:
1. Calculated using data from national sources.
2. Bloomberg LP end-of-period local currency–USD rates are used.
3. Growth rates are calculated from local currency base and do not include currency effects.
4. *Sukuk* refers to Islamic bonds.
5. Sukuk Perumahan Kerajaan are Islamic bonds issued by the Government of Malaysia to refinance funding for housing loans to government employees and to extend new housing loans.
Sources: Bank Negara Malaysia Fully Automated System for Issuing/Tendering and Bloomberg LP.

outstanding *sukuk* (Islamic bonds) at the end of the review period stood at MYR1,041.6 billion on growth of 2.5% q-o-q, spurred by increased stocks of government and corporate *sukuk*.

Issuance of LCY bonds in Q1 2021 jumped 11.7% q-o-q to MYR100.2 billion from MYR89.7 billion in Q4 2020, driven by increased government bond issuance.

Government bonds. The LCY government bond market grew 4.3% q-o-q to MYR889.6 billion in Q1 2021, up from MYR852.6 billion in the previous quarter. The growth was due to the 4.6% q-o-q increase in outstanding central government bonds, which comprised 97.2% of total outstanding LCY government bonds at the end of March. The growth in central government bonds can be attributed in part to the government's additional stimulus package that was unveiled in March to mitigate the impact of the COVID-19 pandemic on the economy. Outstanding central bank bills, which comprised a 0.1% share of total LCY government bonds outstanding, contracted 50.0% q-o-q as some bills matured in March. The outstanding stock of Sukuk Perumahan Kerajaan, which comprised 2.7% of total outstanding LCY government bonds at the end of March, remained unchanged from the previous quarter.

LCY government bonds issued in Q1 2021 surged 81.0% q-o-q to MYR57.0 billion from MYR31.5 billion in the previous quarter, as issuance of government bonds and Treasury bills increased. Issuances of Malaysian Government Securities and Government Investment Issues both increased from the previous quarter.

Corporate bonds. LCY corporate bonds outstanding expanded 1.0% q-o-q to MYR759.3 billion in Q1 2021 from MYR751.9 billion in Q4 2020. Outstanding corporate *sukuk* rose 0.9% q-o-q to MYR614.4 billion at the end of March from MYR608.6 billion in the prior quarter.

The top 30 corporate bond issuers in Malaysia accounted for an aggregate MYR457.3 billion of corporate bonds outstanding at the end of Q1 2021, or 60.2% of the total corporate bond market (**Table 2**). Government institution Danainfra Nasional continued to dominate all issuers with outstanding LCY corporate bonds amounting to MYR74.5 billion. By industry, finance comprised the largest share (51.7%) of the top 30 issuers with MYR236.4 billion in outstanding LCY corporate bonds at the end of March.

Issuance of LCY corporate bonds decreased 25.8% q-o-q to MYR43.2 billion in Q1 2021 from MYR58.2 billion in Q4 2020. The bulk of the issuance during the quarter (MYR28.0 billion) occurred in March as companies frontloaded their financing needs to lock in lower interest rates after there had been upward pressure on bond yields in previous months.

Table 2: Top 30 Issuers of Local Currency Corporate Bonds in Malaysia

	Issuers	Outstanding Amount		State-Owned	Listed Company	Type of Industry
		LCY Bonds (MYR billion)	LCY Bonds (USD billion)			
1.	Danainfra Nasional	74.5	18.0	Yes	No	Finance
2.	Prasarana	37.0	8.9	Yes	No	Transport, Storage, and Communications
3.	Lembaga Pembiayaan Perumahan Sektor Awam	34.2	8.2	Yes	No	Property and Real Estate
4.	Cagamas	29.0	7.0	Yes	No	Finance
5.	Project Lebuhraya Usahasama	28.9	7.0	No	No	Transport, Storage, and Communications
6.	Urusharta Jamaah	27.3	6.6	Yes	No	Finance
7.	Perbadanan Tabung Pendidikan Tinggi Nasional	24.8	6.0	Yes	No	Finance
8.	Pengurusan Air	18.3	4.4	Yes	No	Energy, Gas, and Water
9.	CIMB Bank	14.4	3.5	Yes	No	Finance
10.	Sarawak Energy	13.0	3.1	Yes	No	Energy, Gas, and Water
11.	Maybank Islamic	13.0	3.1	No	Yes	Banking
12.	CIMB Group Holdings	12.6	3.0	Yes	No	Finance
13.	Khazanah	11.9	2.9	Yes	No	Finance
14.	Malayan Banking	11.7	2.8	No	Yes	Banking
15.	Tenaga Nasional	10.3	2.5	No	Yes	Energy, Gas, and Water
16.	Danga Capital	10.0	2.4	Yes	No	Finance
17.	Jimah East Power	9.0	2.2	Yes	No	Energy, Gas, and Water
18.	Danum Capital	8.4	2.0	No	No	Finance
19.	Bank Pembangunan Malaysia	7.2	1.7	Yes	No	Banking
20.	Public Bank	6.9	1.7	No	No	Banking
21.	GENM Capital	6.5	1.6	No	No	Finance
22.	Sapura TMC	6.4	1.5	No	No	Finance
23.	YTL Power International	6.1	1.5	No	Yes	Energy, Gas, and Water
24.	Bakun Hydro Power Generation	5.9	1.4	No	No	Energy, Gas, and Water
25.	GOVCO Holdings	5.7	1.4	Yes	No	Finance
26.	Turus Pesawat	5.3	1.3	Yes	No	Transport, Storage, and Communications
27.	EDRA Energy	5.1	1.2	No	Yes	Energy, Gas, and Water
28.	1Malaysia Development	5.0	1.2	Yes	No	Finance
29.	Jambatan Kedua	4.6	1.1	Yes	No	Transport, Storage, and Communications
30.	Kuala Lumpur Kepong	4.6	1.1	No	Yes	Energy, Gas, and Water
	Total Top 30 LCY Corporate Issuers	457.3	110.3			
	Total LCY Corporate Bonds	759.3	183.2			
	Top 30 as % of Total LCY Corporate Bonds	60.2%	60.2%			

LCY = local currency, MYR = Malaysian ringgit, USD = United States dollar.
Notes:
1. Data as of 31 March 2021.
2. State-owned firms are defined as those in which the government has more than a 50% ownership stake.
Source: *AsianBondsOnline* calculations based on Bank Negara Malaysia Fully Automated System for Issuing/Tendering data.

Energy company Sapura Energy issued the equivalent of MYR6.5 billion in 7-year *sukuk murabahah*, an Islamic bond in which bondholders are entitled to a share of the revenues generated by the assets, under its Multi-Currency Sukuk Programme (**Table 3**). Proceeds from the issuance will be used to settle financial obligations of its subsidiary Sapura TMC. Government-owned public sector home financing board Lembaga Pembiayaan Perumahan Sektor Awam issued eight tranches of *sukuk murabahah* with tenors ranging from 5 years to 30 years and coupon rates ranging from 3.07% to 4.91%. Maybank Islamic also issued *sukuk murabahah* under its Subordinated Sukuk Programme. Proceeds of the 10-year bond will be used for business expansion, general corporate purposes, and other Shariah-compliant activities. During the review period, Cagamas, the national mortgage corporation of Malaysia, issued several conventional medium-term notes to fund the purchase of housing-related transactions from the financial system.

Table 3: Notable Local Currency Corporate Bond Issuances in the First Quarter of 2021

Corporate Issuers	Coupon Rate (%)	Issued Amount (MYR million)
Sapura Energy		
7-year *sukuk murabahah*	Floating	6,504.7
Lembaga Pembiayaan Perumahan Sektor Awam		
5-year *sukuk murabahah*	3.07	275.0
7-year *sukuk murabahah*	3.51	515.0
10-year *sukuk murabahah*	3.85	325.0
15-year *sukuk murabahah*	4.46	600.0
24-year *sukuk murabahah*	4.79	765.0
25-year *sukuk murabahah*	4.81	700.0
29-year *sukuk murabahah*	4.88	100.0
30-year *sukuk murabahah*	4.91	720.0
Maybank Islamic		
10-year *sukuk murabahah*	2.90	1,000.0
Cagamas		
1-year MTN	2.12	55.0
1-year MTN	2.10	400.0
1-year MTN	2.20	175.0
3-year MTN	2.38	55.0

MTN = medium-term note, MYR = Malaysian ringgit.
Notes:
1. *Sukuk murabahah* are Islamic bonds in which bondholders are entitled to a share of the revenues generated by the assets.
2. Multiple issuances of the same tenor indicates issuance on different dates.
Source: Bank Negara Malaysia Bond Info Hub.

Investor Profile

Foreign holdings of LCY government bonds in Q1 2021 jumped to MYR655.0 billion from MYR614.8 billion in Q4 2020, with monthly holdings increasing during the quarter, an extension of the trend of expanded monthly holdings in place since May 2020 (**Figure 2**). A total of MYR16.6 billion in net capital inflows were recorded in Q1 2021, with most of the inflows coming in February. As a share of LCY government bonds, foreign holdings increased to 26.0% at the end of Q1 2021 from 25.2% at the end of Q4 2020. The enthusiasm from foreign investors, especially in March, may be attributed to FTSE Russell removing Malaysia from its fixed-income watch list and retaining Malaysia in its FTSE World Government Bond Index.

At the end of Q4 2020, financial institutions and social security institutions led all investors in LCY government bond holdings with 33.4% and 28.0% of the total, respectively (**Figure 3**). Financial institutions held a larger share at the end of December compared to the same month in 2019, while the share of social security institutions dropped. The foreign holders' share remained the same at 24.9% during the review period. The holdings share of insurance companies increased to 4.9% from 4.7% between Q4 2019 and Q4 2020, while the share of total holdings of BNM surged to 2.3% from 0.6%.

Figure 2: Foreign Holdings and Capital Flows in the Malaysian Local Currency Government Bond Market

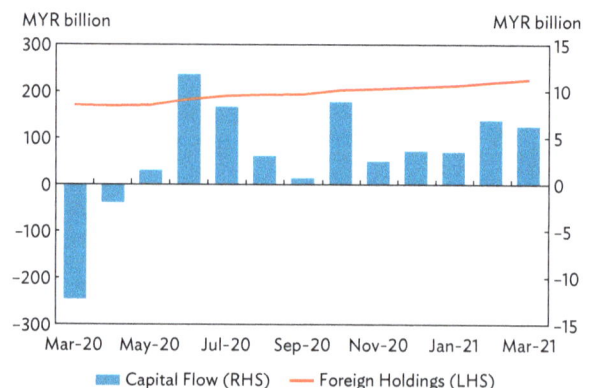

LHS = left-hand side, MYR = Malaysian ringgit, RHS = right-hand side.
Notes:
1. Figures exclude foreign holdings of Bank Negara Malaysia bills.
2. Month-on-month changes in foreign holdings of local currency government bonds were used as a proxy for bond flows.
Source: Bank Negara Malaysia Monthly Statistical Bulletin.

Figure 3: Local Currency Government Bonds Investor Profile

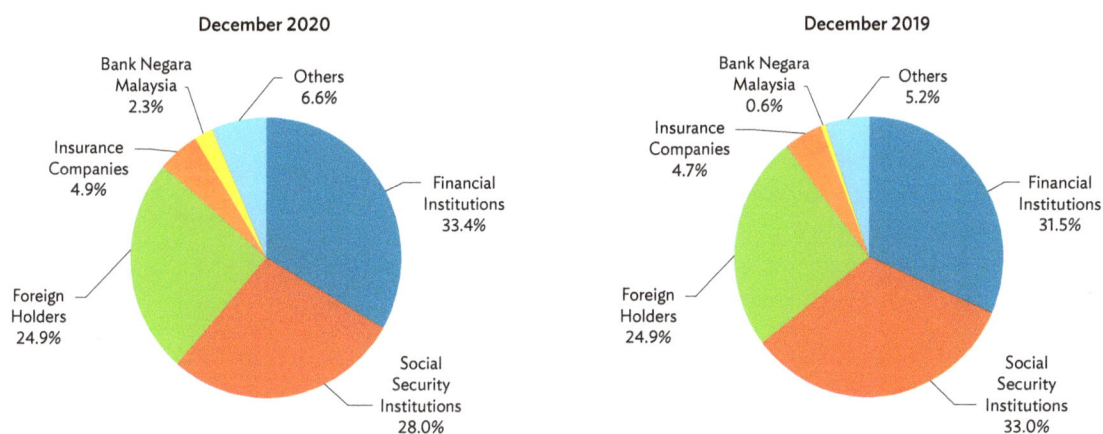

December 2020

- Bank Negara Malaysia 2.3%
- Others 6.6%
- Insurance Companies 4.9%
- Financial Institutions 33.4%
- Foreign Holders 24.9%
- Social Security Institutions 28.0%

December 2019

- Bank Negara Malaysia 0.6%
- Others 5.2%
- Insurance Companies 4.7%
- Financial Institutions 31.5%
- Foreign Holders 24.9%
- Social Security Institutions 33.0%

Note: "Others" include statutory bodies, nominees and trustee companies, and cooperatives and unclassified items.
Source: Bank Negara Malaysia.

Policy, Institutional, and Regulatory Developments

FTSE Russell Removes Malaysia from Its Watch List

On 29 March, FTSE Russell announced that it had removed Malaysia from its fixed-income watch list and retained Malaysia in its FTSE World Government Bond Index. The decision was made in consideration of regulatory enhancements in Malaysia's financial market. When Malaysia was included in FTSE Russell's watch list in 2019, BNM introduced regulations that made its government bond market more accessible to foreign investors by improving secondary market liquidity and facilitating foreign exchange transactions.

Bank Negara Malaysia Liberalizes Foreign Exchange Policy

On 31 March, BNM introduced regulations that provide greater flexibility to export-oriented industries. Effective 15 April, resident exporters can (i) manage the conversion of their export proceeds based on their foreign currency needs, (ii) settle their domestic trades in foreign currency with other residents, (iii) extend the repatriation of their export proceeds without seeking approval from BNM, and (iv) net-off their export proceeds against permitted foreign currency liabilities without seeking approval from BNM. Resident corporates can engage in commodity derivatives hedging with nonresident counterparties. These new regulations aim to attract foreign direct investments to support Malaysia's economic recovery.

Philippines

Yield Movements

The yields of local currency (LCY) government bonds in the Philippines increased for all tenors between 28 February and 15 May, shifting the yield curve upward (**Figure 1**). Yields of bonds with longer maturities (10–25 years) increased the most with average gains of 35 basis points (bps). Comparable yield increases were seen in 1-month to 1-year bonds, which averaged gains of 32 bps. Smaller increases in yields, averaging 13 bps, were observed for securities with 2-year to 7-year maturities. Across the curve, the yield for 25-year bonds increased the most at 48 bps, while 2-year bonds and 7-year bonds had the smallest gains at 12 bps each. The yield spread between the 2-year and 10-year tenors widened during the review period from 178 bps to 189 bps.

The upward movement across the yield curve can be traced to inflation risks as consumer prices are still elevated. The inflation rate in May was 4.5% year-on-year (y-o-y), unchanged from April. The resulting year-to-date average inflation of 4.4% was still above the government's 2021 annual target of 2.0%–4.0%. The implementation of nonmonetary measures by the government, particularly on meat products, aims to temper supply-side inflationary pressure in the coming months. The Bangko Sentral ng Pilipinas (BSP) lowered its 2021 inflation forecast to 3.9% from 4.2%, while it raised its 2022 forecast to 3.0% from 2.8%.

The weak economic performance on the back of subdued economic activity may have also contributed to yield increases. With constrained business operations due to ongoing COVID-19 restrictions, tax revenue has been lower, resulting in expectations that the government will borrow more in the bond market for its funding needs, thus putting upward pressure on yields.

The Philippine economy remained in recession for the 5th straight quarter with GDP contracting 4.2% y-o-y in the first quarter (Q1) of 2021. This was an improvement from the 8.3% y-o-y decline in the fourth quarter (Q4) of 2020, but it was worse compared with the 0.7% y-o-y decline in Q1 2020. All major economic sectors posted declines during the quarter. On the demand side, all components posted declines except for government

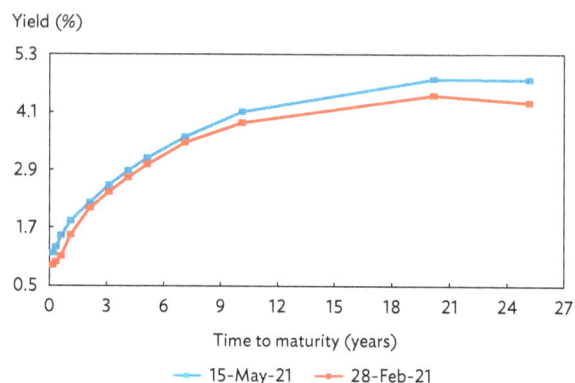

Figure 1: Philippines' Benchmark Yield Curve— Local Currency Government Bonds

Source: Based on data from Bloomberg LP.

expenditure, which grew 16.1% y-o-y. Household expenditure, which contributes about 70% to economic output, declined by 4.8% y-o-y. Recent containment measures in Metro Manila and neighboring provinces is expected to weigh down on GDP performance in the second quarter and act as a drag on recovery. The government reduced its GDP growth target to 6.0%–7.0% in 2021 from the earlier target of 6.5%–7.5%.

The uptrend in domestic yields may also have taken its cue from United States (US) Treasuries, whose yields trended upward on the prospects of a strong rebound in the US economy.

The BSP kept its policy rate steady at 2.00% in its monetary policy meeting on 12 May as it expects inflation to decelerate in the second half of 2021 and settle within the target range of 2.0%–4.0%. The central bank also expects the economy to continue to recover in the coming months, and therefore an accommodative stance is needed to sustain traction. The BSP last reduced its key policy rate in November 2020 by 25 bps, which brought the cumulative rate cut in 2020 to 200 bps.

The Philippine peso sustained its strength against the US dollar despite the economy remaining in recession. The domestic currency traded at 47.8 per US dollar on 15 May, appreciating by 1.6% from 28 February. The appreciation of the peso was driven by inflows from overseas remittances and revenues from business process outsourcing. It also reflected lower demand for imports as economic activity remained constrained.

Size and Composition

The Philippine LCY bond market expanded in Q1 2021 by 6.5% quarter-on-quarter (q-o-q) to reach PHP9,122.1 billion (USD187.9 billion) at the end of March (**Table 1**). Quarterly growth accelerated from 5.3% q-o-q in Q4 2020, driven entirely by the government segment as the corporate segment saw contraction during the quarter. On an annual basis, the LCY bond market expanded 28.4% y-o-y. Government bonds accounted for 82.7% of the total bond market at the end of March, while corporate bonds accounted for 17.3%.

Government bonds. Total LCY government bonds outstanding expanded 8.4% q-o-q to PHP7,542.6 billion in Q1 2021, which was faster than the growth of 7.0% q-o-q in the previous quarter. Treasury bills and Treasury bonds primarily drove the increase, as the government continued to heavily borrow from the local market for its COVID-19 relief efforts and to support economic recovery.

Outstanding Treasury bills and Treasury bonds grew 10.5% q-o-q and 7.2% q-o-q, respectively, on the back of higher debt sales during the quarter, which included

another tranche of Retail Treasury Bonds (RTBs). Securities from the BSP also contributed considerably to the bond market growth, with its outstanding debt increasing 35.2% q-o-q to reach PHP297.5 billion at the end of March. On the other hand, outstanding debt from government-related entities marginally decreased due to bond maturities and no issuances during the quarter.

Total securities issued by the government in the domestic market increased 55.8% q-o-q to PHP2,082.4 billion in Q1 2021. The substantial growth was supported by higher issuance volumes from both the Bureau of the Treasury (BTr) and the BSP.

Treasury bond sales in Q1 2021 reached PHP613.3 billion, more than triple the amount issued in Q4 2020, lifted by the issuance of RTBs in February amounting to PHP463.3 billion. The 3-year RTB issuance comprises the second-largest debt sale to date following the record PHP516.3 billion RTB issuance in August 2020.

Treasury bill issuance amounted to PHP372.6 billion in Q1 2021 on growth of 28.5% q-o-q, reversing the decline of 28.3% q-o-q in Q4 2020. The jump in issuance was due to higher offer volumes from the BTr during the quarter that were fully awarded. The opening of BTr's tap facility to accommodate the demand led to the higher-than-programmed debt sales.

Table 1: Size and Composition of the Local Currency Bond Market in the Philippines

| | Outstanding Amount (billion) | | | | | | Growth Rate (%) | | | |
| | Q1 2020 | | Q4 2020 | | Q1 2021 | | Q1 2020 | | Q1 2021 | |
	PHP	USD	PHP	USD	PHP	USD	q-o-q	y-o-y	q-o-q	y-o-y
Total	7,106	140	8,568	178	9,122	188	6.9	7.9	6.5	28.4
Government	5,526	109	6,956	145	7,543	155	7.5	6.2	8.4	36.5
Treasury Bills	557	11	949	20	1,049	22	14.5	(8.4)	10.5	88.5
Treasury Bonds	4,930	97	5,720	119	6,130	126	6.8	8.1	7.2	24.3
Central Bank Securities	0	0	220	5	297	6	–	–	35.2	–
Others	40	1	66	1	66	1	(0.02)	18.3	(0.01)	65.2
Corporate	1,579	31	1,612	34	1,579	33	5.0	14.0	(2.0)	0.01

( ) = negative, – = not applicable, PHP = Philippine peso, q-o-q = quarter-on-quarter, Q1 = first quarter, Q4 = fourth quarter, USD = United States dollar, y-o-y = year-on-year.
Notes:
1. Calculated using data from national sources.
2. Bloomberg end-of-period local currency–USD rates are used.
3. Growth rates are calculated from local currency base and do not include currency effects.
4. "Others" comprise bonds issued by government agencies, entities, and corporations for which repayment is guaranteed by the Government of the Philippines. This includes bonds issued by Power Sector Assets and Liabilities Management and the National Food Authority, among others.
5. Peso Global Bonds (PHP-denominated bonds payable in USD) are not included.
Sources: Bloomberg LP and Bureau of the Treasury.

The government borrowed more from the market as it ran a budget deficit due to lagging revenue collection and rising expenditure for its COVID-19 pandemic response. On the investor side, the preference for government bonds remained high on the back of the uncertainties brought about by the COVID-19 pandemic. Abundant market liquidity also boosted demand for such safe-haven assets.

The issuance of BSP bills climbed 30.5% q-o-q to PHP1,096.5 billion. The central bank increased its volume offer in Q1 2021 and auctions were all met with good demand except for an auction in February that was undersubscribed. The increase in issued securities during the quarter was indicative of high liquidity in the market.

While government-related entities had no LCY issuance in Q1 2021, the Development Bank of the Philippines returned to the international capital market in March with the sale of a 10-year USD300.0 million bond. The proceeds will be used to refinance its debt of the same tenor that was issued in 2011 and matured on 25 March 2021.

The government plans to borrow PHP3.0 trillion this year to fund its budget deficit. Of which, 85.0% will come from domestic sources and 15.0% from external sources.

Corporate bonds. Debt outstanding in the corporate sector declined by 2.0% q-o-q in Q1 2021 to PHP1,579.4 billion, following a 1.3% q-o-q drop in

Q4 2020. The decline can be attributed to the maturation of bonds offsetting the new issuances during the quarter.

The market shares of corporate bond issuers marginally changed in March 2021 from a year earlier. The banking sector continued to hold the largest share of LCY corporate bonds outstanding at the end of March. Its debt comprised 41.8% of total corporate bonds outstanding, slightly up from 41.2% at the end of March 2020 (**Figure 2**). The property sector had the second-largest share of the market at 23.8%. The banking, property, and "other" sectors saw an increase in their respective shares of corporate bonds compared to a year earlier, while the remaining sectors saw their respective shares decline during the review period.

The aggregate debt outstanding of the top 30 corporate issuers amounted to PHP1,414.1 billion at the end of March, comprising 89.5% of the total corporate bond market (**Table 2**). The banking sector held the largest share of outstanding bonds with PHP633.8 billion or 44.8% of the total LCY corporate bond market. This was followed by holdings firms with PHP296.9 billion (21.0%) and property firms with PHP235.4 billion (16.6%). Ayala Land, BDO Unibank, and Metropolitan Bank were the top three issuers at the end of March with debts of over PHP100 billion each.

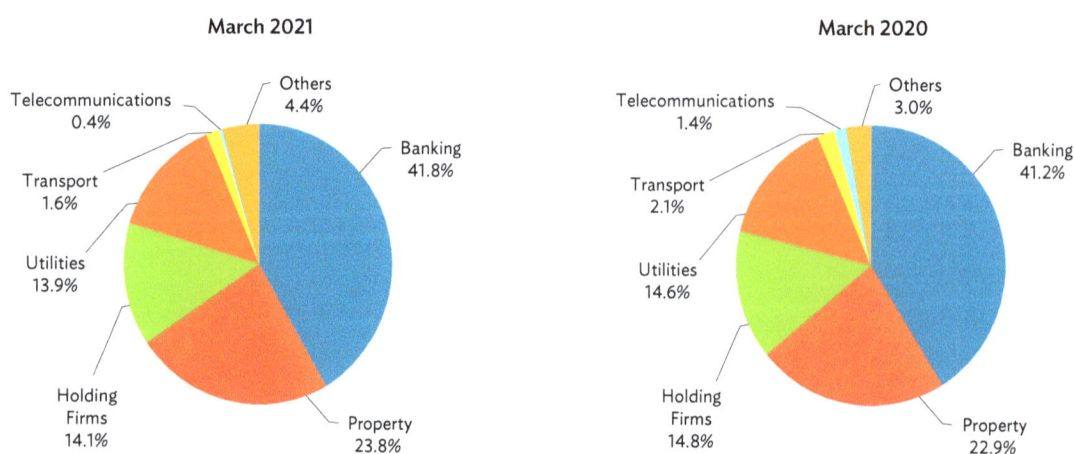

Figure 2: Local Currency Corporate Bonds Outstanding by Sector

Source: Based on data from Bloomberg LP.

Table 2: Top 30 Issuers of Local Currency Corporate Bonds in the Philippines

	Issuers	Outstanding Amount		State-Owned	Listed Company	Type of Industry
		LCY Bonds (PHP billion)	LCY Bonds (USD billion)			
1.	Ayala Land	113.9	2.3	No	Yes	Property
2.	BDO Unibank	109.9	2.3	No	Yes	Banking
3.	Metropolitan Bank	102.8	2.1	No	Yes	Banking
4.	SM Prime Holdings	95.7	2.0	No	Yes	Holding Firms
5.	Bank of the Philippine Islands	86.1	1.8	No	Yes	Banking
6.	SMC Global Power	80.0	1.6	No	No	Electricity, Energy, and Power
7.	Rizal Commercial Banking Corporation	73.1	1.5	No	Yes	Banking
8.	Security Bank	66.3	1.4	No	Yes	Banking
9.	China Bank	61.2	1.3	No	Yes	Banking
10.	San Miguel	60.0	1.2	No	Yes	Holding Firms
11.	SM Investments	58.3	1.2	No	Yes	Holding Firms
12.	Philippine National Bank	52.2	1.1	No	Yes	Banking
13.	Aboitiz Power	48.0	1.0	No	Yes	Electricity, Energy, and Power
14.	Vista Land	43.5	0.9	No	Yes	Property
15.	Petron	42.9	0.9	No	Yes	Electricity, Energy, and Power
16.	Ayala Corporation	40.0	0.8	No	Yes	Holding Firms
17.	Maynilad	28.1	0.6	No	No	Water
18.	Aboitiz Equity Ventures	27.9	0.6	No	Yes	Holding Firms
19.	Filinvest Land	25.8	0.5	No	Yes	Property
20.	Philippine Savings Bank	25.4	0.5	No	Yes	Banking
21.	Robinsons Land	25.2	0.5	No	Yes	Property
22.	Union Bank of the Philippines	24.6	0.5	No	Yes	Banking
23.	San Miguel Brewery	22.0	0.5	No	No	Brewery
24.	East West Banking	16.2	0.3	No	Yes	Banking
25.	Robinsons Bank	16.0	0.3	No	No	Banking
26.	GT Capital	15.1	0.3	No	Yes	Holding Firms
27.	Doubledragon	15.0	0.3	No	Yes	Property
28.	San Miguel Food and Beverage	15.0	0.3	No	Yes	Food and Beverage
29.	Megaworld	12.0	0.2	No	Yes	Property
30.	Puregold	12.0	0.2	No	Yes	Whole and Retail Trading
	Total Top 30 LCY Corporate Issuers	**1,414.1**	**29.1**			
	Total LCY Corporate Bonds	**1,579.4**	**32.5**			
	Top 30 as % of Total LCY Corporate Bonds	**89.5%**	**89.5%**			

LCY = local currency, PHP = Philippine peso, USD = United States dollar.
Notes:
1. Data as of 31 March 2021.
2. State-owned firms are defined as those in which the government has more than a 50% ownership stake.
Source: *AsianBondsOnline* calculations based on Bloomberg LP data.

Corporate bond issuance in Q1 2021 slightly declined by 0.2% q-o-q, which was an improvement from the 53.3% q-o-q drop in Q4 2020. Only five firms raised funds during the quarter, issuing a combined PHP58.9 billion worth of bonds. The weak issuance activity from the corporate sector was due to economic and business prospects remaining gloomy amid the ongoing COVID-19 pandemic and a resurgence of cases. These factors led firms to hold off expansion or issuance plans even as interest rates remained low. **Table 3** lists all issuances in Q1 2021, which were led by the banking sector.

Investor Profile

The investor landscape for LCY government bonds in March was somewhat changed from a year earlier (**Figure 3**). Banks and investment houses, and contractual savings and tax-exempt institutions remained the first- and second-largest holders of LCY government bonds, respectively, at the end of Q1 2021. The market share of banks and investment houses, however, declined to 37.5% from 50.4% during the review period, while that of contractual savings and tax-exempt institutions increased to 35.7% from 23.0%. Government-owned or -controlled corporations and local government units continued to comprise the smallest market share at 0.2%. Changes in ranking based on market shares were seen among the remaining investor groups. Brokers, custodians, and

Table 3: Notable Local Currency Corporate Bond Issuances in the First Quarter of 2021

Corporate Issuers	Coupon Rate (%)	Issued Amount (PHP billion)
China Bank		
3-year bond	2.50	20.00
Rizal Commercial Banking Corporation		
2-year bond	3.20	13.74
5-year bond	4.18	4.13
SM Prime Holdings		
2-year bond	2.46	7.50
5-year bond	3.85	2.50
Aboitiz Power		
5-year bond	3.82	8.00
Century Properties		
3-year bond	4.85	3.00

PHP = Philippine peso.
Source: Based on data from Bloomberg LP.

depositories (9.6%) and BTr-managed funds (8.6%) held the third- and fourth-largest market shares, respectively, overtaking "other" investors (8.5%), which dropped to fifth.

Ratings Update

On 10 January, Fitch Ratings affirmed the Philippines' sovereign credit at BBB with a stable outlook. The affirmation was based on the rating agency's assessment that the Philippines had modest government debt levels relative to peers, robust external buffers, and medium-

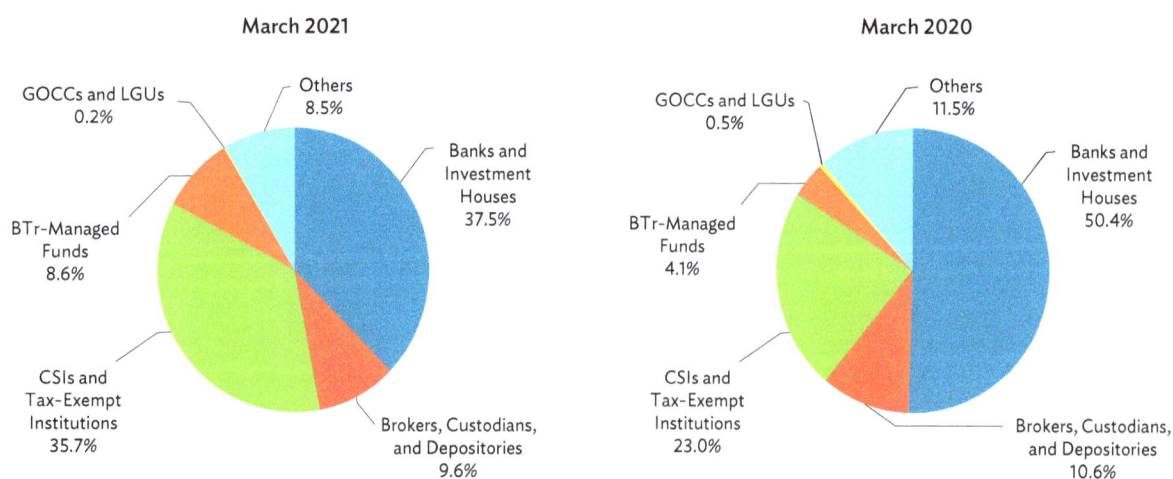

Figure 3: Local Currency Government Bonds Investor Profile

BTr = Bureau of the Treasury, CSIs = contractual savings institutions, GOCCs = government-owned or -controlled corporations, LGUs = local government units.
Source: Bureau of the Treasury.

term growth prospects that remained strong. It also cited risk factors that could negatively affect the credit rating: (i) higher fiscal deficits arising from a reversal of reforms or departure from a prudent macroeconomic policy framework, (ii) failure to return to historically high economic growth rates, and (iii) weakness in external indicators. On the other hand, factors to affect the rating positively include a broadening of the government's revenue base and a strengthening of governance standards.

On 22 April, Rating and Investment Information maintained the Philippines' BBB+ sovereign credit rating with a stable outlook as it expects the economy to recover from the severe contraction, supported primarily by aggressive public investment while accommodative fiscal and monetary policies remain to boost growth. Additional factors cited by the ratings agency that contributed to the affirmation include the government's commitment to maintaining fiscal discipline, the accomplishment of comprehensive tax reforms and various regulatory reforms, the economy's strong external position, and a stable banking sector.

On 27 May, S&P Global Ratings affirmed the Philippines' BBB+ sovereign credit rating with a stable outlook based on the view that the economy will rebound strongly, which will improve the government's fiscal position. Good prospects for the economic recovery are backed by the ongoing vaccine rollout, a strong external account, and fiscal reforms that have made debt manageable. The rating agency noted that it may upgrade the Philippines' credit rating if the economy expands faster than expected and if fiscal consolidation is achieved in the immediate term. Deterioration in these metrics, however, may lead to a downgrade.

Policy, Institutional, and Regulatory Developments

Bangko Sentral ng Pilipinas Increases Net Open Foreign Exchange Limit

In June, the Monetary Board of the BSP approved an increase in the net open foreign exchange position (NOP) limit for banks in response to rising demand for foreign exchange that is underpinned by the increased volume of trade transactions and investments. The NOP limit was raised to either 25% of qualifying capital or USD150 million, whichever is lower. The previous limit was 20% of unimpaired capital or USD50 million. According to the BSP, the increase in the NOP limit is part of a larger set of amendments to the framework for the management of banks' open foreign exchange positions, which aim to make the calculation and measurement of a bank's NOP more risk-based. The amendments will take effect on 1 August 2021.

Bureau of the Treasury Plans to Borrow PHP555 Billion in the Second Quarter of 2021

The BTr is set to borrow PHP555 billion from the domestic debt market in the second quarter of 2021. For April and May, the monthly programmed Treasury bill offerings were PHP100 billion, while Treasury bond offerings were PHP70 billion. In June, the BTr increased its issuance plan by holding more auctions and shifting to a higher offer volume of Treasury bonds. The BTr is seeking to raise PHP215 billion from the market in June, comprising PHP75 billion of Treasury bills and P140 billion of Treasury bonds, through its weekly auctions.

Singapore

Yield Movements

Between 28 February and 15 May, Singapore's local currency (LCY) government bond yields increased for most tenors (**Figure 1**). The shorter-end of the yield curve (3–6 months) declined an average of 2 basis points (bps). Tenors of 1–5 years rose an average of 4 bps, while the 30-year tenor jumped 8 bps. Yields for 10-20 years recorded an average increase of 20 bps. The yield spread between 2-year and 10-year government bonds expanded from 95 bps to 114 bps during the review period.

The yield curve for Singapore's LCY government bonds tracked the movements of the yield curve for United States (US) Treasuries during the review period, with the yields of short-term tenors declining and the yields of long-term tenors increasing. Longer-term US Treasury yields rose on expectations of higher consumer price inflation brought about by fiscal stimulus measures. The low demand for long-term securities can also be attributed to investor cautiousness brought about by uncertainties over the path of the COVID-19 pandemic. Events that may pose challenges are potential vaccine roll out complications and the emergence of new variants of the virus.

In April, Monetary Authority of Singapore (MAS) kept its monetary policy unchanged. The appreciation rate of the Singapore dollar nominal effective exchange rate remained at zero, and the center of the policy band was left unchanged. MAS is optimistic that the economy will exhibit above-average growth this year. However, core consumer price inflation is expected to remain low.

Singapore's economy expanded 1.3% year-on-year (y-o-y) in the first quarter (Q1) of 2021, improving from the contraction of 2.4% y-o-y in the fourth quarter (Q4) of 2020. A bright spot that contributed to Singapore's economic expansion was the growth of manufacturing output. This was partially offset, however, by the construction industry's contraction as social distancing measures inhibited activities in the sector.

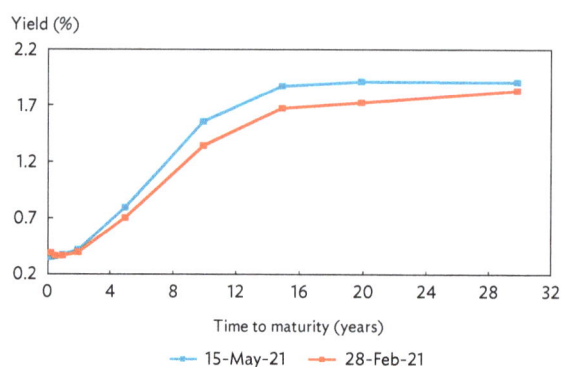

Figure 1: Singapore's Benchmark Yield Curve—Local Currency Government Bonds

Source: Based on data from Bloomberg LP.

The Ministry of Trade and Industry forecasts Singapore's economic growth will be between 4.0% and 6.0% for full-year 2021.

Consumer price inflation in Singapore increased steadily during Q1 2021 from 0.2% y-o-y in January to 0.7% y-o-y in February and 1.3% y-o-y in March. Core inflation, which excludes the cost of accommodations and private transport, was 0.5% y-o-y in March, compared with 0.2% y-o-y in February. Singapore's central bank expects price pressures to gradually pick up as domestic demand improves. MAS projects inflation for full-year 2021 to be between 0.5% and 1.5%.

Singapore was already in Phase 3 of its reopening strategy at the end of December 2020. However, on 8 May, Singapore reverted to Phase 2 (Heightened Alert) due to rising COVID-19 cases. Although not a Circuit Breaker, the government introduced tightened measures to arrest the spread of the disease. Despite the rise in cases, Singapore's vaccination program has been highly successful. Vaccination data from Singapore's Ministry of Health indicated that 2.5 million people have received at least one dose of the COVID-19 vaccine as of 7 June.[10] It is expecting to administer at least one dose of the COVID-19 vaccine to all of its adult population by August.

---

[10] According to Singapore's Department of Statistics, the city-state's population at the end of June 2020 was 5.7 million.

Table 1: Size and Composition of the Local Currency Bond Market in Singapore

| | Outstanding Amount (billion) | | | | | | Growth Rate (%) | | | |
| | Q1 2020 | | Q4 2020 | | Q1 2021 | | Q1 2020 | | Q1 2021 | |
	SGD	USD	SGD	USD	SGD	USD	q-o-q	y-o-y	q-o-q	y-o-y
Total	**461**	**324**	**503**	**380**	**522**	**388**	**2.2**	**11.8**	**3.8**	**13.4**
Government	293	206	330	249	349	260	2.5	14.6	6.0	19.3
SGS Bills and Bonds	188	132	196	148	203	151	2.7	44.8	3.5	8.3
MAS Bills	105	74	133	101	146	109	2.0	(16.5)	9.6	38.9
Corporate	168	118	173	131	173	129	1.7	7.1	(0.3)	3.1

( ) = negative, MAS = Monetary Authority of Singapore, q-o-q = quarter-on-quarter, Q1 = first quarter, Q4 = fourth quarter, SGD = Singapore dollar, SGS = Singapore Government Securities, USD = United States dollar, y-o-y = year-on-year.
Notes:
1. Government bonds are calculated using data from national sources. Corporate bonds are based on *AsianBondsOnline* estimates.
2. SGS bills and bonds do not include the special issue of SGS held by the Singapore Central Provident Fund.
3. Bloomberg LP end-of-period local currency–USD rates are used.
4. Growth rates are calculated from local currency base and do not include currency effects.
Sources: Bloomberg LP, Monetary Authority of Singapore, and Singapore Government Securities.

Size and Composition

Singapore's LCY bond market expanded 3.8% quarter-on-quarter (q-o-q) in Q1 2021 to reach a size of SGD522.2 billion (USD388.3 billion) at the end of March, up from SGD502.9 billion at the end of December 2020 (**Table 1**). On an annual basis, growth accelerated to 13.4% y-o-y in Q1 2021 from 11.6% y-o-y in Q4 2020. The expansion in the LCY bond market was supported by growth in government bonds, which accounted for 66.9% of total LCY bonds outstanding at the end of Q1 2021.

Issuance of LCY bonds in Q1 2021 increased 4.7% q-o-q to SGD226.7 billion from SGD216.6 billion in Q4 2020, driven by rising government bond issuance. This was partially offset by a drop in the issuance of corporate bonds.

Government bonds. The LCY government bond market grew 6.0% q-o-q to SGD349.2 billion in Q1 2021 from SGD329.5 billion in the previous quarter. Outstanding Singapore Government Securities bills and bonds, which comprised 58.2% of total outstanding LCY government bonds at the end of March, increased 3.5% q-o-q. MAS bills, comprising 41.8% of all outstanding LCY government bonds, jumped 9.6% q-o-q.

LCY government bond issuance in Q1 2021 rose 5.1% q-o-q. The growth may be attributed to the government's need to help finance the budget deficit generated by increased spending to address the COVID-19 pandemic. The growth was also due to an increase in MAS bills spurred by the issuance of 1-year floating-rate notes in March in addition to the existing 6-month tenor. MAS issues floating-rate notes to promote the use of the Singapore Overnight Rate Average (SORA) as a benchmark in Singapore's financial market. Issuance of Singapore Government Securities bills and bonds declined to SGD32.2 billion in Q1 2021 from SGD33.5 billion in the previous quarter.

Corporate bonds. LCY corporate bonds outstanding marginally declined 0.3% q-o-q in Q1 2021 to SGD173.0 billion at the end of March, down from SGD173.4 billion at the end of December, as several corporate bonds matured during the quarter and fewer bonds were issued compared to the previous quarter.

The top 30 LCY corporate bond issuers in Singapore accounted for combined bonds outstanding of SGD92.9 billion, or 53.7% of the total LCY corporate bond market, at the end of Q1 2021 (**Table 2**). The government-owned Housing & Development Board remained the largest issuer with outstanding LCY corporate bonds amounting to SGD25.8 billion. By industry type, real estate companies continued to comprise the largest share (47.6%) among the top 30 issuers of LCY corporate bonds with SGD44.2 billion of aggregate LCY corporate bonds outstanding at the end of Q1 2021.

In Q1 2021, issuance of LCY corporate bonds declined to SGD3.7 billion, a contraction of 17.9% q-o-q from SGD4.5 billion in the previous quarter. This marked the third consecutive quarter of decline in corporate bond issuance.

Table 2: Top 30 Issuers of Local Currency Corporate Bonds in Singapore

	Issuers	Outstanding Amount		State-Owned	Listed Company	Type of Industry
		LCY Bonds (SGD billion)	LCY Bonds (USD billion)			
1.	Housing & Development Board	25.8	19.2	Yes	No	Real Estate
2.	Land Transport Authority	9.5	7.0	Yes	No	Transportation
3.	Singapore Airlines	8.7	6.5	Yes	Yes	Transportation
4.	CapitaLand	4.3	3.2	Yes	Yes	Real Estate
5.	Frasers Property	4.0	3.0	No	Yes	Real Estate
6.	United Overseas Bank	3.4	2.5	No	Yes	Banking
7.	Temasek Financial	3.1	2.3	Yes	No	Finance
8.	DBS Bank	2.9	2.1	No	Yes	Banking
9.	Mapletree Treasury Services	2.9	2.1	No	No	Finance
10.	Sembcorp Industries	2.9	2.1	No	Yes	Diversified
11.	Keppel Corporation	2.2	1.6	No	Yes	Diversified
12.	City Developments Limited	2.1	1.5	No	Yes	Real Estate
13.	CapitaLand Mall Trust	2.0	1.5	No	No	Finance
14.	Oversea-Chinese Banking Corporation	1.7	1.3	No	Yes	Banking
15.	Olam International	1.7	1.3	No	Yes	Consumer Goods
16.	Ascendas Real Estate Investment Trust	1.6	1.2	No	Yes	Finance
17.	Shangri-La Hotel	1.5	1.1	No	Yes	Real Estate
18.	NTUC Income	1.4	1.0	No	No	Finance
19.	Suntec Real Estate Investment Trust	1.3	1.0	No	Yes	Real Estate
20.	Singapore Technologies Telemedia	1.2	0.9	Yes	No	Utilities
21.	GuocoLand Limited IHT	1.1	0.8	No	No	Real Estate
22.	Public Utilities Board	1.0	0.7	Yes	No	Utilities
23.	Ascott Residence	1.0	0.7	No	Yes	Real Estate
24.	Singapore Press Holdings	1.0	0.7	No	Yes	Communications
25.	StarHub	0.9	0.7	No	Yes	Diversified
26.	Hyflux	0.9	0.7	No	Yes	Utilities
27.	Mapletree Commercial Trust	0.9	0.7	No	Yes	Real Estate
28.	Keppel Real Estate Investment Trust	0.8	0.6	No	No	Real Estate
29.	Wing Tai Holdings	0.8	0.6	No	Yes	Real Estate
30.	RCS Trust	0.7	0.5	No	No	Real Estate
	Total Top 30 LCY Corporate Issuers	**92.9**	**69.1**			
	Total LCY Corporate Bonds	**173.0**	**128.7**			
	Top 30 as % of Total LCY Corporate Bonds	**53.7%**	**53.7%**			

LCY = local currency, SGD = Singapore dollar, USD = United States dollar.
Notes:
1. Data as of 31 March 2021.
2. State-owned firms are defined as those in which the government has more than a 50% ownership stake.
Source: *AsianBondsOnline* calculations based on Bloomberg LP data.

The Housing & Development Board issued the two largest LCY corporate bonds in Q1 2021, an SGD800.0 million 5-year bond and a SGD900.0 million 7-year bond (**Table 3**). Both issuances were part of the company's multicurrency medium-term note program. Proceeds from the issuances will be used to finance the company's development programs and working capital requirements. Olam International and United Overseas Bank issued callable perpetual bonds in Q1 2021. Proceeds from Olam International's issuance will be used for working capital and general corporate purposes. Promoting the adoption of SORA, United Overseas Bank pioneered the issuance of a capital security with a reset

Table 3: Notable Local Currency Corporate Bond Issuances in the First Quarter of 2021

Corporate Issuers	Coupon Rate (%)	Issued Amount (SGD million)
Housing & Development Board		
5-year bond	0.635	800.0
7-year bond	1.370	900.0
Olam International		
Perpetual bond	5.375	250.0
Surbana Jurong		
10-year bond	2.480	250.0
Boustead Industrial Fund		
10-year bond	7.000	236.0
StarHub		
10-year bond	2.480	200.0
United Overseas Bank		
Perpetual bond	2.250	150.0

SGD = Singapore dollar.
Source: Bloomberg LP.

coupon rate referencing the SORA overnight indexed swap rate. In March, Boustead Industrial Fund issued a bond with the highest coupon rate during the review period at 7.0%.

Policy, Institutional, and Regulatory Developments

Bilateral Investment Treaty with Indonesia Begins

On 9 March, the bilateral investment treaty signed in 2018 by Singapore and Indonesia entered into force. The treaty establishes rules and additional protections for investors and investments in each other's economies. The establishment of the bilateral investment treaty aims to foster a better economic relationship and increase investment flows between Singapore and Indonesia.

Singapore and Japan Renew Bilateral Swap Arrangement

On 21 May, MAS and the Bank of Japan renewed the existing bilateral swap arrangement between Singapore and Japan. Singapore can swap Singapore dollars up to the equivalent of USD3 billion in Japanese yen. Japan can swap Japanese yen up to the equivalent of USD1 billion in Singapore dollars. With the renewal of the arrangement, the two economies will be able to continue to exchange their local currency for US dollars from each other. This gives flexibility to both economies in meeting their liquidity needs, while also promoting financial stability and better economic ties between Singapore and Japan.

Thailand

Yield Movements

Between 28 February and 15 May, Thailand's local currency (LCY) government bond yields showed mixed movements (**Figure 1**). Yields fell an average of 9 basis points (bps) for bonds with maturities of up to 6 years, while yields rose an average of 3 bps for bonds with maturities of 7–9 years. Yields for bonds with maturities from 10 years to 15 years shed an average of 3 bps, while yields of longer-dated bonds with maturities of 16 to 30 years gained an average of 10 bps. Overall, yields fell an average of 3 bps across all tenors. The spread between the 2-year and the 10-year tenors widened to 129 bps on 15 May from 119 bps on 28 February.

The overall decline in yields, particularly at the shorter-end of the yield curve, reflected lingering uncertainties brought about by the prolonged impact of the COVID-19 pandemic on Thailand's trade- and tourism-reliant economy. While the government started its vaccine rollout during the quarter, Thailand's vaccination rate remained low relative to neighboring economies. Programs to revive tourism were thwarted by a third wave of COVID-19 toward the end of the review period.

Declining yields also reflected the lingering weakness in Thailand's economy. GDP contracted 2.6% year-on-year (y-o-y) in the first quarter (Q1) of 2021, an improvement over the 4.2% y-o-y decline recorded in the fourth quarter (Q4) of 2020. Consumption contracted 0.5% y-o-y in Q1 2021, reversing the 0.9% y-o-y growth in the previous quarter as a wave of COVID-19 infections at the end of 2020 prompted containment measures. Government expenditure and gross fixed capital formation rose 2.1% y-o-y and 7.3% y-o-y, respectively. Exports of goods and services contracted 10.5% y-o-y, while imports of goods and services inched up 1.7% y-o-y in Q1 2021. In May, the National Economic and Social Development Council lowered its GDP growth forecast for full-year 2021 to 1.5%–2.5% from 2.5%–3.5% announced in February.

The rise in yields at the longer-end of the curve reflected concerns about the debt burden implied by the government's continued efforts to boost the economy. At the end of March, Thailand's public debt stood at

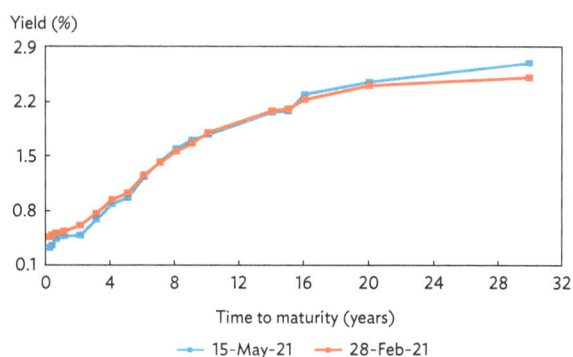

Figure 1: Thailand's Benchmark Yield Curve—Local Currency Government Bonds

Sources: Based on data from Bloomberg LP and Thai Bond Market Association.

THB8.5 trillion, or 53.3% of GDP. The Public Debt Management Office (PDMO) projected the ratio would reach 58.8% of GDP by the end of fiscal year 2021 on 30 September.

Consumer price inflation rose 3.4% y-o-y in April, ending 13 consecutive months of pandemic-driven deflation. The hike was brought about primarily by relatively high oil prices in April compared with a low base a year earlier. Elevated food prices due to supply constraints and the end of a government subsidy on utility bills also contributed to inflationary pressure. Inflation eased to 2.4% y-o-y in May.

The Bank of Thailand's (BOT) monetary policy remained accommodative. On 5 May, the Monetary Policy Committee of the BOT held the policy rate steady at 0.5% to preserve its limited policy space. Since the onset of the pandemic, the BOT has reduced its policy rate by a total of 75 bps.

Size and Composition

Thailand's LCY bonds outstanding totaled THB13,842.4 billion (USD443.1 billion) at the end of March (**Table 1**). The bond market continued to contract in Q1 2021, falling 0.6% quarter-on-quarter (q-o-q) following a 0.7% q-o-q decline in Q4 2020. Contraction in both government and corporate bond segments

Table 1: Size and Composition of the Local Currency Bond Market in Thailand

| | Outstanding Amount (billion) | | | | | | Growth Rate (%) | | | |
| | Q1 2020 | | Q4 2020 | | Q1 2021 | | Q1 2020 | | Q1 2021 | |
	THB	USD	THB	USD	THB	USD	q-o-q	y-o-y	q-o-q	y-o-y
Total	13,169	402	13,923	465	13,842	443	(0.5)	4.1	(0.6)	5.1
Government	9,353	286	10,232	342	10,152	325	(1.0)	2.7	(0.8)	8.5
Government Bonds and Treasury Bills	5,079	155	6,020	201	6,349	203	2.8	6.4	5.5	25.0
Central Bank Bonds	3,492	107	3,365	112	2,911	93	(6.1)	(2.4)	(13.5)	(16.6)
State-Owned Enterprise and Other Bonds	782	24	846	28	892	29	(1.4)	3.1	5.5	14.1
Corporate	3,816	117	3,692	123	3,690	118	0.8	7.9	(0.1)	(3.3)

( ) = negative, q-o-q = quarter-on-quarter, Q1 = first quarter, Q4 = fourth quarter, THB = Thai baht, USD = United States dollar, y-o-y = year-on-year.
Notes:
1. Calculated using data from national sources.
2. Bloomberg LP end-of-period local currency–USD rates are used.
3. Growth rates are calculated from local currency base and do not include currency effects.
Source: Bank of Thailand.

contributed to the decline, with the biggest drop coming from the outstanding stock of BOT bonds partly due to adjustments in the BOT's issuance program. On a y-o-y basis, the growth of outstanding LCY bonds slipped to 5.1% in Q1 2021 from 5.2% in Q4 2020. Government bonds continued to dominate the Thai bond market, accounting for 73.3% of total bonds outstanding at the end of March.

Government bonds. The size of the LCY government bond market stood at THB10,152.5 billion at the end of March, following a 0.8% q-o-q contraction in Q1 2021. The contraction was driven by a 13.5% q-o-q decline in outstanding BOT bonds, which outpaced the growth in outstanding government bonds and Treasury bills, and outstanding state-owned enterprise and other bonds. On an annual basis, the growth of total government bonds outstanding rose to 8.5% y-o-y in Q1 2021 from 8.3% y-o-y in the previous quarter.

Total government bond issuance amounted to THB1,686.6 billion in Q1 2021. Issuance continued to contract, dropping 13.6% q-o-q in Q1 2021 after decreasing 25.6% q-o-q in Q4 2020. Issuance of government bonds and Treasury bills expanded 42.0% q-o-q during the quarter. Issuance of BOT bonds and state-owned enterprise and other bonds saw sizable contractions of 29.0% q-o-q and 19.6% q-o-q, respectively. The BOT adjusted its bond issuance program for 2021 in response to high volatility in the market. To ensure that BOT bonds and government bonds are issued at different points along the yield curve, several tenors of BOT bonds were discontinued to make room for government bond issuance from the

PDMO. These included 6-month bills and 3-year bonds. The adjustments contributed to the drop in BOT bond issuance during the quarter.

Corporate bonds. Outstanding corporate bonds totaled THB3,689.9 billion at the end of March after contracting 0.1% q-o-q and 3.3% y-o-y. The contraction in corporate bonds outstanding was mainly due to a relatively high volume of maturities, as corporate issuance saw robust growth during the quarter.

The LCY bonds outstanding of the top 30 corporate issuers amounted to THB2,164.5 billion at the end of March, accounting for 58.7% of the Thai corporate bond market (**Table 2**). Among the top 30 issuers, food and beverage, commerce, banking, and communication firms held over half of the total outstanding bond stock. The majority of the top 30 issuers were listed on the Thai Stock Exchange, while only four were state-owned firms. Due to sizable issuances during the quarter, CP ALL became the top issuer at the end of March with outstanding debt of THB183.7 billion. Siam Cement, the top issuer in the previous quarter, became the second-largest issuer at the end of March with outstanding debt of THB175.0 billion. Charoen Pokphand Foods, Thai Beverage, Berli Jucker, True Corp, True Move H Universal Communication, and Bank of Ayudhya were the next largest issuers, all with bonds outstanding of more than THB100.0 billion at the end of March.

Issuance of corporate bonds rose 6.4% q-o-q in Q1 2021, reversing the drop of 14.6% q-o-q in the previous quarter as corporates raised debt to lock in low interest rates. Charoen Pokphand Foods issued the largest amount

Table 2: Top 30 Issuers of Local Currency Corporate Bonds in Thailand

	Issuers	Outstanding Amount		State-Owned	Listed Company	Type of Industry
		LCY Bonds (THB billion)	LCY Bonds (USD billion)			
1.	CP ALL	183.7	5.9	No	Yes	Commerce
2.	Siam Cement	175.0	5.6	Yes	Yes	Construction Materials
3.	Charoen Pokphand Foods	139.7	4.5	No	Yes	Food and Beverage
4.	Thai Beverage	125.1	4.0	No	No	Food and Beverage
5.	Berli Jucker	121.6	3.9	No	Yes	Commerce
6.	True Corp	119.4	3.8	No	No	Communication
7.	True Move H Universal Communication	113.0	3.6	No	No	Communication
8.	Bank of Ayudhya	108.8	3.5	No	Yes	Banking
9.	PTT	92.6	3.0	Yes	Yes	Energy and Utilities
10.	Toyota Leasing Thailand	70.9	2.3	No	No	Finance and Securities
11.	Indorama Ventures	69.5	2.2	No	Yes	Petrochemicals and Chemicals
12.	CPF Thailand	68.6	2.2	No	No	Food and Beverage
13.	Minor International	57.7	1.8	No	Yes	Hospitality and Leisure
14.	PTT Global Chemical	51.7	1.7	No	Yes	Petrochemicals and Chemicals
15.	Bangkok Commercial Asset Management	51.2	1.6	No	Yes	Finance and Securities
16.	Banpu	49.3	1.6	No	Yes	Energy and Utilities
17.	Krungthai Card	46.5	1.5	Yes	Yes	Banking
18.	TPI Polene	45.7	1.5	No	Yes	Property and Construction
19.	Frasers Property Thailand	45.6	1.5	No	Yes	Property and Construction
20.	Global Power Synergy	45.0	1.4	No	Yes	Energy and Utilities
21.	Krung Thai Bank	44.0	1.4	Yes	Yes	Banking
22.	Muangthai Capital	41.6	1.3	No	Yes	Finance and Securities
23.	Bangkok Expressway & Metro	38.7	1.2	No	Yes	Transportation and Logistics
24.	Sansiri	38.3	1.2	No	Yes	Property and Construction
25.	ICBC Thai Leasing	37.9	1.2	No	No	Finance and Securities
26.	Land & Houses	37.6	1.2	No	Yes	Property and Construction
27.	dtac TriNet	37.5	1.2	No	Yes	Communications
28.	CH Karnchang	36.9	1.2	No	Yes	Property and Construction
29.	Bangchak	36.0	1.2	No	Yes	Energy and Utilities
30.	TMB Bank	35.4	1.1	No	Yes	Banking
	Total Top 30 LCY Corporate Issuers	**2,164.5**	**69.3**			
	Total LCY Corporate Bonds	**3,689.9**	**118.1**			
	Top 30 as % of Total LCY Corporate Bonds	**58.7%**	**58.7%**			

LCY = local currency, THB = Thai baht, USD = United States dollar.
Notes:
1. Data as of 31 March 2021.
2. State-owned firms are defined as those in which the government has more than a 50% ownership stake.
Source: *AsianBondsOnline* calculations based on Bloomberg LP data.

Table 3: Notable Local Currency Corporate Bond Issuances in the First Quarter of 2021

Corporate Issuers	Coupon Rate (%)	Issued Amount (THB billion)
Charoen Pokphand Foods		
2-year bond	1.75	2.5
5-year bond	2.99	13.1
7-year bond	3.15	4.0
10-year bond	3.60	5.0
12-year bond	3.80	5.4
True Corp[a]		
1-year bond	0.00	2.5
1-year bond	2.72	2.0
1.26-year bond	2.72	0.3
2.75-year bond	3.30	7.4
3.75-year bond	3.85	4.3
4.75-year bond	4.20	2.5
5.75-year bond	4.50	5.8
CP ALL		
5-year bond	2.86	10.0
7-year bond	3.42	6.8
10-year bond	3.95	3.6
15-year bond	4.64	1.5

THB = Thai baht.
[a] Multiple issuance of the same tenor indicates issuance on different dates.
Source: Bloomberg LP.

of corporate debt totaling THB30.0 billion in Q1 2021, comprising bonds with tenors ranging from 2 years to 12 years and carrying coupons ranging from 1.75% to 3.80% (**Table 3**). True Corp was the second-largest issuer during the quarter, with total issuance amounting to THB24.8 billion from bonds with tenors ranging from 1 year to 5.75 years and carrying coupons ranging from 0.0% to 4.50%. CP ALL, a food and beverage firm, was the third-largest issuer with total issuance of THB21.9 billion from bonds with tenors ranging from 5 years to 15 years carrying coupons ranging from 2.86% to 4.64%.

Investor Profile

Central government bonds. Between March 2020 and March 2021, the combined share of the four largest holders of LCY government bonds declined to 89.7% from 91.5% (**Figure 2**). Financial corporations continued to hold the largest share of government bonds, although their share fell to 40.2% at the end of March 2021 from 42.5% a year earlier. In contrast, the share of other depository corporations increased to 20.0% from 15.5% between March 2020 and March 2021. The share held by

Figure 2: Local Currency Government Bonds Investor Profile

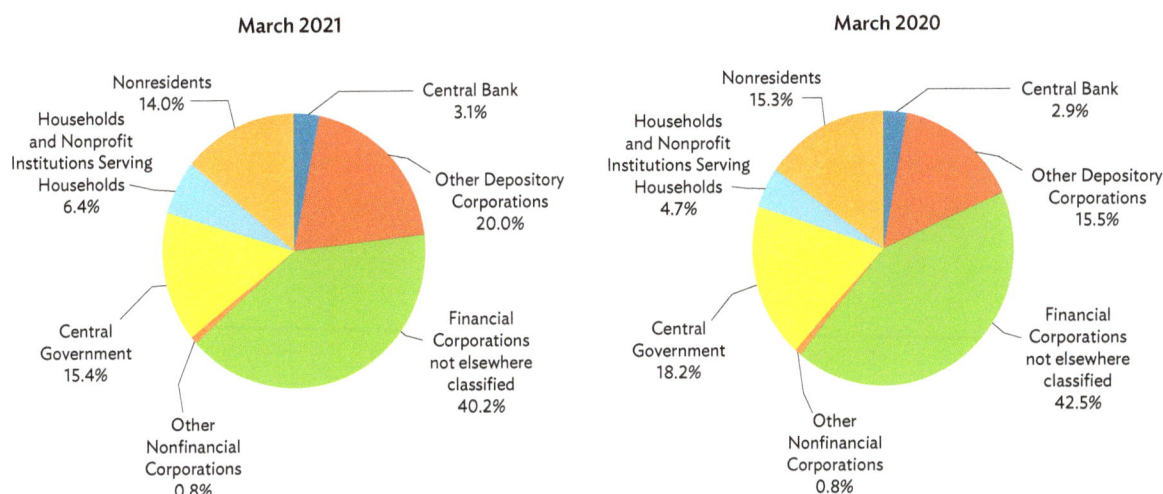

Note: Government bonds include Treasury bills and bonds.
Source: AsianBondsOnline and Bank of Thailand.

the central government decreased to 15.4% from 18.2% during the same period. Nonresidents' holdings inched down to 14.0% from 15.3% due to risk-off sentiment affecting demand for emerging market sovereign bonds.

Central bank bonds. Between March 2020 and March 2021, the combined share of the four largest holders of BOT bonds slipped to 95.6% from 96.1% (**Figure 3**). Other depository corporations held the largest share of BOT bonds, although their share dropped to 38.3% from 49.5% between March 2020 and March 2021. Financial corporations remained the second-largest holder of BOT bonds with 33.3% of total holdings at the end of March 2021, up from 21.7% a year earlier. The BOT's holdings of its LCY bonds decreased to 14.2% from 16.0% during the same period. The central government's share rose to 9.8% in March 2021 from 8.9% a year before. Nonresidents continued to hold a marginal share of BOT bonds at 0.9% in March 2021, down from 1.1% in March 2020.

Foreign investors in Thailand's LCY bond market recorded net inflows of THB4.0 billion in Q1 2021, following net inflows of THB16.8 billion in Q4 2020 (**Figure 4**). Foreign capital flows into the Thai bond market remained volatile in 2021. January saw inflows of THB0.1 billion, followed by outflows of THB4.6 billion in February. March saw inflows of THB8.5 billion, while April witnessed a jump in inflows to THB32.9 billion following the approval of additional relief measures to counter the impact of a new wave of infections.

Figure 4: Foreign Investor Net Trading of Local Currency Bonds in Thailand

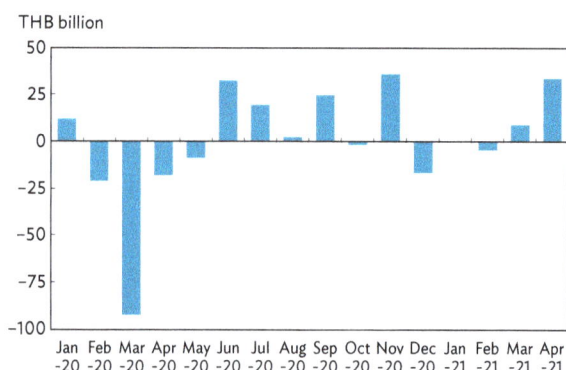

THB = Thai baht.
Source: Thai Bond Market Association.

Figure 3: Local Currency Central Bank Securities Investor Profile

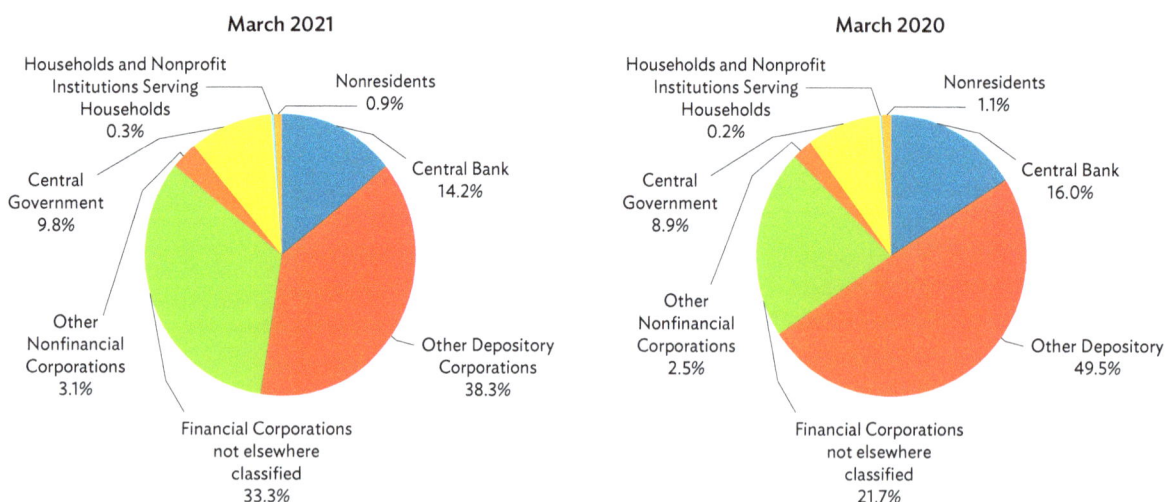

Source: Bank of Thailand.

Ratings Update

In March, Rating and Investment Information, Inc. affirmed Thailand's LCY sovereign credit rating at A– with a stable outlook. The rating was based on the assessment that Thailand's economic fundamentals and fiscal management will remain sound despite an expected slow recovery from the COVID-19 pandemic. The current account balance has maintained a surplus and concerns over Thailand's external position remain small. Thus, the rating agency viewed that the factors supporting Thailand's creditworthiness will remain unchanged. The credit rating agency also affirmed Thailand's foreign currency issuer rating at A– with a stable outlook.

Policy, Institutional, and Regulatory Developments

Bank of Thailand Adjusts Bond Issuance Program for 2021

The BOT adjusted its bond issuance program for 2021 to accommodate changes in market demand and support the government's financing needs for COVID-19 relief measures. The BOT and the PDMO continued to coordinate so that BOT and government bonds would be issued at different sections of the yield curve. In particular, the BOT discontinued the issuance of 6-month bills and 3-year bonds in line with the PDMO's plan to issue 6-month Treasury bills and 3-year government bonds in 2021. The BOT also terminated the issuance of 2-week bills as the need for these short-term bills had declined in recent years. Furthermore, the BOT replaced the Bangkok Interbank Offered Rate-linked floating rate bonds with Thai Overnight Repurchase Rate-linked floating rate bonds to promote the development of the new reference rate.

Viet Nam

Yield Movements

The yields of local currency (LCY) government securities in Viet Nam rose for most tenors between 28 February and 15 May. (**Figure 1**). Yields on 5-year and 15-year bonds increased the most at 4 basis points (bps) and 5 bps, respectively, while those on 1-year and 10-year maturities increased by less than 1 bp each. Declining yields were seen for the 2-year tenor (–8 bps) and 7-year tenor (–0.6 bps). The yield on the 3-year bond was unchanged. The yield spread between the 2-year and 10-year tenors widened from 172 bps to 180 bps during the review period.

The modest general increase in LCY government bond yields signaled that ample liquidity remained in the system and that risk aversion is sustaining the demand for government securities, thereby limiting the increases in rates.

The accommodative monetary policy stance of the State Bank of Vietnam also influenced yield movements. A low-interest-rate environment persists, with the central bank reducing the key policy rate by 50 bps to 4.0% on 1 October 2020.

Inflationary pressure remained relatively weak. The prices of consumer goods in Viet Nam increased 2.9% year-on-year (y-o-y) in May, largely due to higher oil prices in the world market that translated into higher domestic transportation costs. The May figure and the resulting year-to-date inflation of 1.3% were still in line with the government's goal to keep inflation below 4.0% for 2021. Nonetheless, inflationary pressure may build in the coming months as businesses and consumers adapt to the new normal and the global economy recovers, thereby driving up demand.

Viet Nam's economy continued to expand as its GDP grew 4.5% y-o-y in the first quarter (Q1) of 2021. The domestic economy remained resilient despite the resurgence of COVID-19 cases in some areas. The expansion was the same as in the fourth quarter of 2020 but was up from 3.8% y-o-y in Q1 2020. While all economic sectors posted growth during the quarter, the manufacturing sector contributed the most to the overall

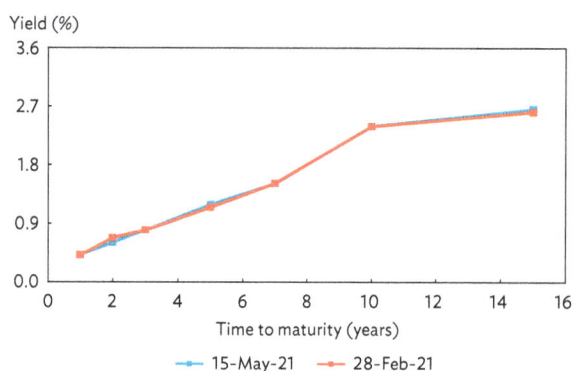

Figure 1: Viet Nam's Benchmark Yield Curve—Local Currency Government Bonds

Source: Based on data from Bloomberg LP.

expansion. The government is targeting annual GDP growth of 6.5% y-o-y in 2021.

The Vietnamese dong was stable against the United States dollar during the review period, trading at VND23,040 per USD1 on 15 May, reflecting only a marginal depreciation of 0.1% from 28 February. The stability of the dong was underpinned by trade surpluses and sufficient foreign exchange reserves.

Size and Composition

Viet Nam's total LCY bonds outstanding slightly declined 0.3% quarter-on-quarter (q-o-q) to VND1,637.3 trillion (USD71.0 billion) at the end of Q1 2021, reversing the previous quarter's expansion of 8.1% q-o-q (**Table 1**). The market contraction was due to lower outstanding government debt even as corporate bonds outstanding increased. Government bonds accounted for a dominant share of Viet Nam's bond market at 82.1% versus corporate bonds with a 17.9% share. On an annual basis, the bond market expanded 19.0% y-o-y in Q1 2021, led by corporate bonds, which grew more than double during the quarter.

Government bonds. The government bond market contracted 1.1% q-o-q in Q1 2021, reducing the government's outstanding debt to VND1,343.5 trillion. A large volume of maturities was seen in government

Table 1: Size and Composition of the Local Currency Bond Market in Viet Nam

| | Outstanding Amount (billion) | | | | | | Growth Rate (%) | | | |
| | Q1 2020 | | Q4 2020 | | Q1 2021 | | Q1 2020 | | Q1 2021 | |
	VND	USD	VND	USD	VND	USD	q-o-q	y-o-y	q-o-q	y-o-y
Total	1,375,700	58	1,642,790	71	1,637,288	71	10.4	14.4	(0.3)	19.0
Government	1,260,477	53	1,358,315	59	1,343,539	58	10.5	15.4	(1.1)	6.6
Treasury Bonds	970,436	41	1,207,228	52	1,199,863	52	(0.9)	5.6	(0.6)	23.6
Central Bank Bills	136,986	6	0	0	0	0	–	–	–	(100.0)
Government-Guaranteed and Municipal Bonds	153,055	6	151,087	7	143,677	6	(5.6)	(9.0)	(4.9)	(6.1)
Corporate	115,223	5	284,475	12	293,749	13	9.9	4.1	3.3	154.9

( ) = negative, – = not applicable, q-o-q = quarter-on-quarter, Q1 = first quarter, Q4 = fourth quarter, USD = United States dollar, VND = Vietnamese dong, y-o-y = year-on-year.
Notes:
1. Bloomberg LP end-of-period local currency–USD rates are used.
2. Growth rates are calculated from local currency base and do not include currency effects.
Sources: Bloomberg LP and Vietnam Bond Market Association.

securities during the quarter, which was accompanied by low or no issuance across government bond segments.

Treasury bonds outstanding declined 0.6% q-o-q to VND1,199.9 trillion in Q1 2021, reversing the 6.9% q-o-q growth in the preceding quarter. The decline came on the back of lower bond offerings and issuance volumes by the State Treasury of Vietnam and was compounded by the large volume of securities that matured during the quarter. The issuance of Treasury bonds decreased by more than 50.0% q-o-q in Q1 2021 to VND39.2 trillion.

Outstanding government-guaranteed and municipal bonds declined 4.9% q-o-q to VND143.7 trillion due to maturities and the absence of issuance in this government bond segment in Q1 2021. There were no outstanding central bank bills at the end of Q1 2021 as the State Bank of Vietnam continued to support liquidity in the market.

Corporate bonds. Corporate bonds posted growth of 3.3% q-o-q in Q2 2021, lifting the total outstanding amount to VND293.7 trillion at the end of March. The increase, however, was slower compared to the growth of 13.5% q-o-q in the previous quarter. The slowdown in growth can be traced to lower issuance volume from the corporate sector due to regulations that raised standards for corporate bond issuance to promote transparency and fairness in the market.

The aggregate bonds outstanding of the top 30 LCY corporate issuers amounted to VND199.9 trillion, or 68.1% of the total corporate bond market, at the end

of March (**Table 2**). The top 30 corporate issuers were mostly from the banking industry with cumulative outstanding bonds equal to VND107.0 trillion, or more than half of the top 30's outstanding bonds. Property firms were the next most prolific issuers with VND44.7 trillion in bonds outstanding, or 22.4% of the top 30's total debt. The Bank for Investment and Development of Vietnam was the single-largest issuer with outstanding debt of VND22.0 trillion at the end of Q1 2021.

Issuance from the corporate sector in Q1 2021 amounted to VND18.6 trillion, down from VND45.6 trillion in the fourth quarter of 2020. Debt issuance from property firms dominated the list of new corporate bonds with sales amounting to VND12.8 trillion, which accounted for about 70.0% of total issuance in Q1 2021. There were 32 corporate bond issuers in Q1 2021, 17 of which are property firms. Notable bond issuances during the quarter were mainly from the property sector, led by Vingroup with cumulative issuance of VND4.4 trillion from three tranches of 3-year bonds (**Table 3**).

Investor Profile

Insurance firms and banks together held nearly all government securities outstanding at the end of December 2020, accounting for a combined share of 99.3% (**Figure 2**). The insurance sector held 54.1% of government bonds outstanding, slightly down from 54.7% at the end of December 2019, while the banking sector held 45.2%, up from 43.9% during the same period. The remaining outstanding bonds were held by

Table 2: Top 30 Issuers of Local Currency Corporate Bonds in Viet Nam

	Issuers	Outstanding Amount		State-Owned	Listed Company	Type of Industry
		LCY Bonds (VND billion)	LCY Bonds (USD billion)			
1.	Bank for Investment and Development of Vietnam	22,023	0.95	Yes	Yes	Banking
2.	Masan Group	16,900	0.73	No	Yes	Finance
3.	Ho Chi Minh City Development Joint Stock Commercial Bank	12,248	0.53	No	Yes	Banking
4.	Vinhomes Joint Stock Company	10,890	0.47	No	Yes	Property
5.	Lien Viet Post Joint Stock Commercial Bank	10,600	0.46	No	Yes	Banking
6.	Tien Phong Commercial Joint Stock Bank	9,649	0.42	No	Yes	Banking
7.	Vietnam Prosperity Joint Stock Commercial Bank	9,150	0.40	No	Yes	Banking
8.	Vietnam International Joint Stock Commercial Bank	9,050	0.39	No	Yes	Banking
9.	Vietnam Joint Stock Commercial Bank for Industry and Trade	8,850	0.38	Yes	Yes	Banking
10.	Saigon Glory Company Limited	8,000	0.35	No	No	Property
11.	Sovico Group Joint Stock Company	7,550	0.33	No	Yes	Diversified Operations
12.	Orient Commercial Joint Stock Bank	7,535	0.33	No	No	Banking
13.	Vingroup	5,425	0.24	No	Yes	Property
14.	Asia Commercial Bank JSC	5,300	0.23	No	Yes	Banking
15.	Vinpearl	5,080	0.22	No	No	Hotel Operator
16.	Vietnam Technological and Commercial Joint Stock Bank	5,000	0.22	No	No	Banking
17.	Bac A Commercial Joint Stock Bank	4,640	0.20	No	Yes	Banking
18.	Phu My Hung Corporation	4,497	0.19	No	No	Property
19.	Ho Chi Minh City Infrastructure Investment Joint Stock Company	4,390	0.19	No	Yes	Construction
20.	Nui Phao Mining and Processing Co., Ltd.	4,310	0.19	No	No	Mining
21.	NoVa Real Estate Investment Corporation JSC	4,207	0.18	No	Yes	Property
22	Vincom Retail	3,050	0.13	No	Yes	Property
23.	Vietnam Maritime Joint Stock Commercial Bank	2,999	0.13	No	Yes	Banking
24.	Tuong Minh Investment and Real Estate Company Limited	2,950	0.13	No	No	Property
25.	TNL Investment and Leasing Joint Stock Company	2,926	0.13	No	No	Property
26.	Phu Long Real Estate Joint Stock Company	2,800	0.12	No	No	Property
27.	Binh Hai Golf Investment and Development Joint Stock Company	2,745	0.12	No	No	Leisure
28.	Masan Resources	2,500	0.11	No	No	Manufacturing
29.	Hoan My Medical Corporation	2,330	0.10	No	No	Healthcare Services
30.	Refrigeration Electrical Engineering Corporation	2,318	0.10	No	Yes	Manufacturing
	Total Top 30 LCY Corporate Issuers	**199,912**	**8.67**			
	Total LCY Corporate Bonds	**293,749**	**12.74**			
	Top 30 as % of Total LCY Corporate Bonds	**68.1%**	**68.1%**			

LCY = local currency, USD = United States dollar, VND = Vietnamese dong.
Notes:
1. Data as of 31 March 2021.
2. State-owned firms are defined as those in which the government has more than a 50% ownership stake.
Sources: *AsianBondsOnline* calculations based on Bloomberg LP and Vietnam Bond Market Association data.

Table 3: Notable Local Currency Corporate Bond Issuances in the First Quarter of 2021

Corporate Issuers	Coupon Rate (%)	Issued Amount (VND billion)
Vingroup[a]		
3-year bond	Floating	1,860
3-year bond	Floating	1,515
3-year bond	Floating	1,000
Nhat Quang Property Development Corporation		
3-year bond	–	2,150
Smart Dragon Investment JSC		
3-year bond	–	1,900
Masan Group		
3-year bond	Floating	1,400

– = not available, VND = Vietnamese dong.
[a] Multiple issuance of the same tenor indicates issuance on different dates.
Sources: Vietnam Bond Market Association.

security companies, investment funds, offshore investors, and other investors. Foreign investors held 0.6% of government securities at the end of December 2020, which remained the smallest foreign holdings share among all emerging East Asian economies.

Ratings Update

On 1 April, Fitch Ratings affirmed Viet Nam's sovereign credit rating at BB and raised the outlook to positive. The rate affirmation and improved outlook were based on Viet Nam's strong economic performance as it was able to maintain positive growth despite the pandemic, largely because of success in containing its COVID-19 outbreak;

an improvement in public finances; and a strong external finance position on the back of a current account surplus and rising foreign exchange reserves. Sustained high economic growth, further improvement in public finances, and sustainable fiscal consolidation over the medium-term could lead to a rating upgrade, while a deterioration of these conditions could be rating-negative.

On 21 May, S&P Global Ratings retained Viet Nam's sovereign credit rating at BB and upgraded the outlook to positive. The rating agency noted that the decision was based on Viet Nam's impressive economic achievements and policy reforms, and measures in response to the negative impacts of the pandemic. S&P Global Ratings expects that Viet Nam will continue to enjoy a firm economic recovery, supported by its robust macroeconomic fundamentals, well-managed public debt, and flexible fiscal policy.

Policy, Institutional, and Regulatory Developments

Ministry of Finance Lists Market Makers

Viet Nam's Ministry of Finance released Decision No. 2290/QD-BTC, which lists market makers for the debt market effective 1 January–31 December 2021. The market markers for 2021 comprise 17 commercial banks and securities firms, up from only 13 in 2020. The entities have the right to participate in the bidding of government bonds, act as the main guarantor organization for the

Figure 2: Local Currency Government Bonds Investor Profile

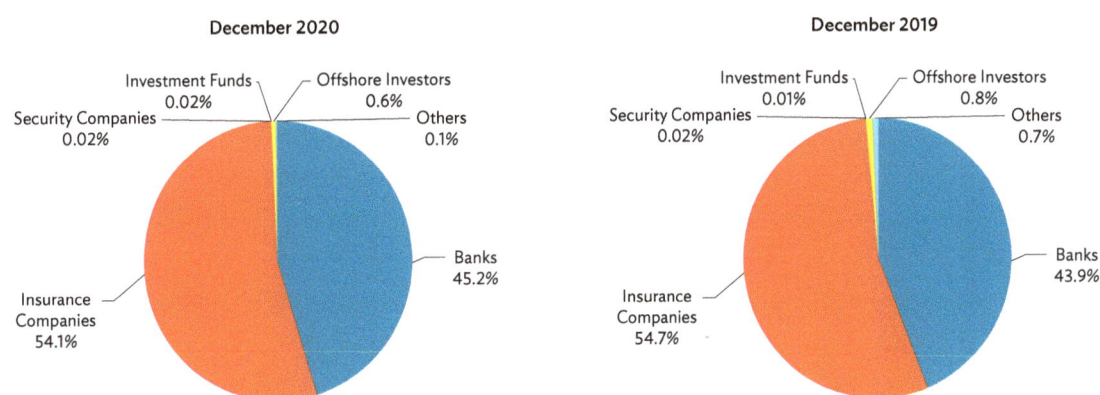

Source: Viet Nam Ministry of Finance.

issuance of government bonds, and provide inputs for drafting new policies for the bond market. The Ministry of Finance will evaluate the entities toward the end of the year if they can maintain their status as market makers.

State Bank of Vietnam Issues Regulation to Control Credit Quality in Risky Sectors

In May, the State Bank of Vietnam issued Official Dispatch No. 3029/NHNN-TTGSNH to credit institutions and foreign bank branches, instructing them to implement strict control over the quality of credit in sectors with potential risks such as real estate and securities. High-risk credit areas include investments in corporate bonds, securities credit, real estate, build-operate-transfer, and consumer loans. For corporate bonds, issuance from the real estate sector has rapidly increased in volume, with almost none having any collateral. This risks the formation of a property bubble that could inflict huge losses on investors when the bubble bursts.

www.ingramcontent.com/pod-product-compliance
Lightning Source LLC
Chambersburg PA
CBHW042036220326

41599CB00045BA/7475